Orphans of Empire

ORPHANS of EMPIRE

The fate of London's foundlings

HELEN BERRY

OXFORD
UNIVERSITY PRESS

OXFORD

UNIVERSITY PRESS

Great Clarendon Street, Oxford, OX2 6DP,
United Kingdom

Oxford University Press is a department of the University of Oxford.
It furthers the University's objective of excellence in research, scholarship,
and education by publishing worldwide. Oxford is a registered trade mark of
Oxford University Press in the UK and in certain other countries

Published in the United States of America by Oxford University Press
198 Madison Avenue, New York, NY 10016, United States of America

British Library Cataloguing in Publication Data
Data available

Library of Congress Control Number: 2018950679

ISBN 978-0-19-875848-8

Printed and bound in Great Britain by
Clays Ltd, Elcograf S.p.A.

This book is dedicated to
Mary Bamsey
(1914–2014)
and to the mothers of lost children everywhere

PREFACE

At Russell Square tube station in central London, throngs of tourists gather daily, straight from their hotel breakfasts or discharged from long-distance coaches, and move off in packs towards Covent Garden. If they only took a moment and headed north-east in the opposite direction, they would find instead a much quieter corner, a seven-acre park known as Coram's Fields just a few streets away. If it is a fine day, there will be the sound of children playing. The observant eye may spot a curious sign ('Adults may only enter if accompanied by a child'). This green playground, with its children's centre, nursery, and city farm, was once the site of the London Foundling Hospital. It was built upon fifty-six acres of land in Lamb's Conduit Fields, purchased for the princely sum of £7000 in 1742 from the earl of Salisbury. All that survives today is a small colonnade, since the rest of the building was demolished in the 1920s. Nearby is the Foundling Museum, where the interior of some of the original Hospital has been preserved, complete with the valuable art work that was donated by famous artists of the day. Here in the Museum it is possible to stand in the reconstructed room, replete with fine wooden panelling and moulded ceiling, where poverty-stricken mothers brought their infants in a desperate attempt to have them admitted to the Hospital. The spectacle of their misery has been imagined by countless visitors, recreating the public drama that was described by Georgian commentators in vivid detail.

This book relates the history of what happened to those infants who gained admission by chance to the London Foundling Hospital, and who survived long enough to go out into the wider world. Their stories are set within the context of Britain's imperial history from the mid-eighteenth to the mid-nineteenth centuries, exploring the social, economic, and political forces that were behind the establishment and funding of the Hospital's mission during the first 100 years of its existence. This is not a history of empire as told by military historians, but it explores instead the ways in which British imperial ambitions abroad shaped society at home. It reveals how empire shaped the fortunes and life chances of the very poorest members of society. This book sets out to explore how the dynamics of political, cultural, and economic forces shaped Georgian society, particularly in relation to maritime trade and warfare, and the interconnections between the charitable deeds and interests of the governing elite and the fortunes of the poor. It explores what living in London, the great metropolis at the centre of what was rapidly becoming the world's leading superpower, meant for poor children at the mercy of charitable institutions. The eighteenth century witnessed new experiments in social welfare sponsored by the ruling elite through a combination of charity and direct government investment, among which the London Foundling Hospital was one of the most expensive and ambitious schemes. The Hospital was a voluntary response to the growing problem of urban poverty, an unprecedented venture for the English that had consequences, intended and unintended, not just in London but throughout the nation for all concerned in the enterprise. Its influence extended globally in the pattern of the philanthropy it modelled among the rich and powerful, and among working communities in the life courses of the children it raised. Understanding this phenomenon will require a certain amount of openness to rethinking the motivation on the part of those who sought to 'do good' in their own time, and a nuanced understanding of the complicated motivations for people to engage in charitable works, both in the eighteenth century and today.

The sources of evidence relating to those whose lives depended upon charity are extremely difficult to piece together in the archives. First-hand accounts written by society's poorest members who often had little or no literacy are almost non-existent, so the fragments that document their lives are usually mediated through others: the accounts of clerks, court scribes, and commentators. The voices of orphaned and abandoned children are very difficult to hear in modern times: recovering them from almost 300 years ago is almost but not quite impossible. The history of George King, a former foundling who wrote a detailed autobiographical account of his life, is woven through the narrative of this book, a single, precious thread. Other foundling voices join his in smaller, broken whispers. Together, they tell the story of what it was like to be raised without knowing the name you were given at birth, nor the identity of your parents, during the century before Queen Victoria came to the throne.

CONTENTS

LIST OF FIGURES

Whether 'tis Nobler in the minde to suffer
The Slings and Arrowes of outragious Fortune,
Or to take Armes against a Sea of troubles,
And by opposing end them.

William Shakespeare, *Hamlet* (first fol., 1623),
Act III, Scene 1

CHAPTER 1

Empire

THE PUBLIC OPENING of Trafalgar Square, one of London's most famous landmarks, on 1 May 1844 was not a great success. Building work had begun as far back as the 1820s to clear and develop the site, which was formerly occupied by the Royal Mews. The outlandishly extravagant monarch George IV had his horses moved to Buckingham Palace, leaving the premises empty, but progress on developing the site over the next two decades was slow. The leading architect of Regency style, John Nash, developed the south side of the square, but he died in 1835 before the work was completed. It was then decided that the square would be named after the Battle of Trafalgar in commemoration of Admiral Lord Nelson's famous victory in October 1805. Plans for the new National Gallery on the north side were criticized for their lack of grandeur, whose architect William Wilkins also died before the work could be completed. By the 1840s a new architect,

Charles Barry, had been appointed, and the scheme became more costly and grandiose, with the addition of fountains, four granite plinths for sculptures, and pedestals for lighting. An extra committee was formed to commission a monument to Nelson, who had died a hero's death at Trafalgar, but it took two years for them to decide how public subscriptions towards the cost of the monument could best be organized and managed. Eventually, an open competition was held. It was won by the architect William Railton, who produced a design for a monumental column topped by a statue of Nelson and flanked by four bronze lions. Charles Barry publicly declared his dislike of the winning scheme, and there was further widespread condemnation. The famous Trafalgar Square statues of lions by Sir Edward Landseer were not finished until the 1860s. Further delay this time was caused by Landseer's insistence on sketching from a real lion's corpse obtained from London Zoo, which decomposed before the artist had time to finish his drawings.

Amid this tortuously slow progress, there was recognition that the surviving veterans of the Battle of Trafalgar should be honoured. During the late spring and summer of 1844, *The Times* announced that a grand ceremony and dinner would be held at public expense for the men who had fought at Trafalgar, and at Nelson's other great battles—Copenhagen, Cape St. Vincent, Tenerife, and the Nile.[1] Some months later, the newspaper reported that this plan had been cancelled following complaints ('earnest solicitations') from local tradesmen that such an event would harm their businesses. The alternative suggestion was that a ceremony would be held at Greenwich Hospital, a naval school and charitable foundation which housed former seamen. The plan was to present each of the veterans who had served alongside Nelson with a medal and a gift of money.

And so, some miles away from Trafalgar Square, south of the River Thames, in the grand Painted Hall at Greenwich Hospital, approximately 350 elderly 'Trafalgar men', former seamen who were the survivors of that famous battle, assembled on the morning of 2 April 1845. The boys of the naval school marched on the parade ground in full regalia, to the sound of a military band that played 'God Save the Queen'. Inside, under the vaulted magnificence of the Painted Hall, the veterans were called forward in turn by name, many with missing limbs and wooden legs that marked their sacrifice for the nation. One by one, each was solemnly presented by the governor with a medal and gratuity of ten shillings in tribute to his service. The medal bore Nelson's effigy and an inscription of the admiral's famous message, signalled to his men on the eve of the Battle of Trafalgar: 'England expects every man will do his duty'. On the reverse, there was an engraving of the 'Nelson Pillar' (known to us today as Nelson's column) with the words 'To commemorate the opening of the Nelson Testimonial, Trafalgar-square, 21st October, 1844'. On the commemorative medal, Trafalgar Square was depicted in its idealized, completed form, not showing the reality of bare hoardings and empty plinths. *The Times* reported that not only did the elderly heroes 'look healthy', but they were universally praised for their 'orderly behaviour'.[2] Media attention that day was focused on the heroic deeds of Admiral the Rt. Hon. Sir Robert Stopford, governor of the Greenwich Hospital, the seventy-six-year-old former naval commander who had served with Nelson and, it was reported, 'almost' saw action at Trafalgar. At the upper end of the hall were the governor, lieutenant-governor, officers, and their friends, seated together with assembled dignitaries behind a high table flanked by the Union Jack and flags of the Admiralty.[3]

Another, somewhat less celebrated, invitee that day was George King, a former ordinary seaman, now nearly sixty years of age. Unlike many of the dignitaries who were present, he had actually taken part in the Battle of Trafalgar when he was just eighteen years old.[4] George King was remarkable in that, unlike many of the rank-and-file sailors below decks, he was able to read and write, and so compiled his own arresting account of his experience of active service. On that fateful day he was eyewitness to 'great slaughter' at Trafalgar, but extraordinarily by his own account he 'never received a Wound'.

The truth was that George King had been fighting to survive against the odds all of his life, for as an infant he had been given up to be raised in the London Foundling Hospital. His is the only detailed autobiography by a foundling child born and raised in the eighteenth century, and as such provides some of the few surviving clues as to what it was like to have been brought up in an institution founded for 'orphaned and abandoned children' over 250 years ago. George was an 'orphan of empire', someone whose parents had died or who had abandoned him (thereby effectively orphaning him, since very few children left at the Foundling Hospital were ever reunited with their birth families). George's precarious life as a pauper infant was 'saved for the nation' via a publicly sponsored charity whose main purpose was to boost the workforce at home and manpower for the armed forces abroad in order to further Britain's imperial mission. Almost no one at the time nor subsequently knew of George King's story, nor his heroic service to his country. He surpassed expectations of the kind of modest, useful life that the Foundling Hospital's supporters had planned for the poor children in their care by fighting at one of the most iconic

4

battles in British history.[5] His remarkable autobiography is a vital part of the story that will be told for the first time in this book. But the exceptionalism of his life can only be fully appreciated if we uncover as much as it is possible to know about the thousands of other children who were raised in the Foundling Hospital, and expose some of the myths about what happened to them, where they were sent to work, and what they experienced of life's 'Slings and Arrowes of outragious Fortune'.

In order to understand how and why the lives of poor children like George King came to be deemed worthy of saving for the nation, we need to go back a century earlier, to the year 1720, and the politics and power relations that shaped the lives of ordinary women and men living at the epicentre of a rapidly expanding British Empire. In this year, a financial scandal rocked the City of London, the ramifications of which led to the rise to power of Sir Robert Walpole, who became *de facto* Britain's first prime minister. Overspeculation had led to inflated share prices in the South Sea Company, which had seemed a safe bet for investors since it was effectively underwritten by leading British government ministers. In fact, rumours proved to be correct that the company's claim to a trade monopoly on the *asiento* (the right to the trade in slaves with South American colonies) was entirely spurious. There was widespread reporting of the subsequent panic at the Royal Exchange when the 'bubble' burst, leading to bankruptcy and even suicide of speculators whose life savings vanished. Among those who lost a fortune was Sir Isaac Newton, whose mathematical genius could not defend him against the vicissitudes of stock market gambling.[6]

As first lord of the treasury, Walpole had unprecedented command of the intricacies of the financial markets (and indeed of a 'vast spoils system' of bribery that was spectacularly corrupt, even by Georgian standards).[7] By 1722, he had re-established investor confidence in City institutions, and united the office of prime minister with first lord of the treasury, a dual title held by the British prime minister to this day.

The events known as the South Sea Bubble illustrate just how much the governance of Britain had come to be linked to the fortunes of the City of London and the creation of a so-called 'fiscal-military state', where both government and trade were organized to support and expand a growing overseas empire. In the late seventeenth and eighteenth centuries Britain emerged as 'the military *Wunderkind* of the age'. As historian John Brewer has observed:

> Dutch admirals learnt to fear and then admire its navies, French generals reluctantly conferred respect on its officers and men, and Spanish governors trembled for the safety of their colonies and the sanctity of their trade.[8]

This was far from being an era of peace and stability, as it has sometimes been portrayed. Britain was engaged in a series of continental European wars, starting with the Nine Years' War under William III against France in the 1690s, and continuing with the Wars of Spanish Succession (1701–14), Austrian Succession (1740–48), and the Seven Years' War (1756–63). These conflicts were waged often for dynastic reasons that reflected struggles for supremacy between Catholic France and her Protestant neighbours in Europe. At the end of the seventeenth century, a new Anglo-Dutch alliance was fostered by William III, Prince of Orange and former *Stadhouder* of the United Provinces, whose seizure of the English throne in 1688/9 was a coup against the Catholic incumbent, James II. William's successor, Queen Anne, died in 1714, and the throne passed to a new Hanoverian dynasty of experienced military princes, George I and George II, who strengthened Britain's alliances with Protestant German states. Britain's assertion of her military strength enabled defence of the maritime trade which in turn brought prodigious wealth to rival other European colonial powers. During the reign of George III, the Royal Navy became the 'senior service' among British forces, and by 1805, the Navy was the last line of resistance against the combined forces of their only maritime rival, the combined fleet of French and Spanish ships under the command of Napoleon Bonaparte.

The growth of British imperial ambition over the course of the eighteenth century would not have been possible without bankrolling by the City of London. In 1694, the newly formed Bank of England brokered enormous loans that enabled successive monarchs to wage war against continental European powers. In order to service the national debt, parliament levied taxes via customs and excise duties and paid interest to the stockbrokers, merchants, and bankers in the City of London who profited from government loans. The loans in turn paid for a vast network of bureaucratic offices operating on behalf of centralized government, procuring supplies to equip a standing British Army and Navy with everything it needed, from transportation and arms, to clothing, food, billeting costs, leather for horse saddles, and boots for the men. They also distributed wages to pay battalions and squadrons by newly professionalized ranks of officers, as well as rank-and-file sailors and soldiers, and the civilian trades that were needed to support the activities of the armed forces, such as shipbuilders, rope makers, tanners, blacksmiths, and carriers for transportation of troops and supplies. In the Nine Years' War, 76,000 men were mobilized, rising to 92,000 during the War of Spanish Succession.[9] By 1794, the total number of Naval seamen and Marines had reached 86,000, with an additional 62,800 'volunteers' (many of them press-ganged), of whom half were able seamen. Though these numbers fluctuated, depending upon whether the country was preparing for war or scaling back operations during peacetime, they give some idea of the scale of the logistical task in terms of manpower alone.[10]

The exercise of military and naval power in pursuit of territorial gains was seen as unashamedly desirable to the ruling elites of eighteenth-century Britain. The Georgian world-view was one of 'mercantilist' ideology. Unlike modern neoclassical economic theory, which rests upon the idea that economic growth is potentially infinite, mercantilism was predicated upon the empire builder's world-view, which centred on territorial land grab and colonization as a means of gaining control of the world's resources. Britain wanted a greater share of power in international relations, particularly in the ongoing rivalry with her near neighbour, France. Proponents of mercantilism deemed it necessary to wage war in order to expand the empire and protect British interests. This brought prosperity to the mother country, siphoning more and more raw materials and labour from imperial rivals, and safeguarding an ever-increasing British share of colonial territories and global maritime trade. Wars were usually enacted via complicated and shifting networks of alliances with other European powers, such as the Grand Alliance between Britain, the Holy Roman Empire, the Dutch Republic, and the Duchy of Savoy. The War of Spanish Succession brought strategic territorial gains for the British Navy via the acquisition of Gibraltar and Minorca (and hence access to the Mediterranean), and trade advantages for British merchants in the granting of exclusive rights to the slave trade in Spanish America.

The foundations of Britain's empire were in the New World, and went back to the late 1500s—the colonies of the eastern seaboard counties of what is now the United States, which grew out of settlements in New England during the Elizabethan era. Subsequent acquisitions in the West Indies provided further trading advantages (British dominion over Jamaica, for instance, dated back to 1655). This was the origins of the 'triangular trade' in slaves from West Africa, bought and sold in return for British manufactured goods and transported on the horrific 'middle passage' across the Atlantic to work on sugar and cotton plantations. For as long as this continued, the myth could be sustained that the 'first British empire' in the west was mutually beneficial to Britain and her dominions, based upon shared cultural ties (a common language and Protestant religion) and tacit consent won through mutual trading interests, since the American colonies were the prime market for British exports. The reality was somewhat different, however: the American colonies were beginning to assert their right to self-government and showed signs of questioning their obligations to the 'old country', specifically their obligation to pay taxes to Westminster.[11]

The Seven Years' War (1756–63) showed both the strengths and weaknesses of Britain's imperial policy at this time. It has been called 'the most dramatically successful war the British ever fought', viewed from the perspective of the eighteenth-century establishment. The British Navy, working in alliance with their new allies, the Prussian army, conquered Canada and drove the French out of most of their Indian, West African, and West Indian territories. The charismatic orator and Whig politician Charles James Fox trumpeted the success of British efforts in parliament 'Observe', he said, 'the magnificence of our metropolis—the extent of our empire, the immensity of our commerce and the opulence of our people.'[12] But behind the swagger were growing concerns about how to govern such a vast empire. After 1763, Britain controlled a swathe of territory on the North American continent from New Brunswick in the north to Florida in the south, with other gains in the Caribbean and Senegal, which were crucial to the development of the slave trade. The footholds of Britain's 'second empire' in the east were planted on the Indian sub-continent, with French interests routed in trading posts at Bombay (Mumbai), Madras (Chennai), and Calcutta (Kolkata). The character of the British Empire after 1763 changed profoundly. Westminster was now presented with the conundrum of how to govern peoples with whom there could be no pretence of shared culture or mutual interests: 70,000 French-speaking, Catholic Québécois inhabited a new British province created at the Treaty of Paris that ended the Seven Years' War. The limited ability of the British Army to enforce rule should any of His Majesty's new subjects wish to rebel was already becoming apparent. The North American colonies would soon test their right to independence. After 1763, the question of how sufficient manpower could be mustered to sustain British colonial rule, by force if necessary, troubled both the Westminster parliament and the reigning monarch, George III.

Against this backdrop of British colonial expansion through trade and military conquest, the nation's prosperity centred upon London as the nation's largest port. The area east of the Tower of London that teemed with quays, wharfs, dockyards, and warehouses employed about a quarter of the city's workforce, an *entrepôt* for the import, national distribution, and re-exportation of foreign manufactured goods, raw materials, and comestibles such as tobacco, rice, tea, coffee, and sugar. The port of London also handled the export of domestically produced manufactured goods from all parts of the British Isles. London was also the largest centre of industrial production in Europe. The 'dirtiest' trades were confined to the poorest neighbourhoods downriver, through the East End and Isle of Dogs, which teemed with workshops, tanneries, breweries, tallow makers, glasshouses, and metal foundries.

One very visible sign to contemporaries of Britain's trading links with her overseas colonies and the rest of the world was that the Thames was a 'continued Forest of Ships of all Nations', as one foreign visitor commented The riverbanks were crowded, flanked with the masts of vessels so closely packed that from a distance it was difficult to work out where the docks ended and dry land began.[13] Londoners breathed air that was thick with coal dust. The majority of coal was brought via coastal shipping from the 'black Indies' of north-east England and was used to provide fuel in people's homes.[14] Many working men were employed in building-related trades, such as brickmakers, plasterers, painters and carpenters, roofers, and metalworkers producing rivets, tacks, and nails. Then there were the skilled trades, such as stonemasons, and semi-professional occupations such as surveyors and amateur architects. Construction sites were everywhere, and were always noisy, often noisome. Hundreds of workmen were employed in fabricating grand squares, erected with palatial scale to reflect the social and political ambitions of the nobility; other smaller ventures aimed at providing accommodation for prosperous households, funded by small-scale speculation and private investment in building properties that were then rented out to many different tenants. Only the very rich had their own kitchens: a few victualling establishments had rudimentary plumbing; none had proper sanitation. In his poem *Trivia* (1716), the leading satirist of the age, John Gay, who lost both of his parents by the age of ten, fancifully imagined the life of an orphaned London bootblack. The boy was conceived by the goddess Cloacina (a play on Cloaca, the main sewerage drain of ancient Rome), the personification of Fleet Ditch, a stinking open sewer.[15]

As early as 1700, London was fast becoming the largest metropolis in Europe, with over half a million inhabitants. The City of London and its surrounding parishes were part building site, part vision of neoclassical elegance, part slum, swallowing the green fields to the north and west.[16] When the earl of Salisbury sold the land upon which the Foundling Hospital was built, nearby Powis Place was connected with Lamb's Conduit Fields by means of a country gate from the gardens of Powis Wells, where spa water refreshed passers-by: 'How pleasant it is after drinking the Waters to ramble in the fields amongst the Cows', reminisced one contemporary, of an area that was rapidly absorbed into the metropolis.[17] Towards the West End were the newly laid-out squares, providing elegant and spacious dwellings for the rich, and ornate shops purveying luxury goods to supply their households. In the City, St Paul's Cathedral, Sir Christopher Wren's grandiose Baroque confection completed in 1711, rapidly became a landmark of British national confidence. The London skyline was also spiked with Hawksmoor church spires, whose rich endowments brought prestige to their patrons, the prosperous City merchants.

But for those urban dwellers whose eyes were drawn towards the mud rather than up towards the heavens, everywhere, for those who cared to look, were the signs of growing urban poverty. Paintings of eighteenth-century London by the Venetian artist Canaletto give prominence to the fine new streets and classical vistas of magnificent buildings. But they are like modern snapshots that give the illusion of experiencing views of famous landmarks in elegant desertion, when the reality is being jostled in the uncomfortable crush of a thronging crowd (Figures 1.1 and 1.2). Eighteenth-century London was teeming with humanity, and poverty was never far from politeness. This was particularly the case in the arterial thoroughfares that supplied a constant stream of people and goods, and in the dark backstreets and alleyways untouched by the Great Fire. The urban poor were a vital part of the ebb and flow of commercial life; numberless itinerant vendors, street criers, labourers, and odd-jobbers earned a precarious living. Illness, disability, and unexpected misfortune could tip such workers and their families into destitution. It was common practice for genteel people to keep separate accounts of the small coins given daily to beggars. As each shop closed for the day in the smarter parts of town, whole families bedded down for the night in the 'bulks' or wooden benches in the street, or in the haylofts,

FIGURE 1.1 An idealized view of eighteenth-century London. Canaletto (Giovanni Antonio Canal), *London: The Thames from Somerset House Terrace towards the City*, c.1750–1. Oil on canvas (1079 mm × 1880 mm).

stables, reeking middens, or dunghills where some degree of animal warmth could be found. In the early 1700s, parliament issued a series of severe penal codes in response to the petty larceny, assaults, shoplifting, and housebreaking that were associated with the desperate and the destitute.[18] Transportation to the colonies, branding, and imprisonment in a foul gaol were the common punishments for the poor and hungry. The gallows at Tyburn overshadowed the lives of those whose options were few.

Throughout the Georgian period, contemporaries realized that the growth of London was remarkable, although the poorer parishes tended to fare worst in terms of overcrowding and filthy living conditions. The cause of this population growth was not the fertility of Londoners. Many eighteenth-century commentators believed, not without some foundation, that the reproductive capacity of its citizens had been enfeebled by venereal disease.[19]

MISERIES OF LONDON.

FIGURE I.2 The reality: London's streets were crowded and chaotic, as depicted by a leading satirist of the age. Thomas Rowlandson, *Miseries of London*, 1807. Hand-coloured etching (292 mm × 400 mm).

The endemic presence of syphilis in the adult population certainly harmed fertility, although the fatal virulence of this sexually transmitted disease, which was first brought during Elizabethan times to England from South America, declined over the course of the 1700s. Other endemic diseases such as smallpox were not fatal to adults, but sufferers could have sickly infants who were unlikely to thrive in the absence of large-scale inoculation and effective medical treatment.[20] During the eighteenth century, infant mortality was in decline, but there was still a shockingly high peak of 450 deaths per 1,000 live births in the 1740s, falling to 250 per 1,000 by the 1770s, and 200 by 1800.[21] In spite of these overall improvements, by the end of the century relatively low levels of hygiene and nascent understanding of obstetrics still meant that many pregnancies ended with the death of either the mother, the unborn child, or both.

Everyone would have known someone who had perished in labour or had lost a child at or after birth. Miscarriage, stillbirth, and neonatal fatalities were often the by-products of poor nutrition and rudimentary obstetric and neonatal care. For a woman who haemorrhaged as a result of protracted labour, further bloodletting by doctors or the administration of 'cures' and poultices might actually hasten death. Many poorer women were cared for exclusively by midwives who relied upon traditional wisdom and first-hand experience. Midwives were often adept in handling complications such as breech births, but their options were few without the aid of modern medicines and surgery. Wealthier women of fashion were beginning to favour 'man-midwives', whose qualifications, licensed by the Royal Colleges, did not prevent bawdy contemporary commentary about the probings of male doctors into the female domain of gynaecology and obstetrics. In the second half of the eighteenth century, male obstetricians were starting to bring new techniques to the birthing chamber, but the use of new surgical instruments such as forceps delivery aroused many terrors, and were associated with desperate last-ditch attempts to save both mother and baby in cases of protracted labour.[22]

After 1750, the rise of the 'culture of sensibility' (which prized emotional expression and sincerity over polite formality) and its close kin, the Romantic movement, much beloved of artists and poets, placed new emphasis on emotional bonding between mother and child. Breastfeeding became fashionable among ladies of the social elite, but in general this was seen as normal practice only among working-class women. The practice of 'wet nursing' extended to orphaned and abandoned infants, farmed out at the expense of parish officials to be suckled by women who offered variable amounts of neglect. The foundling infants who are at the centre of this story were treated in ways that would be regarded as barbaric today, but such measures as feeding them on water and gruel from a dangerously young age, or experimental mixtures of 'pap' made from flour and dirty water, were not unusually reckless in the context of the day.[23]

High mortality rates among adults, children, and infants were a by-product of living in Georgian London. Weekly lists were published in the Bills of Mortality of those who suffered disease and death, litanies of the fatal conditions that often resulted from poor sanitation, inadequate medical care, and the easy contagion and filth of city life. Another restriction on population growth among Londoners was the relatively late age of marriage, which on average was in their mid- to late twenties for both single men and women. This was compounded by the relatively high proportion of people living in the metropolis at the start of the 1700s who never married, which was as many as one in ten of the population.[24] But neither high death rates, nor preference for the single life among a sizeable proportion of the population, hindered London's remarkable growth. The main cause of this was the magnet that it offered in terms of economic opportunity; the chance to enter domestic service in a household, learn a trade, and make money in countless other ways led to massive rural–urban migration from within the British Isles. Between 1750 and 1801, nearly 400,000 people migrated to London and the two neighbouring counties of Middlesex and Surrey. At the same time, 380,000 people moved out of a dozen rural counties, including Cambridgeshire in the south-east and the North Riding of Yorkshire. These areas experienced an even more catastrophic shrinking population in the first half of the nineteenth century, losing over 1 million people.[25] Successive waves of immigration from continental Europe into London, particularly refugees from religious persecution such as French Huguenots, and German Protestants from the Palatine region, added to the populousness of certain East End parishes. Immigrant communities also brought valuable skills that added to the industrious economy of the Capital, such as silk weaving and metal working.[26]

The young men and women who arrived from around the British Isles and from overseas had high hopes, seeking if not their fortunes then at least the chance to build up some savings so they could learn a trade, marry, and have a better life. As they walked the streets of London, they would have noticed that young faces outnumbered old. Average life expectancy was somewhere in the mid- to late thirties, so 'old' included anyone who made it past their fortieth birthday.[27] Removed from the communal scrutiny of the smaller face-to-face communities that were the mark of English rural life, apprentices notoriously ran wild, getting into binges of fraternal drinking and visiting prostitutes in the dark, furtive streets around Covent Garden, or the notorious 'stews' of Southwark. For unmarried girls, migration to London for a period of time in service, placed in the household with at least one other servant, was a common experience. While these young men and women 'at their own disposal' in London were perhaps freer than their rural cousins to choose an active role in courtship, the young women were also at greater risk of unwanted pregnancy and destitution. Terminology that would have been familiar to people at the time was that this was 'making shift' (that is, 'just about managing', sometimes described retrospectively by historians as a 'makeshift economy' to describe the hand-to-mouth existence of vagrants and other migrant people in crowded London and Middlesex parishes. Eighteenth-century parish poor relief has been called 'a rough and ready welfare system in miniature', in which 'benevolence, moral reform and economy marched together'.[28] It was also a 'mixed economy of welfare' in which parish relief operated alongside other institutional forms of help such as charities, guilds, and religious foundations, with a great deal of overlap in terms of who administered the relief and by what means.[29] In addition to parish doles, livery companies in the City of London issued regular hand-outs of bread, fuel, and clothing, and the City of London was the official guardian for those children whose fathers had been citizens of London but died before the children married or came of age. In such circumstances, an 'orphans' fund' was accessible to the few who met these conditions.[30]

Up to the mid-eighteenth century, one of the greatest evils facing the poorer ranks of society was the 'gin craze'. The appetite for cheap and noxious spirits consumed by the dram in drinking dens in the poorest neighbourhoods grew almost unchecked by parliament. Famously the artist William Hogarth featured health and prosperity on his imaginary 'Beer Street', which was built on good English ale, in contrast to the consumptive and murderous chaos of 'Gin Lane' (Figures 1.3 and 1.4) There was growing public awareness of the social problems that attended drunkenness caused by cheap gin. Crime, child neglect, and public disorder caused by gin that could be witnessed in the streets of London. Magistrates had warned the government as early as the 1720s that gin drinking was 'destructive of the lives, families, trades, and businesses...of the lower, poorer sort of the people', and constables calculated that over 6,000 houses and shops were selling spirits in the area outside

FIGURE 1.3 Good order and England's prosperity. William Hogarth, *Beer Street*, 1751. Engraving (560 mm × 450 mm).

FIGURE 1.4 Hogarth's famous depiction of the evils of gin drinking was published as a pair with *Beer Street*. Hogarth's graphic illustration of the effects of poverty and the sale of unlicensed spirits upon infants and children contributed to the passing of the Gin Act in 1751. William Hogarth, *Gin Lane*, 1751. Engraving (390 mm × 321 mm).

of the city walls in London, judged to be an underestimate given the difficulty in detecting all outlets in this 'pernicious' trade. Particular concern was expressed about the effect upon the children of the poor 'born weak and sickly, and often look shrivel'd and old...Others again daily give it to their children'. Neglected children became a burden on their parishes and turned to beggary and theft to make a living.[31]

Many social reformers, notably some who were inspired by their non-conformist Christian faith, such as Presbyterians, Baptists, and Quakers, campaigned for improvements to the conduct and morality of populations in London and urban areas of the 'inner empire' of the British Isles. Their campaigns mirrored at home the activities of those who planned for the betterment of society through the promotion of Christianity in the 'outer empire' (Britain's overseas colonial and dependent territories) in far-flung locations such as North America. Societies for the Reformation of Manners, encouraged by Queen Mary in the early 1690s, became especially popular among zealous non-conformists in Middlesex and the East End of London, a movement that also produced the Society for the Promotion of Christian Knowledge (SPCK). Reforming magistrates, at odds with the more easy-going morals of the population at large, took it upon themselves to hunt down and punish whoremongers, drunkards, Sabbath-breakers, and gamblers, whose numbers were legion.[32] Lobbying by Hogarth and many others for government intervention to place a tax upon gin and regulate the sale of spirituous liquors eventually led to an Act of Parliament in 1751. This social reform, undertaken by a reluctant administration, brought marked improvements to the fortunes of the London poor.[33]

Another response to the growing crisis of urban poverty was to produce industrial-scale solutions that were an alternative to 'outdoor relief' offered by parishes. In the wake of Charles Dickens's *Oliver Twist* (first published as a serial between 1837 and 1839) many people imagine it was the Victorians who invented workhouses, but in fact these institutions were familiar to the Georgians over a century earlier. The invention of the parish workhouse coincided with the growing centralization of state mechanisms to fund the fiscal-military state whose imperialist ambitions were reliant upon extracting maximum labour efficiency from its population.[34] As historian John Brewer has commented, 'even the most humble of [British] subjects became part of an economic order whose scope and complexity rendered it liable to fiscal measurement and vulnerable to wartime disruption'.[35]

The first workhouses appeared in the 1720s: by the mid-eighteenth century, London provided a range of institutions for the 'indigent poor', and almost seventy parish workhouses. Larger ones, like that of St Martin-in-the-Fields, accommodated 300 to 400 inmates mid-century, rising to 800 by the 1780s.[36] Before the New Poor Law of 1834, when the Victorians instituted workhouses in every town, of a size that was industrial in scale and organization, there were a small number of these notorious institutions, particularly in London. Before the nineteenth century, many parish workhouses were populated with the most vulnerable members of society: orphans, the sick, disabled, and elderly parishioners. Recent research has questioned whether 1834 marked as great a change in the approach to dealing with the problem of urban poverty as has sometimes been assumed.[37] This seems plausible, since outdoor relief continued in many parishes until the twentieth century, and elderly parishioners were still claiming their cherished rights to parish settlement in the lead-up to the First World War. Attitudes towards the 'undeserving' poor certainly hardened during the era of Samuel Smiles and his doctrine of self-help shaped many Victorian ratepayers' assumptions. But the idea that those who fell upon hard times had only themselves to blame had a much older lineage, dating back to Elizabethan times, and was certainly familiar to the Georgians.

Complementing parish relief in the eighteenth-century 'mixed economy of welfare' was help from charitable institutions funded by private subscription and donation. These had arisen out of religiously motivated Christian concerns to educate poor children, and look after women and children, the sick, the elderly, and the destitute. The Elizabethan founders of charity schools in the late 1500s had demonstrated the potential for combining private benefaction and public good. In response to the alarm at the number of beggars and 'masterless men' on the streets of London in Shakespeare's day, successive Lord Mayors took control on behalf of the City of London of four royal hospitals, which before the Reformation had been attached to monasteries. Of these, St Bartholomew's and St Thomas's were for the sick and elderly, and Bridewell was for vagrants and bankrupts. The mission of Christ's Hospital, founded in 1552, was to 'take oute of the streates all the fatherless children and other poor men's children, that were not able to keep them'. Over time, the practice of leaving foundling infants at Christ's Hospital was at first rationed, then discouraged altogether, since they constituted an additional burden upon local ratepayers, even though they may not have been born there.[38] These institutions continued to flourish in the eighteenth century, with the addition of new charitable foundations such as Magdalen Hospitals for the reform of prostitutes, Lock Hospitals specializing in venereal disease, and Lying-In Hospitals where expectant mothers could be safely delivered of their babies, and became the charities of choice for genteel and polite citizens.[39]

By the late seventeenth century, there was a new vogue for setting up charity schools. Charitable institutions funded by private subscription and donation became fashionable when Christian concerns to educate poor children, and look after women and children, the sick, the elderly, and the destitute, coincided with the growing centralization of the state.[40] It was in this context that Captain Thomas Coram, a man of honest but humble origins, came forward with a scheme that would help to solve London's growing social problems, and provide the manpower that was so desperately needed to sustain British imperial ambitions across the globe.

CHAPTER 2

'My Darling Project'

I N SEPTEMBER 1740, an elderly Thomas Coram took up his quill pen with an uncertain hand and began a letter to a clergyman friend in Boston, New England about matters closest to his heart. He was not a fluent writer, finding it difficult to achieve the quality of expression and penmanship that was expected of a gentleman in his day. He apologized frequently for his lack of education ('I am no Judge in Learning I understand no Lattin, nor English nither, well').[1] Thomas began this particular letter in the autumn of 1740 by breaking the news that Eunice, his beloved American wife of forty years, had recently died after a long illness ('By her Death I am bereaved of one of the best of Wives'). In his public life, he had a tendency to become embroiled in conflict, but Eunice had been one of the few people with whom he could live in peace. Her widower testified that she had always been a sincere Christian 'of an humble meek and Quiet Spirit' and 'never once

gave me Cause to be angry with her'. Theirs had been a close relationship but they had never had children, and Eunice devoted her
life to caring exclusively for her husband. Whenever he reflected
upon grief and death, Thomas had a stock phrase which he used to
comfort himself and others: he prayed that God would 'Sanctify
this Stroke to me'. His wife's death was a blow, but one to which he
submitted like any other loss, since it was brought about by divine
providence.[2] He believed it was also providential that his childless
state enabled him to devote his energies to causes that were well
beyond the purview of private, domestic concerns.

Having delivered the heartrending news of his wife's passing,
Coram introduced to his correspondent the subject of 'my Darling
project', the cause that had preoccupied him for the best part
of eighteen years: 'the Establishment of ... the Hospital for the
Maintenance and Education of Expos'd and Deserted Young
Children', commonly known as the Foundling Hospital. It was said
that he had been inspired to do something to help the infant poor
of London having seen 'exposed and deserted' babies in the public
streets on his daily walk from Rotherhithe to the City.[3] Whether or
not this was true, it captured something of the shockingly poor conditions into which many of London's most vulnerable citizens were
born, and the story resonated with many of the charity's donors.

The idea of a foundling hospital had been discussed in the public
prints for many years before Thomas Coram's philanthropy and
determination brought the project to fruition. It was widely known
among educated Londoners that cities such as Florence, Paris, and
Lisbon had institutions that took in abandoned infants, with babies
'found' (hence 'foundling') outside places set up for this purpose.
They were admitted without discrimination, since the primary

concern of these 'hospitals' (a name applied to charities in general as well as to places for curing the sick) was baptism and the saving of souls.[4] As early as 1713, Richard Steele (co-editor of the *Spectator*, the most influential periodical published before modern times) had written in favour of 'a Provision for Foundlings', an institution to care for children who 'for want of such a provision are exposed to the Barbarity of cruel and unnatural Parents'.[5] 'Multitudes of Infants', Steele claimed, had been murdered 'by those who brought them into the World', being either ashamed at their illegitimate birth, or unable to provide for their upkeep. Institutional neglect rather than murder had long been the English way of dealing with unwanted infants and children.[6] By the late 1600s, abandonment of infants was an increasing social problem; as many as 1,000 were left on the streets to fend for themselves every year in London alone.[7] Georgian England presented almost unimaginable hardship for the poor, and those parents who were barely surviving themselves had few choices. To eighteenth-century commentators, it seemed that the number of cases of child neglect and abandonment were getting worse, prompting cries for something to be done.

Thomas Coram's world-view was shaped as a footsoldier of empire, a well-travelled man of relatively humble origins who was used to undertaking huge and ambitious projects in the interests of the British state. An experienced mariner, administrator, schemer, and colonist, he shunned the fashions that had so many of his contemporary Londoners in thrall, with no time for periwigs or fancy waistcoats. His famous portrait by the artist William Hogarth, executed in 1740 (the same year that Coram's wife died), shows that the septuagenarian Coram wore not a false wig but his own thick, white hair. His ruddy complexion and pleasant but careworn face told of a life of hard work. Thomas's garb was the sensible brown, worsted cloth that denoted a sturdy yeoman farmer or trusted head steward of a country estate. In one hand he holds tightly to a glove (which since this was the mark of a gentleman was perhaps a witty comment by the artist that Coram had the gentry 'in his clutches'), and in the other the precious Royal Charter granting permission to build the Foundling Hospital, a project that took him seventeen years to realize (Figure 2.1). Even in old age, Coram had the energy of a much younger man, and boasted of his rude health and ability to walk 10

FIGURE 2.1 The Foundling Hospital's founder, Thomas Coram. A plain-speaking and passionate advocate for social reform, he also alienated powerful men who were used to more polite and deferential treatment. William Hogarth, *Captain Thomas Coram*, 1740. Oil on canvas: full-length portrait (2387 mm × 1473 mm).

or 12 miles a day. Like many Georgians, he was constantly devising new schemes of improvement and lobbying influential men in order to improve efficiency, save money, and place Britain's prosperity upon a surer foundation.

Thomas Coram was born during the reign of Charles II, in or around the year 1668, and was a native of Dorset, the son of obscure but honest folk (or, as Coram put it himself, 'Famelies of Strict hon'r and honesty and always of Good Reputation amongst the better sort of people'). He had been given the honorary title of 'Captain' following a lifetime of working as a shipwright and procurer of supplies for His Majesty's Navy, and he had risen in the world upon his merits. As a young man in his twenties, he had lived in Taunton, Massachusetts, working in the shipyards. He then moved to Boston and became a ship's master, engaged in the procurement of timber and other supplies for the Navy. In 1704 he promoted an Act of Parliament to encourage tar manufacture in the British Atlantic seaboard colonies of North America. He argued passionately with anyone who would listen that this would provide employment, save money on expensive imported tar from Sweden, and procure an essential supply for rendering British ships watertight.[8] By 1720, the year of the South Sea Bubble, he had returned to London to work at the Admiralty, where not long before Samuel Pepys the famous diarist had forged his career. By 1732, he had proved his worth to the king's ministers to the extent that George II appointed him one of the trustees of the newly formed state of Georgia, charged with devising a system of colonization. He took a keen interest in British concerns in Nova Scotia for its rich stocks of

cod and timber, and in Maine, where he had proposed a scheme
(ultimately without success) for the settlement of discharged soldiers
from the War of Spanish Succession.[9] Later in life, his enterprises
included lobbying for the foundation of a bank that would assist
New Englanders travelling to London, and in the supply of mis-
sionaries to the outposts of Britain's emergent 'second empire' in
India. Coram dedicated his life to being a good patriot. He was
wedded to the creation of a fiscal-military state dedicated not only
to expanding Britain's colonies, but to promoting the education
of 'heathens' in the Christian faith. For him, the British imperial
project was as much about saving souls as about increasing national
prosperity. Coram and many of his contemporaries had no qualms
about this twofold mission.[10]

Concerns over respecting the other cultures of indigenous peoples
tended not to cross the minds of eighteenth-century Britons, although
the treatment of Native American tribes troubled Coram, who lobbied for their compensation for damage done by British settlers to
their lands.[11] Some of Coram's enterprises succeeded, and an equal
number failed, but he was indefatigable in his ambition to use all of
his energies in being useful and profitable to his country. Coram was
judged by Horace Walpole, MP, the youngest son of Prime Minister
Sir Robert Walpole, to be 'the honestest, the most disinterested, and
the most knowing persons about the plantations'.[12] His tireless and
forthright lobbying for the schemes about which he was so passionate
was conducted in the salty language of the shipyard, which earned
him a reputation in polite London circles for plain-speaking and
unvarnished honesty. His arguments, it was noted following his
death in 1751, were *'nervous'* (that is, full of feeling) 'tho' not *nice'*,
with the additional disadvantage in political and diplomatic circles

that his ideas were 'founded commonly upon *Facts*'. In an age when polite circumlocution was required to get on in the world, Thomas talked 'plain Sense, his Eloquence [was] the Natural Language of the Heart', qualities that won him many friends, and not a few enemies.[13] His few surviving letters confirm that he was indeed forthright: perhaps his Christian faith as well as his own idea of common sense gave him the boldness to tell uncomfortable truths to powerful men. One of the few surviving examples of his original handwriting is a hastily scribbled note to the duke of Newcastle, begging to be admitted to the ducal presence in order that Coram could disclose 'some pernicious Frauds and abuses Continually practised in some of the Northern Parts of New England greatly to ye Prejudice of the Crown and preventing the Increase of Settlements in those parts'. Coram as he wrote this was waiting impatiently (adding a footnote '[I'm] Now in the Hall'), frustrated at the hindrance to the development of His Majesty's North American colonies that these alleged frauds were presenting.[14] His habit of plain speaking had led to his ejection from the governing board of the state of Georgia, and was a foretaste of the difficulties that lay ahead in his greatest charitable project, the London Foundling Hospital.

The obstacles that Thomas Coram faced in getting his charity up and running were legion. Apathy and a prevailing *laissez-faire* attitude characterized the reaction of the ruling elite to social problems. There were objections that an institution established to take care of the problem of abandoned children, including illegitimate ones, would encourage idleness among the labouring poor (since people would not have to work to maintain their children), promote immorality (by encouraging extramarital sex, since any resulting illegitimate baby could be sent to the Foundling Hospital), and be a disincentive to marriage. More subtly, some argued that it might be a 'great inconvenience...to the government to breed up a set of people so unconnected by any ties of relation or friendship'. Not having experienced family life, they would feel no investment in society, so the argument went, and they would be so badly raised that there would be little hope that they would ever become 'useful members of society'.[15] Coram tried to win sponsors but failed at first. 'I found it was Impossible to be done', he complained in later years, not mincing his words as was his customary manner:

> I could no more prevaile on any Arch Bishop or Bishop or Nobleman Britain or Foreigner or any other Great Man...to speak to the Late King [George I] or his present Majesty on this affair than I could have prevailed with any of them...to have putt doun their Breeches and present their Backsides to the King and Queen in a full Drawing room.[16]

Having tried and failed repeatedly to secure the backing of the great and good, Coram resorted to 'round about Wayes' to make it happen. Timing was critical. The Anglo-Irish poet Jonathan Swift was an influential commentator on the social ills of Dublin, which he witnessed as Dean of St Patrick's Cathedral. In 1729, he launched an outspoken attack on the endless discussion (but little action) on the problem of child poverty by publishing his *Modest Proposal for Preventing the Children of Poor People from Being a Burthen to Their Parents or Country and for Making Them Beneficial to the Publick*. This vitriolic pamphlet captured exactly the tone of public debates about the benefits and drawbacks of helping destitute but unwed mothers. His satire exposed the hypocrisy of a Christian society that did little to help the poor, but which enjoyed prolonged debates over the morality of sanctioning sexual 'vice', and abstract calculations about the public utility of human life. With a deliberately provocative intention, Swift's proposed solution in the *Modest Proposal* was to fatten up infants as a delicacy for the tables of the rich, thus making them 'useful'.

Perhaps shamed into action, in the following year, the Dublin parliament decreed that all foundling children should be admitted to the workhouse, which was henceforth to be known as the Foundling Hospital and Workhouse of the City of Dublin. Archbishop Boulter, Primate of All Ireland, was the first chairman of the Governors, who resolved to adopt the practice commonly used on the Continent for receiving babies anonymously into orphanages, with no questions asked about whether they had been born in wedlock. They found that the tried and tested methods for anonymously handing over infants to orphanages across Europe differed from city to city. In Italy alone, there were many different systems, developed over centuries since the foundation of medieval charitable orphanages. In Venice, abandoned newborns were left in a little boat, accessed through a discreet and narrow alley; in Naples, a revolving wheel was set up, enabling the baby to be deposited outside of the orphanage and spun inside without the person leaving the baby being seen. At the famous *Ospedale degli Innocenti* in Florence, a basin for depositing babies of the type used to hold holy water in churches was placed in an arcade beyond the orphanage walls. The Dublin Foundling Hospital chose to adopt its own version of these systems by placing a revolving basket at their gate.[17]

Swift's shock tactics in Ireland, and the launch of the Dublin Foundling Hospital, doubtless contributed to the increasing pressure upon English authorities to undertake a similar campaign of improvement to alleviate the condition of poor infants and children.

Another influential voice for change was Rev. Thomas Bray, a reforming clergyman and founding member of the Society for the Promotion of Christian Knowledge (SPCK). Like Coram, Bray's first-hand experience of empire building and reform had been forged in the American colonies. Coram knew Bray personally, and had a similar wish to convert both English colonists and Native Americans to Christianity. Via the philanthropic ventures and fundraising activities of the SPCK, Bray had succeeded in establishing over 1,400 charity schools by the 1720s using funds from multiple benefactors. His approach was similar to 'joint stock' ventures that made the schools more likely to succeed, since they were not reliant upon a single charitable donor.[18] The clergyman had also written a pamphlet concerning the foundation of a hospital for orphans and foundlings, which had so impressed Coram that he donated a copy to Harvard University Library. In this work, Bray had noted the influence of 'Princesses and Dutchessess, and other Ladies of the Prime Nobility' in establishing such an institution in Paris in 1640.[19] In Georgian England, many seekers after patronage knew that high-born women could exert considerable influence with their husbands and male relatives, and their choices as charitable donors in their own right were highly strategic. Doing good works was of a piece with the expectations of a pious Christian woman, particularly in relation to those charities that supported the plight of destitute women and children.

Having been given the brush-off by the powerful men he had approached to help his foundling cause, it is not surprising therefore that Coram, in his own words, 'bethought himself at last of applying to the Ladies'. This change of tactics brought immediate success. Coram's breakthrough moment was to secure the support of Charlotte Finch, the young duchess of Somerset, as the first signatory to a petition addressed to George II, urging the King to approve a charter that would establish the Foundling Hospital. The duke of Somerset had been the patron of Henry Newman, a native of New England and secretary of the SPCK, whose interests and social circles brought him into Thomas Coram's close acquaintance. The Somersets were of a rank and wealth to place them above suspicion with regard to the duchess's support for the cause.[20] She was followed as a signatory by Ann, duchess of Boulton, who also enlisted her mother-in-law. A roll-call of twenty-one fashionable and aristocratic women followed, most of whom were the daughters of dukes, marquesses, earls, or barons.[21]

The willingness of elite women to sign up to Coram's petition reflected the tenets of Christian charity deemed appropriate for their own sex, but also had personal resonance. Some had husbands who were well-known womanizers with many illegitimate children by different mistresses, while others had first-hand experience of unorthodox family arrangements. The dowager duchess of Bolton, *née* Henrietta Needham, also an early signatory, was herself the illegitimate daughter of the duke of Monmouth, the bastard son of Charles II. Aristocrats had their own moral codes that were different from those of the gentry and middling sorts, but it would be wrong to imply that their own experiences of sexual betrayal and illegitimacy gave them special identification with the cause of 'foundlings'.[22]

The illegitimate granddaughter of a king might as well have been living on a different planet to the bastard offspring of the London poor, their worlds were so different. What mattered to Coram was that aristocratic women were highly influential, well connected, and of impeccable reputation, married to powerful and wealthy men with direct access to political power, both at court and in parliament.

Once he had secured the backing of influential female patrons, Coram took advantage of the new mechanisms that existed in the City of London to centralize fundraising. He set up an arrangement with a banker in Charing Cross to establish an account so that funds could be raised to pay for drafting the Royal Charter, which he publicized as being supported by 'some great Ladies', the Lord Mayor of London, an alderman, and the duke of Bedford. Renewing his efforts in the mid-1730s with a second petition to George II, he used the availability of printing presses in the metropolis to advertise the charity by printed letter and in the newspapers, sending invitations to 'Ladies of Quality' in their country estates, and hoping to attract benefactors from the middle ranks of society (the professions and wealthy merchants in particular) through the association of the charity with prestigious names:

> Several Ladies of Quality and Other Persons, having Earnestly recommended the erecting and supporting an HOSPITAL for FOUNDLINGS, in or near *London*, where it is so much wanted, to prevent the frequent Murders of innocent Children at their Birth, by the Hands of their own Parents, to hide their Shame, beside other fatal Consequences, as breeding up Thieves, Robbers, Murders &c. to the great Reproach of the *British* Nation...It is therefore humbly recommended to compassionate

and well dispos'd Persons, to assist by their Bounty in defraying the said Expence [*of drawing up a Royal Charter*] . . . for bringing so necessary an Establishment to effect.[23]

Some 'weak persons' (mostly ladies, Coram observed somewhat ungratefully) had argued that such a foundation would be 'a promotion of Wickedness', the implication being that widespread promiscuity would result from providing the means of raising bastard children without consequences. 'They who admitted the evil questioned the remedy, and doubted whether it might not prove greater than the disease', as one Victorian commentator later observed.[24] Coram had appealed directly to 'Learned men of the universitys' to write something that would convince potential benefactors that the Foundling Hospital would not be an incentive to vice, but they 'all excused themselves'. The support of noblewomen had galvanized their male relatives into action, but royal assent was still required.

In 1737, Coram's petition to George II put in unequivocal terms the cause for which he had lobbied for so long. Using powerful rhetoric, Coram played upon the elite's worst fears about the widespread moral and social degradation among the urban poor that they glimpsed on the occasions that they strayed beyond the safer confines of privilege. If not deliberately murdered at birth by unfeeling parents, foundlings might be given over by the parish to 'wicked and barbarous Nurses' who would starve and neglect them, or be given up to gangs of beggars who might deliberately disfigure their bodies in order to gain more sympathy from charitable passers-by. The petition even succeeded in the royal household and was received with particular sympathy by Queen Caroline, a shrewd and intelligent woman who had much influence with her husband. Her close circle of ladies-in-waiting included Sarah, Duchess of Richmond, her lady of the bedchamber, who was a signatory to the Foundling Hospital petition. The Queen showed a particular interest in the cause, to the extent that she requested particulars of the running of the Paris Foundling Hospital.[25]

Though it took him nearly two decades, it is remarkable that Thomas Coram, a man of modest social rank and few polite manners, eventually succeeded, having negotiated the complex web of personal and familial ties of allegiance and patronage through which power was mediated in eighteenth-century elite circles. But there were more frustrations: lawyers obfuscated in drawing up the Royal Charter, and the death of the Queen in November 1737 delayed things further. George II received a list of 375 potential Governors, about half of whom expressed a wish to be active in the governance of the Hospital rather than merely titular or honorary signatories. The Royal Charter for the foundation of the Hospital was finally granted in October 1739. Now in his seventy-third year, and with an understandable degree of pride, Coram declared 'I am Strong and pretty Successful'. He recorded in his own words that the Royal Charter was passed ('I got an Act of Parliament for Confirming and enlarging the Powers therein Granted'). The extraordinary scale and success of Coram's fundraising efforts were evident: 'We have between 5 and 6000 pounds in Cash paid in, 326 annual Subscriptions and [£]2300 Legacies not yet received'. Thomas had personally secured the signatures or consent of 172 out of the 375 men nominated to the Privy Council as Hospital Governors.[26]

The newly appointed Foundling Hospital Governors drew prestige from their aristocratic members under the leadership of the first president, the duke of Bedford, and created a general council of eminent patrons who were happier to lend their names and make donations than to attend numerous meetings. Thomas Coram was frustrated that the delay in starting to construct purpose-built premises was hindering further donations. The Governors went to some trouble to find temporary premises for the Hospital: an early offer of rented accommodation at Montague House had come to nothing. Once the charity had found suitable temporary accommodation in Hatton Garden, the necessary arrangements were made to appoint nurses, a physician, an apothecary, and servants, and to purchase linens, infant clothing, and basic furniture. Finally, Coram's vision for a Foundling Hospital would be realized.

On 4 March 1741, the Governors of the London Foundling Hospital approved a public advertisement that announced the details of how the first infants would be admitted:

> On Wednesday 25th of this instant March at eight at night and from that time until the house is full, their house over against the charity school in Hatton Garden will be open for children under the following regulations: that no child exceed in age two months nor shall have the French Pox [syphilis] or disease of like nature; all children to be inspected and the person who brings it to come in at the outer door and not to go away until the child is returned or notice given of its reception. No question asked whatsoever of any person who brings a child, nor shall any servant of the Hospital presume to enquire on pain of being dismissed.[27]

For the Georgians, the idea of female virtue and virginity was something for the respectable ranks of the 'middling sorts' (the forerunners of the Victorian middle classes) to obsess over, particularly in the novels of the day. For working women, having an illegitimate child was regarded more as bad luck or misfortune, perhaps the result of sex following the promise of marriage, in which the couple chanced their luck. In the face of unexpected disaster, such as the man losing his employment, or being seized by a press gang, setting up a household became impossible for couples, and many poverty-stricken unmarried women who had consummated a relationship on the promise of marriage were left holding the baby.[28] Separation from an infant for whom they could not provide was a desperate decision for a new mother, and the process took place under the cover of darkness. It is highly likely that the stigma of sexual shame was less of a pressing issue for them than the emotional distress of separation from their newborns.

Word quickly spread that the Foundling Hospital was open, and crowds thronged at the gates on the night of 25 March. The first admissions took place in the presence of assembled Governors and dignitaries, including that first night the duke of Richmond and Captain Coram himself. The voices of the stricken mothers who gave up their infants on that night and hundreds like it subsequently are hard to recover. Some fragments of their testimonies, preserved from the time when the Hospital later introduced a policy of receiving written accounts of the circumstances of mothers, give some idea of their predicament:

The most humble Petition of Mary Cole, seduc'd & reduc'd...the Person who is the Cause of my Misfortunes has deceiv'd me and is gone abroad, by the best Intelligence I can have. He made me a promise of Marriage, with many Vows and Protestations, before I unhappily yielded to his Solicitations, by which I am now brought to this Miserable Condition, depriv'd of the Esteem and regard of my friends, and relations, destitute of many Necessaries...Having no dependence (when able to work) but my daily Labour, and not able to provide for my Child.[29]

On the first night that the London Foundling Hospital opened, thirty children were admitted, eighteen boys and twelve girls. 'The Expressions of Grief of the Women whose Children could not be admitted were Scarcely more observable than those of some of the Women who parted with their Children', noted the Secretary, who recorded the proceedings that day, adding 'a more moving Scene can't well be imagined'. Of those who witnessed first-hand the moment when mothers surrendered their newborns to the Hospital authorities, 'none went away without shewing most Sensible Marks of Compassion for the helpless Objects of this Charity and few (if any) without contributing something for their Relief'.[30]

Further newspaper advertisements informed the public upon which days infants were to be taken into the Hospital in batches of twenty. Numbers grew even greater over time, so that eventually folk thronged from early in the morning on admission days, in numbers that the Governors had not foreseen. To the crush was added the gathered crowd of paying visitors who came to watch the spectacle of admission day, distinguished by their fashionable dress from those they had come to view (Figure 2.2). Mothers arrived with their babies in such numbers that a ballot was soon introduced, administered by means of a bag containing white and black balls.

FIGURE 2.2   Admission day at the Foundling Hospital. Crowds of paying visitors came to watch the spectacle of admission day, distinguished by their fashionable dress from those they had come to view. Nathaniel Parr, *An Exact Representation of the Form and Manner in which Exposed and Deserted Young Children Are Admitted into the Foundling Hospital*, 1749. Engraving (560 mm × 620 mm).

Bearing their newborn babies, each woman stepped forward in turn to draw a ball from the bag. If the mother chose a white ball at random, her child would be admitted. The baby was taken from her immediately and an inspection was carried out by a nurse and an apothecary to make sure that the infant was free from infectious disease and under two months of age. If all went according to plan, the mother would not see her baby again. A black ball meant she was turned away with her baby, while a red ball placed the mother in an anteroom, waiting to see whether her turn would come if an infant admitted with a white ball was later rejected.

This spectacle had a peculiar drama and poignancy for the genteel spectators, but from the perspective of the pauper mothers who had only recently given birth, this lottery system was just another layer to the element of chance that governed their lives. The local authorities in Holborn and neighbouring parishes feared that women who were 'blackballed' would abandon their babies and cause additional expense to the parish ratepayers. They therefore posted additional watchmen and constables to be vigilant near the gate. Though this proved an unnecessary precaution for the majority, on 1 April 1741, the authorities apprehended and sent to Bridewell Prison a disappointed woman who had left her baby behind in the street to be taken to the parish workhouse.[31]

At the moment of separation, mothers left tokens with their babies, usually an everyday item such as a key, a charm or button, a broken coin, or even a hazelnut, so that they could identify their child should they ever be in a position to come and reclaim them (Figure 2.3). The Governors had promised that 'If any particular marks are left with the child great care will be taken for their preservation'.[32]

The use of identifying tokens was a well-known practice adopted by the London Foundling Hospital, and had a deep history rooted in the ancient world and in Catholic orphanages across Europe that is worth dwelling on in some detail. Many of these tokens survive today, and provide a tangible and immediate connection between the children given up to be raised in the Hospital, their parents, and the fact that we can view and perhaps even handle them. How we understand and interpret what these tokens meant to the mothers

FIGURE 2.3 In a custom adopted from other foundling hospitals on the continent, mothers left a token with their babies—a key, a charm or button, a broken coin, c.1700s.

who surrendered their babies, never to see them again, is fraught with emotion (both theirs and our own) and difficulties in reaching across over 250 years of separation between them and us.

Love and care for human infants might appear to be a universal value, but attitudes towards babies have varied over time, shaped by social and cultural practices and economic conditions. Spiritual belief played a role in determining the fate of infants, since they embodied cultural ideas and practices surrounding fertility, both of land and people. In communities with a small settler population, largely rural, such as colonial New England, barrenness was stigmatized and child abandonment was less common: survival was a priority and all hands were needed to grow food and increase the labour force.[33] The practice of sacrificing newborns as offerings to appease angry and vengeful gods can be traced to prehistoric times in Europe, Asia, and Oceania. Exposure of unwanted babies was certainly known to the ancient Greeks and Romans, particularly if infants were suffering from disabilities, or if they had the misfortune to be born female. Such practices were not considered murder since these tiny fatalities resulted from supposedly natural causes, such as dehydration and hypothermia. Cultural familiarity with the exposure of infants gave rise in classical antiquity to stories about lost children and their dramatic recovery that were well known to educated Europeans in later generations, and it is here that we find the origins of the association between tokens and identifying 'lost' infants.

The famous pastoral tale *Daphnis and Chloe* was much beloved of bad painters and poets of the eighteenth century, when frolicsome love stories between shepherds and shepherdesses were in vogue. Set on the island of Lesbos in the second century AD, the eponymous duo are abandoned as infants with identifying tokens (a motif that recurred time and again in the history of foundlings, both real and imagined), but are rescued by a shepherd and a goatherd, and raised in idyllic simplicity as childhood companions. They innocently fall in love and overcome obstacles, including the heroine Chloe's abduction by sailors and rescue by the god Pan. The pair's true identities are soon discovered, and they are able to marry, having been reclaimed by their respective parents, who turn out conveniently to be high-born and wealthy. Another ancient Greek story known as the *Aethiopica* (the 'Ethiopian Tale') by Heliodorus, an epic romance dating to the third or fourth century, was well known to Renaissance scholars across Europe. Chariclea, a female infant, was abandoned. This time, the 'token' left with the baby was a cloth embroidered by her mother. After a series of adventures, during which time Theagenes, a nobleman, falls in love with her, the cloth's mysterious 'Ethiopian characters' are deciphered and reveal the girl's true identity as no less than the daughter of Persinna, queen of Ethiopia. The queen had given up her fair-skinned child for fear she would be suspected of adultery, since she and her husband were dark-skinned, although ancient medicine supplied a plausible rationale for this quirk of fate.[34] In both of these tales, the moment of recognition (*anagnorisis*) becomes the vehicle for uncovering the central plot in the drama, which relies upon uncovering the mysterious 'true' identity of an orphaned or abandoned child, hinging upon the possibility of surprise and the satisfying moment of revelation which would have restored the 'natural' social order and a sigh of relief amongst the audience.

From the eleventh century, Catholic religious orders had cared for the poor, foundlings, and orphans, and had used a system of tokens as identifying markers, a practical solution in centuries when literacy levels were almost non-existent among the poor. One such foundation was established in 1070 in Montpellier, France, run by an order known as the *Hospitalarii Sancti Spiritus* (hence 'hospital' meant not just 'a place for the sick' as in modern times, but a place of hospitality and succour).[35] In early thirteenth-century Rome, Pope Innocent III was moved by the plight of sick infants thrown into the River Tiber to perish. By the end of the thirteenth century there were more than 100 'hospitals' of the *Ordre Hospitalier du Saint-Esprit* across Europe, including foundations in France, Italy, Belgium, Switzerland, Germany, Poland, Ireland, and Spain. Several of these institutions, originally at Florence, and then at Amsterdam and Paris, had adopted the practice of preserving identifying tokens with infants upon admission, and influenced the London Foundling Hospital Governors to adopt a similar system.[36]

The variety of tokens left with infants at the London Foundling Hospital is astonishing, and often deeply moving. Up until the late 1750s not all babies were received with tokens, and those who were had a range of objects left with them. Later, the vast majority of tokens were in the form of textiles. When admissions were at their height in the late 1750s and early 1760s, identifying snippets of cloth were removed from the infant's clothing by the Hospital authorities. These have been described by historian John Styles as the most significant surviving textile collection from the eighteenth century, with some 5,000 individual items documenting the everyday clothing of pauper women.[37] Sometimes they were drab remnants of clothing, linsey-woolsey (a mixture of linen and wool), cambley or fustian (coarse woollen cloth), the workaday dress of the poor recycled as baby clothes. The collection includes more luxurious fabrics—highly coloured and expensive slips of silk, satin, or high-quality linen decorated with flowers or patterns. Perhaps these signified better-off mothers fallen upon hard times, but more likely the mother of an illegitimate baby could simply be the servant of a well-to-do woman who had benefitted from her mistress's hand-me-downs. Tokens could even be colourful and elaborate: silk ribbons, a 'cockade' rosette for a little boy resembling the badge on a soldier's hat, or a 'top-knot' bunch of ribbons to adorn the head of a small infant girl. Ribbons were common love gifts between courting couples and suggested a strong emotional bond between mothers and their infants.[38] The clothing samples (or even sometimes a complete baby's cap or tiny sleeve) were neatly pinned to the bureaucratic billet (admission form) with its formulaic typeface and checklist ticked to show the items that the baby was wearing upon admission (Figure 2.4).[39] Whatever personal tokens had been left with the baby as a mark of distinction, whatever handcrafted embroidery lovingly wrought to identify the child with its own name and personality, these were removed once he or she was taken in, and each foundling was placed in identical clothing to the others.[40]

Some infants had already been baptised before they were admitted, as explanatory notes left with some babies indicated. But whatever name had been given to the child before entry to the Hospital was also immediately replaced. He or she now belonged to the Hospital, and was entered into the general registers, baptised by a Church of England minister with a new name that was symbolic of their new life under the guardianship of the Hospital's Governors. The pragmatic rationale was that double baptism (a heretical practice in some theological circles) was preferable to none at all. The first two infants to be admitted were baptised with the names Thomas Coram and Eunice Coram. The little boy, about two weeks old, was 'cleanly dressed, wrapped in a red cloak'. It was 'numbered 18 in the general register', since each foundling was given a serial

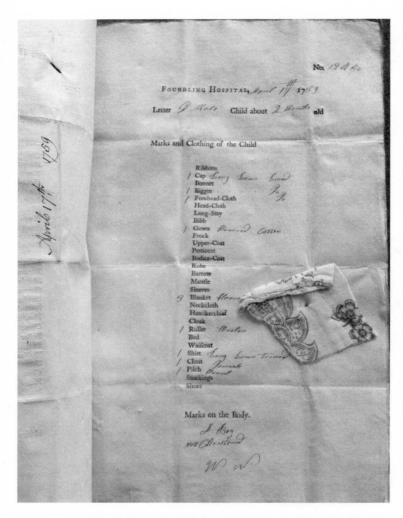

FIGURE 2.4 Descriptions of each infant admitted to the Foundling Hospital were recorded in the billet book, with samples taken of the clothing the infant was wearing on the day they were taken in. This page records a boy admitted at about two months old on 17 April 1759, wearing a flowered cotton gown. He had not been christened, and was given the number 12,450.

number to aid identification. Parish workhouses also had a system for administering serial numbers upon admission, but these were usually not in strict order, and workhouse record keeping was patchy by comparison. Foundling Hospital clerks were few in number, but highly efficient, executing their duties with a great deal of care, no doubt mindful of their accountability to the Hospital's powerful Governors.[41]

Sadly, neither of the infants Thomas and Eunice survived for long, although other babies were named in honour of the Foundling Hospital's founder and his wife, some of whom did survive.[42] Other dignitaries lent their names to infants admitted: Sarah and Charles Richmond were named after the duke and duchess of Richmond, and babies were also baptised William and Jane Hogarth. Bestowing a grand name such as George Grenville (who became prime minister in the early 1760s) or John Montagu (after the duke of Montagu) started as an honorific with regard to the respected patrons of the Hospital, but the practice was stopped when some of the children later claimed they were related to their namesakes. Instead, the whimsies of godparents and clergy started to be indulged. A Clarissa Harlowe, named after the heroine in Samuel Richardson's famous novel *Clarissa* (1748), appears in the general register, as does a David Garrick, named after the famous actor and theatre impresario.

There is a parallel in the fanciful names given to foundlings and the common eighteenth-century practice of naming African slaves after the heroes and heroines of classical antiquity. 'Dido' was a contemporary case in point, a woman of African descent born into slavery and raised as a ward of Lord Mansfield at Kenwood House.[43] While foundlings were not born into slavery, and their ethnicity generally meant that they could 'pass' invisibly in a way in which black people on the streets of Georgian London could not choose to do, distinctive names marked them for life. The ridicule suffered by one young lad apprenticed by the Hospital to a paper-maker in York who laboured under the name of Augustus Caesar can only be imagined.[44] During the 1750s and early 1760s, as nominal flights of fancy by the educated were overtaken by the practicalities of naming a large number of children, more everyday names were given to foundlings, such as Mary Hall (no. 17,664) and Daniel Clutterbuck (no. 18,841). There is some evidence that a small number of the infants admitted as foundlings were black or born of mixed-race parents, although caution is needed when interpreting documents in this regard since the description as 'a black boy' could mean a boy with black hair. Other contemporary terms such as 'negro' or 'mulatto' are less ambiguous, such as the 'mulotta Boy, with Black Hair' admitted in March 1755, who was baptised with the name Henry Agincourt.[45] Mary Lamas was admitted in October 1758 and was returned to the Hospital suffering from smallpox in October 1763. She was apprenticed in January 1768 to William Frankling of Leadenhall Street, described as 'a black cook in the West India trade'. Mary herself may have been black or mixed race, although there is no description of her appearance in the documentation from when she was admitted to the Foundling Hospital as an infant. It is also ambiguous whether her master was himself black, or whether his job was to cook for the slaves onboard a slave ship (hence 'black cook').[46] Catherine Beecher, who worked as a Hospital servant, was said to be 'a beautiful Girl with a countenance truly Egyptian', a parallel with the biblical Pharaoh's daughter or even Cleopatra. These comparisons were often used to describe girls and women of African descent, though to describe them in this way meant that their heritage was as undifferentiated in the eyes of English commentators as Shakespeare's 'Moor'.[47] Ideas about racial identity changed in the course of the eighteenth and early nineteenth centuries. with a growing pseudo-scientific literature on supposedly inherent differences between ethnicities increasingly used to justify white racial superiority. It was not until 1819 that applicants to the Hospital for a child's admission had to state whether 'the child is of colour'.[48]

Giving each baby a name upon admission to the Hospital stripped him or her of another vestige of their identity, just as their clothes and tokens left by their mothers were taken away. There is evidence many of these infants were neither unwanted nor unloved. Sometimes maternal love was expressed through handwritten notes left with babies at the Hospital. If a woman was able to write, or could persuade someone to write it for her, there might be a note giving the circumstances of the child's birth, his or her given name, and the promise that the baby would be reclaimed one day. A typical example is the note left with foundling no. 8,959: 'Florella Burney Born june the 19: 1,758: In the Parish off St. Anns SoHo. Not Baptize'd, pray Let porticulare care be take'en off this child, As it will be call'd for Again'.[49] Any promise that the child would be 'Call'd for again' was to prove a futile hope for the vast majority of parents: fewer than 200 children were reclaimed alive before the mid-1800s, usually by their birth mothers. Many who returned to claim their children discovered that they had died in infancy.[50] Two of the first babies admitted died even before they could be baptised, 'too weak to Suck, or receive Nourishment'.[51]

The fragments of detail about the circumstances of birth also tell us more about the personal stories behind the formal, bureaucratic details of admission. A letter left with child no. 6,527 on 4 December 1757 read 'This little Innocent is the darling offspring of an unhappy but truly virtuous woman by the fondest husband who is born of a good family and may one time or other be able to show his gratitude to this noble charity'.[52] Before 1757, where some indication was given of whether the babies' parents were married, a surprisingly high proportion—as many as one third—of infants admitted in the early years of the Hospital's operation were declared to have been born to married couples. Whether this is accurate is impossible to prove.[53] An important principle for the Hospital's Governors was that no baby should be turned away on the grounds of illegitimacy or 'bastardy', according to the contemporary terminology. Furthermore, no inquiry would be made as to whether the mother, if single, was an 'honest' woman who had temporarily lapsed into sexual 'immorality' or been seduced.[54]

In the early years, with approximately £600 provided annually by public charitable donation, the Foundling Hospital Governors anticipated that admissions would have to be kept low, rationed by selective admission. Over time, conditions for admission were further altered and amended. When war broke out with France in 1793, the orphans of soldiers and seamen killed during active service were welcomed into the Hospital, a patriotic endeavour that elicited an additional grant for their maintenance from the Secretary of War.[55] It also became possible to have a 'sponsored' baby admitted with payment of a fee of £100, a large sum which aroused suspicions that this mechanism could be used by the rich to pass off the evidence of their adulterous or premarital affairs, although in practice only about two admissions per year were secured in this way up to 1801, when it was banned by the General Court.[56] As we shall see, for a time there was no cap on admissions at all, with disastrous consequences.

The temporary premises in Hatton Garden served their purpose while the new Foundling Hospital building was under construction. Designed by the architect Theodore Jacobsen, the new Hospital in Bloomsbury presented an imposing Georgian edifice on what was then the outskirts of London, encircled by high walls, as monumental and impressive as any military academy (Figure 2.5). By 1745, the west wing was completed, accommodating 192 children, sleeping two to a bed. From January 1750 to December 1755, over 2,500 children were brought to the Hospital on admission days. Out of these, fewer than 800 could be taken in, with over two thirds turned away.[57] From 1741 to 1757, between 20 and 200 babies were admitted in this way each year.

Having been inspected, admitted, stripped of any 'verminous' clothing, issued with a serial number, and baptised, the babies were sent almost immediately to a wet nurse outside of the Hospital. Since this entailed being transported out of London, a temporary stay in the infirmary might have been needed to ensure the child would survive the journey. Most children admitted before the late 1750s were from London and were sent to wet nurses in rural parts of the home counties. The prevailing medical opinion of the time was that foundlings would be more likely to thrive if sent away from London to be breastfed by countrywomen. In an era when there was a growing fashion for 'natural' childrearing, when even gentlewomen were known to breastfeed their babies, contemporaries commented

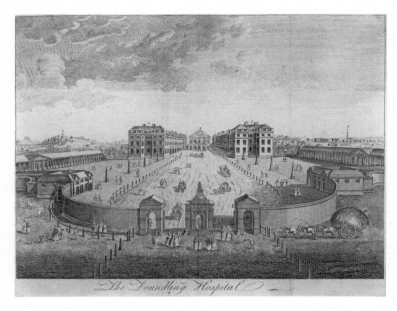

FIGURE 2.5   The London Foundling Hospital, an imposing Georgian edifice encircled by high walls, as monumental and impressive as any military academy. *The Foundling Hospital*, c.1750–80. Engraving (196 mm × 257 mm).

approvingly that the Hospital's regime followed 'Dr Cadogan's *Essay upon Nursing*', a childrearing manual first published in 1748 under the auspices of the Foundling Hospital on how to raise infants from birth until the age of three. Dr William Cadogan, appointed physician to the Hospital in 1754, saw the charity as an opportunity to improve childrearing practices. 'In my Opinion', he declared, 'this Business has been too long fatally left to the Management of Women, who cannot be supposed to have proper Knowledge for such a Task'. The doctor advocated breastfeeding, and the avoidance of swaddling and other practices that restricted children's movement, which included the wearing of shoes.[58]

In the first twenty years of the Hospital's admissions, some locations in the home counties and the south east were especially popular destinations for sending infants to be wet nursed, particularly Surrey, Middlesex, Essex, Hertfordshire, Berkshire, and Kent, where babies could be sent quickly via a relatively well-developed road network. Some of the infants were sent further on wagons to wet nurses in Yorkshire, Staffordshire, and Somerset, although this would have been a perilous journey for weaker babies.[59]

The Foundling Hospital Governors appointed a network of men and women to act as voluntary local inspectors, leading citizens in their local community such as clergymen and charitable gentlewomen ('Ladys or Gents of easy Fortunes & humane dispositions') who made arrangements for the wet nurses to be found and vetted for their good character and honest reputations.[60] They also wrote to the Governors for advice on health matters relating to the children, employed local doctors, and arranged for babies' clothing to be supplied. The nurses they recruited were likely to be tenant farmers' wives, or the wives of agricultural labourers who had already given birth to several children, and who could demonstrate their ability to care for and nourish infants. The women had probably given birth within the previous year, since most babies were weaned before the age of one, and they were able to prolong lactation by continuing to suckle a foster baby. Many of these 'wet nurses' were despatched to collect infants in person from London, bearing notes that testified to their 'exceeding good Character' and 'a fit person to intrust with the care of a Child of your hospital'.[61] Records show that wet nurses could take on more than one foundling at a time, and that they were paid a premium of 10 shillings by the Hospital for keeping the infants alive and well cared for.[62]

The first three years of a foundling's life were precarious and depended upon whether they were breastfed by a woman who cared for them, and raised with at least some nurturing and attention alongside the other children in cottagers' families. Some spent their early years in materially slightly better circumstances, raised in the families of the parish clerk, school master, shoemaker, or tailor. Others were removed several times to different foster mothers, owing to 'the Sluttishness, or Poverty of the Nurses', discovered by the inspectors. In general, though, as a result of regular inspections, and better pay which made it possible for the nurses to have a good diet, the survival rates were better than for foundling infants than those sent out to parish wet nurses under the Poor Law system.[63]

Between the first baby's arrival in 1741 and the end of the eighteenth century, a total of 18,539 infants were carried through the gates of the London Foundling Hospital and received into its care, with roughly an equal number of boys admitted as girls.[64] Of these, two thirds perished in infancy or early childhood. One survivor, however, was foundling no. 18,053, received on 10 November 1787. He was baptised with a new name, George King, alongside another infant boy, foundling no. 18,050, who was given the name Henry Rivington. Though they were quickly processed through the admissions system of the Hospital and sent on their separate ways to different wet nurses, years later they would be reunited, and would come to regard one another as best friends, perhaps even surrogate brothers.

By the end of his life, Thomas Coram could take satisfaction from the fact that he had lived to see his plan put into action and the first infants admitted via the Foundling Hospital's makeshift accommodation. Having personally championed the grant of a Royal Charter that permitted the foundation of the Hospital, and successive Acts of Parliament to establish the legality of its operation, the energies he had expended upon his 'darling' project had spread over nearly two decades. His portrait by William Hogarth took pride of place at the centre of the Foundling Hospital, and it was said that foundlings reciting the Lord's Prayer thought that it referred to him when they prayed to 'Our Father in Heaven'. Coram proved to be the visionary who galvanized the formation of the charity, rather than the person who could influence the government of the Hospital with the diplomacy and tact required to run the charity on a day-to-day basis. He was ejected from the Board of Governors over an indiscretion regarding his loose talk about the role of two Governors in a scandal involving the alleged drunkenness of the chief nurse, Sarah Wood. In future, the Governors resolved that any allegations against its staff should be made to the General or House Committee collectively, which oversaw the management of the Hospital, rather than spreading tittle-tattle via any one Governor. The charity was sensitive to its public reputation since it depended upon private donations and had to be seen to be acting with the highest degree of probity. It operated as the first example of an incorporated organization of its kind, and showed a remarkable degree of impartiality in setting out the unimpeachable standards that were expected of its Governors. Coram had been indiscreet and had to go, no matter that he was the founding father of the hospital. The views of Morris Lievesley, later secretary to the Hospital and an incurable gossip, coloured later interpretations of Coram's unceremonious ejection from the institution he had created:

> It is scarcely possible to believe that Gentlemen of Education assembled within the walls of the Hospital to carry out works of charity should lose sight of that object and permit the most hateful passions of hate and Jealousy to infuriate their Minds alike injurious to their moral character and the best interests of the Institution. Coram the great the good Founder was driven out of his own temple of mercy by Cabal.[65]

The pity of it was that Coram was marginalized within the organization he had founded; an elderly man of a lower social status than the Governors, lacking their mutual ties of education and high-born family connections, he had become an embarrassment to them, if not an outright hindrance. Coram was not re-elected to the General Committee in May 1742, and his attempts to influence the decision-making process about the plans for the new Hospital building were sidelined. Many admired this 'Advocate for the Helpless and the Unborn' who pursued the case of every deserted child as if it were his own, his plain speaking, and persistence for the cause. But it was difficult to be on a committee with someone of whom it was observed 'what he thought he spoke, what he wished he declared, without Hesitation', and ultimately he was ostracized.[66]

Coram was headed for old age in poverty. Having spent his own money in promoting his favourite causes, he was now a widower of small means, living in humble lodgings. In 1749, his supporters raised a subscription to support him with a generous pension of 160 guineas a year. He no longer attended meetings of the two governing bodies of the Foundling Hospital, the General Committee, and

General Court, preferring instead to attend the happier occasions of baptism in the Hospital chapel, where he stood as godfather to twenty foundlings. The national value of his tireless campaigning was recognized in the subscription of the Prince of Wales to his pension fund. It suited the sentimentality of later commentators to imagine Coram's last days spent distributing gingerbread to the children 'with tears in his Eyes', himself the recipient of charity in his dotage. In fact, right up to his death in March 1751, he continued his relentless lobbying for varied schemes such as the creation of a vagabond hospital and colonizing Nova Scotia with ex-soldiers from the War of Austrian Succession.[67]

Thomas Coram was buried with considerable ceremony in the chapel of the newly built Foundling Hospital premises in Bloomsbury. The charter of the Hospital with its royal seal was carried before the coffin on a cushion of red velvet, and the establishment character of the service itself was underscored by the presence of the choirs of St Paul's Cathedral and Westminster Abbey. A patriot to the end, the Governors mourned his passing and gave him his due. An inscription in the Foundling Hospital chapel made explicit Coram's dedication to public causes and the greater good of the British empire:

CAPTAIN THOMAS CORAM,
whose name will never want a monument,
so long as this Hospital shall subsist,
was born in the year 1688;
a man eminent in that most eminent virtue,
the love of mankind:
little attentive to his private fortune,
and refusing many opportunities of increasing it,

his time and thoughts were continually employed
in endeavours to promote the public happiness,
both in this kingdom, and elsewhere;
particularly in the colonies of North America;
and his endeavours to were many times crowned
with the desired success.[68]

But the dukes and earls who did him honour must have appreciated that they were now at liberty to conduct their business in the
gentlemanly manner to which they were accustomed, free from
the interference of this common man whom death alone could
persuade to know his place.

CHAPTER 3

A Fashionable Cause

THE PLIGHT OF lost and abandoned infants inspired many
wealthy and respectable members of elite Georgian society
to dig into their pockets to help fund an enterprise that was
both wildly ambitious and hopelessly expensive, in more than mon-
etary terms. In the eighteenth century, foundlings had a particular
cultural resonance, inspiring plays, poems and novels, comedies
and satires. Children whose parents and birthplace were unknown
became the focus of debates over questions of lost identity in era of
unprecedented change. The rapid growth of London and provincial
towns throughout the British Isles, and encounters through overseas
trade and imperial expansion, brought prosperity and better standards of living for a growing number of people. There had never been
a more industrious age, full of scientific exploration and techno-
logical innovation, by no means confined to London but hot-housed
in Scottish universities and centres of industrial production in the

Midlands and northern England. The so-called British Enlightenment found its proponents in Edinburgh, home of the philosopher David Hume and the founding father of modern economics, Adam Smith. The Midlands was home to the Lunar Society, the brilliant coterie surrounding Erasmus Darwin (grandfather of Charles), known for their scientific innovations and philosophical experiments.[1] But there were trade-offs too, with some commentators fearing that change was happening too fast, wrecking traditional rural life. Some warned that the church was losing its authority, and that the young who migrated to live in the metropolis were in danger of corruption, lacking guidance from their elders and betters. Other commentators feared that materialism was becoming a national obsession, to the detriment of honour and Christian morality. The Newcastle clergyman Dr John Brown blamed the British loss of Minorca in 1756 upon 'a *vain, luxurious, and selfish EFFEMINACY*', which he claimed was caused by a decline of national morals and devotion to luxury. The cause of this tirade was the unfortunate Vice-Admiral John Byng who had retreated from Minorca in 'placid despondency' when threatened by the French without putting up a fight, an ignominious surrender for which he was shot on his own quarterdeck.[2]

A growing obsession with sustaining British imperial might coincided with the first era of the novel as a literary genre. The tastes of the age found expression in the most popular novel of the eighteenth century, Samuel Richardson's *Pamela; or, Virtue Rewarded* (1740). Richardson's many imitators drew upon the theme of female foundlings to emphasize their heroines' precarious virginity, with titles such as *The Female Foundling: or, Virtue, Truth and Spirit Opposing Every Difficulty* (1751).[3] At a time when value was placed upon female honour and chastity among the middling sorts and ruling elite, the prospect of vulnerable virgins with no male 'protector' to safeguard their honour presented the largely female novel-buying public with a horrifying, sometimes thrilling, prospect. These evolved into racy tales with few literary aspirations, such as *The Perjured Lover, or the History of Thomas Beaumont, an Oxford Student, and Miss Lucia Bannister* (1790), whose illicit liaison results in a love child that 'is got into the Foundling Hospital'. The destitute heroine takes to drinking and 'dies of a Consumption', her promising young lover killed in a drunken brawl, 'and confesses it is Divine Justice for having been guilty of Seduction and Perjury'.[4]

These themes were not invented by the authors of Georgian bodice-ripping novels: they had an ancient ancestry that was rediscovered in the eighteenth century among educated readers schooled in classical literature. Legendary tales of lost and abandoned babies whose identities were unknown were familiar to the educated Georgian elites who sponsored the Foundling Hospital project. Such tales from antiquity conjured fantasies and desires about free will, self-determination, and destiny. Across time and place, foundlings appeared in biblical stories and classical literature from the ancient civilizations of Greece and Rome. They seemed to embody all of human potential, with none of the normal constraints of family expectations, such as a fixed place in society or pre-determined identity. The idea of the foundling raised the seductive possibility of complete autonomy and individual freedom, but also the terror of utter abandonment, anonymity, and alone-ness in the world. Modern psychoanalytic theory would later propose that fantasizing about unknown origins is the means by which a child accommodates the reality of the low status of her parents (and by extension her own identity and prospects) as well as the feelings of rivalry with siblings. The prospect for each of us that we might not be 'ordinary' but the foundling offspring of royal parents is *the* fundamental 'drama' of adolescence.[5]

Human societies had long speculated about 'nature versus nurture' in examining what constitutes a person's character traits from birth. Without the baggage of inheritance, foundlings could be full of limitless potential and could rise on their own merits to become anything they set their minds to. This was by no means a modern phenomenon: the legendary twin founders of Rome, Romulus and Remus, were supposed to have been saved from perishing as abandoned infants by being suckled by a she-wolf. But throughout history foundlings could also be seen as 'cuckoos in the nest' when taken into adoptive families, and the carriers of fearful taboos, particularly the stigma of illegitimacy and sexual shame of the parents who had conceived them. Foundlings could go far, but they could also arouse hatred and ostracism, fearfully objectified as 'strangers within', the bearers of atavistic, incestuous desire. Oedipus was supposed to have been a foundling—left to die as an infant on a mountainside, but rescued by shepherds and raised in a royal household, his destiny the double doom of patricide and maternal incest. In pre-modern times, before the compulsory registration of births, marriages, and deaths, the possibility that someone might actually marry close kin within the 'degrees of prohibition' forbidden in the Bible was more plausible than today, but it was a rare occurrence, something that happened more in the imaginations of literary authors than in real life.[6]

Debates about what society should do to help abandoned pauper children can be found in what is probably the most famous account of a foundling's life in eighteenth-century literature. Out of the 189 literary works with 'foundling' in the title published after 1739, a remarkable 132 of these are accounted for by the various editions of Henry Fielding's phenomenally successful novel *The History of Tom Jones, a Foundling*. This was first published in 1749, ten years after the Royal Charter was granted for the London Foundling Hospital, and it was a sell-out success, with 10,000 copies sold in the first year alone. The plot hinges upon the discovery of an abandoned infant in the bed of Squire Allworthy, a good-hearted, childless widower who lives with his sister Bridget, described as an 'old maid', unmarried and 'somewhat past the age of thirty'. Allworthy embodies the benevolent country gentleman, the leading citizen in his neighbourhood whose Christian charity and kindliness inspire him to found a hospital. His compassion for the abandoned babe is immediate—he demands that his housekeeper, Mrs Deborah Wilkins, should take care of the child and should find a nurse for it the very next day. Mrs Deborah, by contrast, urges Allworthy to 'send out your warrant to take up the hussy its mother', and expressing her wish to see her 'committed to Bridewell, and whipt at the cart's tail' for her sexual misconduct. 'Indeed', continued the fifty-two-year-old virgin housekeeper, who had never so much as seen a man without his coat, 'such wicked sluts cannot be too severely punished'. In the character of Miss Deborah and several other neighbourhood gossips, both male and female, Fielding is unsparing in his satire upon the self-appointed neighbourhood morality police ('Faugh! How it stinks. It doth not smell like a Christian... I would have it put in a basket, and sent out and laid at the churchwarden's door. It is a good night, only a little rainy and windy'). Allworthy's sister, Miss Bridget, other gossips of the neighbourhood, and the local parson, Rev. Mr. Thwackum, at various times agree with Miss Deborah's sentiment that 'it is, perhaps, better for such creatures to die in a state of innocence, than to grow up and imitate their mothers; for nothing better can be expected of them'. Foundling Tom Jones grows up to be a ladies' man, who lets down his kind adoptive father, and habitually falls into bad company, but his failings are human ones. Fielding shows how time and again those around the lad are quick to conclude he was 'born to be hanged' and that his moral failings are owing to his origins as a 'beggarly bastard'. Tom has more moral courage than Capt. Blifil, who marries Allworthy's sister for her money and propagates the perverse idea that to be charitable is un-Christian. For all his good-heartedness, Squire Allworthy is charitable to the point of gullibility, easily swayed by conniving neighbours, and negligent in allowing his sister's foolish marriage.[7]

The characters in *Tom Jones* rehearse many of the arguments that were raised for and against the Foundling Hospital enterprise, and Fielding's sympathies as a patron of the Hospital are expressed in his depiction of sceptical and foolish gossips whose inhumanity towards Tom is indicative of their wider prejudice against foundlings as 'living monuments of [sexual] incontinence'.[8] The ancient Greek and Roman practice of exposing infants to certain death had come to be regarded as barbaric by the eighteenth century, but some ambivalence towards procreation of unwanted children remained. In England, as in other parts of Europe, a large family could be regarded as a blessing from God, but only within the sanctity of marriage, and then only if children could be supported without being a burden upon the parish ratepayers who would otherwise pick up the burden of paying for unwanted children.[9] Fielding was a vocal supporter of the Foundling Hospital, 'A Design so truly humane and charitable, that one cannot help wondering [why] it has been delayed so long'. After the success of *Tom Jones*, whose original title was *The Foundling*, Fielding became a reforming Middlesex magistrate. He energetically pursued a programme of social betterment for the urban poor, including founding the Bow Street Runners (constables who were a prototype for the metropolitan police). Fielding also underwent a personal reformation: having got his cookmaid Mary pregnant, he married her and legitimized their son William.[10]

The device of a 'lost' child whose identity is discovered, or the fateful destiny of an illegitimate infant, was not just fertile territory for fictional plots. Historical archetypes and Western European ideas about foundlings also influenced many other cultural forms, from the architecture of the Hospital's buildings, to the visual arts that adorned its public rooms, and the musical life and concerts with which the Hospital became associated. Across the continent of Europe, there were precedents for providing a rich cultural endowment along with the practical help offered to foundlings via charitable institutions. The first secular organization for the care of children, *Ospedale degli Innocenti* in Florence, was founded in the fifteenth century by a wealthy Prato merchant, Francesco Datini. His legacy paid for a foundling hospital designed by the great Renaissance architect Brunelleschi, and was endowed with valuable works of art, including bas-relief sculptures of infants by Andrea della Robbia, and paintings of the Christ child by Botticelli and Ghirlandaio.[11]

With the opportunity to start from scratch, the design, layout, and furnishing of the London Foundling Hospital were set to rival any produced in Catholic Europe, and provide clues about the motivations of those patrons who made the enterprise possible. Their money went into realizing a British utopian vision of order, creating a world of rational utility, hygiene, and Protestant morality. Their ambition was to create something distinctly different from both the Catholic piety that attended orphanages on the continent, and to provide and orderly space for London's poor children, away from the chaotic, crime-ridden, and dirty slums of St Giles and other poor neighbourhoods where bastard children were conceived and born. The high walls around the Hospital marked out the orderly regime within. From the outside, the Hospital buildings were dignified with a 'stately...plain, useful and austere' aspect. The main part of the Foundling Hospital comprised for the most part bare corridors and functional wards, sick rooms and outbuildings to accommodate the routine life: the charitable upbringing of thousands of children.[12]

Inside the Hospital, a picture gallery in the west wing and luxurious court room where the Governors met provided a setting for some of the finest artists of the eighteenth century to showcase their talents (Figure 3.1). In the council room where the Hospital's aristocratic patrons held their meetings, the sculptor William Wilton executed an ornate plasterwork ceiling and panelled walls embellished with fine mouldings. John Sanderson contributed a marble-topped table, and a carved mantelpiece was presented by the mason J. Devall. Both Sanderson and Devall displayed their names prominently on their work, advertising in the hope of future commissions from the Governors and genteel visitors to the Hospital.[13] The room also received a gilded oval pier-glass carved

FIGURE 3.1   A reconstruction of the luxurious court room, one of the main public rooms of the Foundling Hospital, where the Governors met, provided a setting for some of the finest artists of the eighteenth century to showcase their talents. *The Foundling Hospital: The Interior of the Court Room,* [undated, nineteenth century]. Engraving (105 mm × 142 mm).

with extravagant foliage, in fine Rococo style. To the modern eye, the juxtaposition of opulence in the spaces where the Foundling Hospital's rich patrons gathered, and strict austerity in the children's dormitories and communal areas, is almost obscene. There were many similar examples, however, in other institutional settings where the European elite demonstrated that, in their world, charity, power, and patronage went hand in hand.

The theme of orphaned and abandoned infants presented rich territory for literary and artistic inspiration in Judeo-Christian cultural traditions. Most famously, there was the biblical story of

FIGURE 3.2 Saving foundlings for the nation was given biblical precedent in the art on display at the Foundling Hospital, and evoked sympathy from public donors. William Hogarth, *Moses Brought before Pharaoh's Daughter*, 1746. Oil on canvas (1727 mm × 2083 mm).

Moses, the Hebrew baby abandoned in a basket to avoid the slaughter of the Israelites' first-born sons, and found among the bulrushes by Pharaoh's daughter. The moment when the child Moses was handed over by his nurse (his natural mother) was depicted in a monumental painting donated to the London Foundling Hospital by William Hogarth (Figure 3.2). Hogarth had ambitions to found a 'British School' of artists whose talent would compete with their continental European counterparts, boasting that he could rival the perfection of Van Dyck in portraiture. He was also a passionate supporter of philanthropic ventures and through his art was a compassionate documenter of the plight of ordinary folk. Like their personal friends Thomas and Eunice Coram, William Hogarth and his wife Jane were childless, their energies devoted instead to public service and improving the lives of the poor. Hogarth's paintings and engravings reveal his interest in everyday beauty and decay, the riot and revelry of election days, street carnivals, and executions. His work was deeply humane and political in character, depicting the dignity of ordinary people, as much as the follies of the world, and its love of luxury and vice. His spectacular life-size portrait of Coram, gifted *gratis* to the Foundling Hospital in May 1740, received universal approval.

In France, it was Louis XIV who had founded the *Hôpital des Enfants-Trouvés* ('hospital for found children') but Britain, with its constitutional monarchy, eschewed the swagger of an absolutist 'Sun King'. Instead, the subject of Hogarth's portrait, in the idiom of an emperor but the clothing of a stout merchant, was a study of Coram in dignified and humble modesty (Figure 2.1). Hogarth also helped to create an identity and distinctive culture for the Hospital in other ways: by designing the children's uniform, the shield over the doorway, and in 1747 a new coat of arms, a naked child flanked on one side by an allegorical figure of many-breasted Nature, and on the other Britannia, a reminder that the charity was founded in the national interest as a patriotic endeavour (Figure 3.3). There was no Latin inscription (which would have been inaccessible to the general public and to most children): instead, the one-word motto accessible to all read 'HELP'. The engraving of this coat of arms appeared on some of the letterheads of documents associated with the Hospital, and as a motif on other items owned by the institution, including the silver patten and chalice used in the Hospital chapel for communion.[14]

73

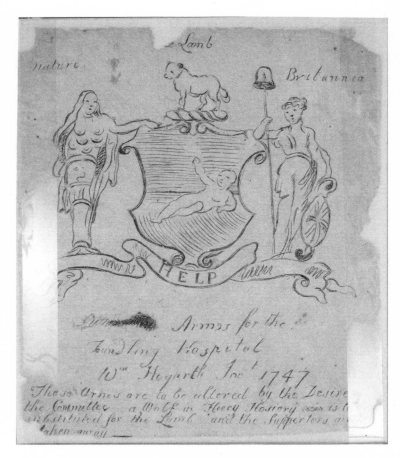

FIGURE 3.3 A naked child flanked on one side by an allegorical figure of many-breasted Nature, and on the other Britannia, a reminder that the charity was founded in the national interest as a patriotic endeavour. William Hogarth, *Emblem of the Foundling Hospital* (1747). Original drawing for the Letterhead for the Foundling Hospital (4³⁄₈ × 8¼).

Hogarth was made a governor from the earliest days of the charity, and had been present to witness the admission of the first infants.

Other historical and allegorical paintings adorned the council room, donated by Hogarth's contemporaries Joseph Highmore, Frank Hayman, and James Wills, connected via the St Martin's Lane Academy for artists. Their common theme was biblical texts dealing with children and charitable giving, including Wills's depiction of *Little Children Brought to Christ* following the saviour's famous dictum 'Suffer the little children to come unto me'.[15] Fifteen artists who donated works were made Governors of the Hospital in 1746, and an annual meeting of the Governors was held on 5 November on the anniversary of the Gunpowder Plot, to underscore the patriotic and Protestant character of their endeavours. At these meetings, proposals to add to the collection were considered, with the expectation that new works would be donated by the artists 'without any expence to the Charity'.[16] The Foundling Hospital soon amassed an impressive private art collection which became a visitor attraction in its own right.

A series of eight 'roundels' in the council room, small circular paintings placed between the biblical canvases on display, emphasized the place of the Foundling Hospital among London's pre-eminent charitable institutions. These were executed by the young Thomas Gainsborough, who went on to find fame as a leading society portrait artist, Edward Haytley, Samuel Wale (a founding member of the Royal Academy), and Richard Wilson. They depicted St Thomas's and St George's, medical hospitals; Greenwich Hospital for former seamen and Chelsea Hospital for veteran soldiers; 'Bedlam' (Bethlem Hospital for the mentally ill); and Christ's and Charterhouse which catered for orphaned boys, each depicting their fashionably dressed, polite patrons. The sick, the elderly, the 'mad', the infirm, discharged former servicemen, and children were all worthy recipients of polite benefaction. For the price of a charitable donation, it was possible to join the ranks of worthy notables who condescended to lend their help to these causes. The Foundling Hospital soon became the first public art gallery in London, appearing in numerous tourist guides and handbooks for curious visitors with detailed descriptions of the paintings on display. One such handbook, *The Curiosities of London and Westminster* (1783), provided a detailed guide of the works of art on display, and drew attention to a fine painting, 'sea-piece of the English fleet in the Downs'. In the course of the late eighteenth and nineteenth centuries, the charity amassed a collection that featured maritime scenes and famous British victories at sea, such as Thomas Luny's *Action off the Coast of France* (1779) and John Singleton Copley's *Siege of Gibraltar* (1788). Though often overlooked today in favour of works by Hogarth and his contemporaries, the imposing canvases depicting naval battles were displayed in the public rooms of the Foundling Hospital and remain visual and prominent reminders of the founder and Governors' close association with trade and empire.

The addition of a chapel to the Foundling Hospital in 1747 provided for worship and the habit of regular piety that the Governors wished to instil in its charges. The chapel was also a public space and an important venue for generating donations for the work of the Hospital. Not only could wealthy patrons attend divine service and witness the pathos of the neatly dressed foundling children singing hymns; they could also attend some of the most fashionable concerts held anywhere in eighteenth-century London (Figure 3.4). Georg Friedrich Handel was the most influential composer of the

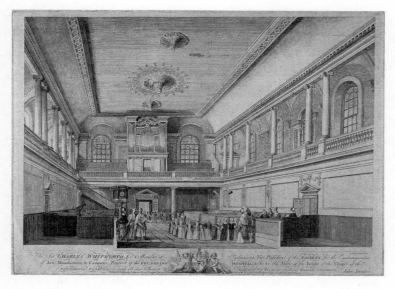

FIGURE 3.4 The Foundling Hospital Chapel, one of the leading venues for sacred music in Georgian London, where Handel's *Messiah* was performed annually as a benefit concert. John Sanders, *Foundling Hospital, Holborn, London: interior of the chapel*, 1774. Etching (341 mm × 493 mm).

eighteenth century, his compositions dominating London performances of sacred and secular music until his death in 1759. A German by birth, he found a permanent home in England after the succession of the Hanoverian dynasty in 1714, numbering both George I and George II as his patrons. For many years an annual benefit concert took place in a performance of the *Messiah* in the Hospital chapel, his most enduringly popular composition. All of London society turned out to hear these performances, conducted by the composer himself and played upon the organ that Handel donated to the Foundling Hospital. Handel never married and had no children: the main beneficiary in his will was his male servant. His legacy to the Foundling Hospital was considerable, since he bequeathed to the Governors the original manuscript of his famous *Messiah*, and wrote *The Foundling Hospital Anthem* especially for public performance to raise money for the charity.[17]

The cultural endowment of the Foundling Hospital was more than a luxurious afterthought. Endowment and patronage by famous artists and composers provided valuable income, and overlaid what was a controversial enterprise associated with illicit sexual conduct and the raising of bastard infants with an air of cultured respectability. Charity was not merely about putting Christian values into practice; it was of a piece with the eighteenth-century vogue for polite culture. An essential prerequisite for this was the quality of civic virtue, founded upon a code of conduct that self-consciously emulated the supposed probity and law-abiding character of the citizens of ancient Rome.[18] The number of individuals in England holding peerages was no more than 1,003 in the entire eighteenth century. Even if Scottish and Irish peers, baronets, and knights are added to this total, the composition of the social elite in Britain remained a tiny fraction, less than 1 per cent, of the total population. They were a small, closely intermarried oligarchy of men and women who exercised complex networks of patronage, exerting influence over their social inferiors and making strategic alliances among their peers whilst maintaining a tight stranglehold on power and privilege.[19] The neoclassical architecture of the Foundling Hospital, its list of aristocratic patrons, and its cultural endowments underscored the social respectability of its mission to save the 'innocents'. This was legitimized and sanctioned by scripture, but patronage of the

Foundling Hospital became a mark of kudos which brought further social, economic, and cultural benefits. Governors who attended court and General Committee meetings forged deeper ties of allegiance and confraternity in their mutual support for the Foundling Hospital cause. The artists who gave their services for free did so knowing that their work would be viewed approvingly by the Governors and elite visitors, possibly leading to further commissions and enhancing their reputations. As some modern analysts have observed of nineteenth-century philanthropy, the question was not whether donors were *primarily* motivated to 'do good': there was a profound, often unarticulated understanding that different kinds of capital (social, cultural, and economic) were interchangeable. Building prestige in one area (such as charitable giving) enhanced reputation (Christian benevolence, humanitarian mercy) and brought other mutual benefits, including what today would be called 'networking opportunities' with a rich peer group of powerful patrons who safeguarded and promoted one another's interests in business and politics.[20]

One of the most crucial aspects of the Foundling Hospital project that lent its patrons credibility was its patriotic mission to expand the nation's manpower, as conceived from the outset by Thomas Coram. Among the Governors of the Foundling Hospital were the leading politicians of the day whose interests were indistinguishable from those of the British Empire. For example, William Legge, 2nd earl of Dartmouth, was vice-president of the Council of the Foundling Hospital for half a century. He was also a member of the Cabinet and President of the Board of Trade at the time of fierce debates surrounding the British government's right to tax the colonies when they did not return members of parliament to Westminster. Protests at the Stamp Act culminated in the Boston Tea Party (hence the rebels' cry 'no taxation without representation' as tea was despatched into Boston Harbour), a decisive moment that precipitated the rebellion of the American colonies. An evangelical Christian, Dartmouth was esteemed by George III as a man of integrity. His missionary zeal for supporting charities in Britain was matched by his enthusiasm for good works in the colonies. In 1766, as a trustee of Eleazar Wheelock's charity school in Connecticut, he met Samson Occum, the first Native American pupil. Wheelock wanted to move the school further north into New Hampshire, and to find favour with the trustees he named it Dartmouth College after the 2nd earl.[21] Dartmouth's portrait, executed in 1757 by the leading society artist Sir Joshua Reynolds, adorned the walls of the picture gallery in the west wing of the Foundling Hospital. The combination of dedication to a patriotic and fashionable charitable cause and imperial values that typified the British ruling elite were also embodied in John Russell, 4th duke of Bedford, an anti-Walpole Whig. The duke's foible was said to be 'speaking upon every subject and imagining he understood it', although he proved himself to be an able minister, who as secretary of state had significant political influence.[22] Russell became first lord of the admiralty in the 1740s, but it was perhaps fortunate that the socially eminent but often absentee council devolved to others the business of bringing the planned hospital to fruition.

The grandees of the Foundling Hospital's council, like the earl of Dartmouth and duke of Bedford, delegated the operational responsibility for the day-to-day running of the Hospital to a General Committee, composed of a practical and professional group of men skilled in public administration. These included Arthur Onslow, speaker of the House of Commons, who was well known for his astonishing organizational powers and mnemonic abilities. Onslow famously memorized the ancient precedents and byzantine procedures that governed the rules of parliamentary conduct, as well as hundreds of MPs' names. He brought an unimpeachable probity to the speaker's role, an honesty which had hitherto been lacking in that particular office. Other able professionals on the governing committee were the eminent doctors Richard Mead, who pioneered the smallpox vaccination, and Sir Hans Sloane, the polymath whose private collections and philanthropic ventures enabled the foundation of the British Museum. Taylor White, a barrister and judge on the Northern Circuit, proved to be an able treasurer from 1745 to 1772, during which time he attended around 3,000 General Committee meetings.[23]

The organization of the Foundling Hospital mirrored the way in which the British political system had achieved a balanced constitutional settlement, blending traditional landed interests and those of merchants and professional men, both Anglicans and non-conformists. In contrast to the portrait of the 2nd earl of Dartmouth that emphasized the vice-president's status and power, there was a rather more modest portrait on display at the Foundling Hospital by Joseph Highmore. Highmore was the self-made son of a coal merchant, an artist much beloved of the prosperous middling sorts for his ability to execute honest yet sympathetic portraits without pretension. His subject, Thomas Emerson (Figure 3.5), was a merchant whose wealth derived from the sugar plantations in the colonies: his refineries in London brought him a vast fortune on the back of African slave labour. A man of non-conformist religious conviction

FIGURE 3.5 Thomas Emerson was one of the Foundling Hospital's leading patrons and Governors. He left a fortune to the charity that was earned on the back of African slave labour. Joseph Highmore, *Thomas Emerson*, 1731. Oil on canvas (1220 mm × 1454 mm).

(that is, a Protestant but not a member of the established Church of England), Emerson had a particular concern for women and children's causes, and seems to have shown an unusual level of sympathy for the plight of women 'ruined' by unscrupulous men. He left annuities for his sister and a female servant which specified in his will that their incomes were to be protected from their husbands. Such paradoxes were frequent in eighteenth-century society, where acceptance of human slavery could sit alongside Christian faith and charitable compassion for others. John Newton, famous for penning the words of the hymn 'Amazing Grace', was a slave trader, and many

Quaker families (otherwise famed for their love of social justice) were slave owners. The autobiography of Oludah Equiano, a former slave who visited England, documents that he was at one time owned by a devout Quaker, Robert King.[24] Emerson, like Coram, Hogarth, and Handel, was himself childless, but in his role as Governor he found ways of influencing the organization of the Foundling Hospital. This included the separation of girls and boys through the provision of an east wing, which he funded himself. Since the Hospital was a legally chartered body it could receive legacies and endowments, of which Emerson's was a notable example. When he died in 1745, the Hospital was the main beneficiary of his estate, which amounted to £12,000, the equivalent of approximately £2.4 million today.[25]

Emerson's benefaction is just one example of how, via its patrons, the charity had ongoing and close connections both with the slave trade and the 'first British empire' in the Americas. The Foundling Hospital also had numerous links with the so-called 'second empire' in the east. In 1769, the secretary, Thomas Collingwood, invited the former commander-in-chief of British forces in India, Major-General Robert Clive ('Clive of India'), to be appointed steward for the Hospital's annual anniversary dinner, a gathering of the charity's most eminent patrons.[26] Collingwood was also charged with the administration of a large donation from an East India Company Bengali merchant to the Foundling Hospital, the so-called Omichund bequest, which was beset by legal difficulties. 'Omichund', who died in December 1758, was Amir Chand, a merchant and major trading partner of the British in Bengal and closely associated with the campaign by Lord Clive to secure British interests in the region via the East India Company. By the 1730s, Chand had become the company's leading supplier, living in Calcutta in princely style, where he amassed a fortune of £450,000. He died without issue, and bequeathed most of his estate to a Sikh shrine, but his legacy to the Foundling Hospital and Magdalen Hospital in London were indicators of the extent to which he had appropriated the customs and causes of the British ruling elite.[27]

The Foundling Hospital, like other charities in the eighteenth century, relied upon the ties of obligation, patronage, and mutuality that engaged the wealthiest sections of society with the commercial interests of the middling sorts. Lords and merchants, titled aristocrats, and prosperous philanthropists were bound together by a common rhetoric of Christian charity and imperial mission. These ties fostered mutual interest between members of the social and political elite and brought men from disparate walks of life into overlapping circles. The Foundling Hospital enterprise was part of a public sphere in Britain that was beyond the divisions of party politics and other potentially divisive factors. Women, and people of different ethnic and religious backgrounds within the empire, could even become part of this collective endeavour (the champions of Coram's vision included aristocratic women, Sikh donors, and non-conformist Christians). Private philanthropic ventures such as the Foundling Hospital charity brought together diverse interests, such as joint-stock companies and charities, and helped foster wider social cohesion. Some historians argue, plausibly, this contributed to Britain's avoidance of the violent revolutions witnessed in France in 1789 and other parts of Europe as the nineteenth century progressed. It also helped to create the necessary conditions for the economic boom of the Industrial Revolution that gave Britain competitive advantage in becoming the world's first modern industrial nation.[28] More recently, these debates have been given new force in relation to the political controversy in Western countries over whether welfare is a 'luxury' that hinders economic growth.[29] However, the kind of social cohesion witnessed in eighteenth-century British society, the 'Greatness' for which some are today nostalgic, came with attitudes that would be objectionable to most twenty-first-century people: inequality of different classes and genders, lack of social mobility for those below the rank of the middling sorts, unapologetically imperialist attitudes towards other races and creeds, and a paternal form of patriarchy that endowed men with God-given authority over women, children, servants, and even African slaves.

These debates about empire and the questionable value placed upon human rights in the eighteenth century are no better illustrated than through one of the Foundling Hospital's most influential Governors, Jonas Hanway (Figure 3.6). Apart from Thomas Coram, Hanway exerted the single greatest influence on the course of the history of the London Foundling Hospital, and the British government's policy on welfare and poor law reform, before modern times. In an age of extraordinary adventurers, Hanway was one of the most extraordinary of all. Born in 1712, the generation after Thomas Coram, as a young man Hanway lived in Lisbon and experienced first-hand the trials of earning his living as a merchant at the outbreak of war with Spain in 1739. He removed to the Russia Company which had a monopoly of trade with that country and the Middle East, where he became embroiled in a rebellion in Persia at the time of an uprising against the shah. A practical man and a constant innovator and improver, another

FIGURE 3.6 Jonas Hanway, a governor of the Foundling Hospital. Hanway founded the Marine Society, which avoided some of the pitfalls of raising abandoned infants from birth, and did more than any single person to calculate the economic and human costs of poverty in the eighteenth century. James Bretherton, *Jonas Hanway*, c.1770–80. Etching (214 mm × 161 mm).

of Hanway's singular distinctions was that he was the first gentleman to carry an umbrella on the streets of London.[30]

At the outbreak of war with France in 1756 (termed the Seven Years' War in retrospect, or French-Indian War in Canada and North America), Hanway was back in England. He soon began to direct his considerable energies towards philanthropy and public policy. He addressed the major concern of the British government: how to find enough manpower to engage in large-scale military campaigns. Hanway's family had close connections with the Navy and with government office, although they were moderately well-off, professional men rather than established gentry. His outlook was profoundly influenced by his travels, including his twelve years in Portugal where he learned of the philanthropic *Santa Casa da Misericordia*, a charitable brotherhood that cared for orphans and found them apprenticeships. 'I love an honest man', wrote Hanway, 'whether he be a Methodist, or a papist, a Jew or a Mahommedan.' There were limits to his modern-sounding toleration, however, since at heart he believed that the government should foster the supremacy and strength of Britain and the Church of England. Following his expression of affection and tolerance towards those of other faiths, he added, 'I wish they were all true Christians'.[31]

Such were the values that underpinned Hanway's particular strain of 'Christian mercantilism', a popular ideology among men of his class at this time which argued the logic of the interdependence of church and state, and the need to exclude those of other faiths from full citizenship. Hanway's advocacy of free trade was designed to remove obstacles primarily to British trade and prosperity. 'Commerce', he argued, 'is the link by which men are united in love', which he believed would produce 'a connexion and harmony... among the whole race of mankind'.[32] His philosophy was shared by many of his peers. The merchants of the Russia Company numbered many of the evangelical philanthropists who ran the leading charities of the day: half of the company's governing court were also Governors of the Foundling Hospital, as were five out of eight of the founders of the Magdalen Hospital for 'fallen' women.[33]

Hanway began his career as a political lobbyist by writing pamphlets that engaged in controversial topics of national concern, such as the naturalization of Jews and a defence of the monopoly of the Levant Company, both of which were of material concern to his own trading interests. He began to engage in writing political polemics that were a characteristic feature of the media in Georgian England. The last systematic attempt to censor or control the English press was marked by the lapse of the Press Act in 1695, allowing a proliferation of newspapers, periodicals, and all manner of popular satires, cartoons, and scurrilous publications in the course of the century that followed. Foreign visitors from other parts of Europe thought the English press remarkable for its ability to launch direct attacks upon powerful men. Considering treason remained a capital offence, and libel could be severely punished. These were often issued under the guise of satire without mentioning names, and under a veil of author anonymity, but the reading public could see through these thinly veiled attacks upon authority with ease.[34]

Writing in this polemical tradition, which is the origins of our modern parliamentary lobbying system, Hanway penned lengthy and influential treatises that expressed the necessity of investment in improving the condition of Britain's poor as an essential requirement for imperial expansion and prosperity. Mounting a defence of the Foundling Hospital, he wrote:

> As the true foundation of riches and power is the number of working poor, every rational proposal for augmentation of them merits our regard. The number of people is confessedly the national stock: the estate, which has no body to work in, is so far good for nothing; and the same rule extends to a whole country or nation...considering our extensive commerce; the smallness of this island compared with His Majesty's dominions abroad; and the formidable neighbour who is ever meditating our limitations [France] we had need to promote population by all rational and pious means.[35]

For Hanway, Christian humanitarian concerns about the suffering of the poor were indivisible from the imperative to save lives in the national interest, a view of the value of human life that might appear distasteful to modern eyes, but which had its own logic in an era of global conflict between European powers, notably Britain's ambition to overcome France, her main imperial rival.

The outbreak of the Seven Years' War in 1756 began as a skirmish in North America between British and French troops, but threatened to split European alliances and jeopardize British over-seas, including access to the most important trading routes in the Mediterranean, the West Indies and the Americas, Africa, and the Indian sub-continent. It is with good reason that it has been called the first truly global conflict. Britain forged an alliance with Prussia, squaring up to the combined might of the French and Austrian forces, and the Spanish, who became embroiled in the conflict after

1759.[36] Following the loss of Minorca in 1756, British officers pursued much more aggressive engagement with enemy forces, reversing humiliation with victories against French troops in Quebec under General Woolf, who lost his life in the process, and at the naval blockade of the port of Brest, resulting in the near destruction of the French navy at Quiberon Bay.[37] Victory at the Battle of Minden in August 1759 by Britain's Prussian allies added to the growing swell of military triumphalism in the press. The then secretary of state William Pitt (later created Earl of Chatham) was convinced that the British Navy's destiny was global supremacy, a view shared by the new king, George III, who succeeded to the throne at the age of twenty-two in 1760, and who was the first Hanoverian monarch to consider himself first and foremost to be British.

Protecting British interests via these campaigns was expensive in terms of both manpower and resources. In his *Thoughts on the Duty of a Good Citizen with Regard to War and Invasion* (1756), Jonas Hanway signalled his warning to the British government that 60,000 troops would be needed to reverse the nation's military fortunes. In the same year, he qualified for election to a governorship of the Foundling Hospital by donating £50 to the charity. His election on 12 May was timely: just a few weeks earlier, in March 1756, the Hospital had petitioned parliament for a public subsidy to enable them to meet public anxiety that the nation would be unable to muster enough able-bodied troops to fight the French. Hanway's election as a governor was three weeks after parliament agreed to fund the admission of all infants, at whatever cost, from 1 June to the end of the year, provided that none should be turned away.

Hanway's arrival as a governor coincided with a rapid scaling up of the Foundling Hospital's activities. The charity went from being primarily a London-based operation to an ongoing national concern during the period that became known as the General Reception when parliament granted funding directly to the charity, from June 1756 to March 1760.[38] An astonishing 5,510 children were received between June 1756 and the end of December 1757 alone, with perhaps exaggerated reports of babies being brought in pannier baskets from all over provincial England. Tales began to circulate in the press of those who had perished being abandoned at the roadside and others admitted in a pitiful and 'dying condition'.

Struggling to meet demand and to maintain what had previously been a fairly efficient system, the Hospital's Governors set up six satellite institutions at Ackworth in North Yorkshire, Chester, Shrewsbury, Aylesbury (Bucks), Westerham (Kent), and Barnet (formerly Hertfordshire). The location for the branch hospitals depended upon the network of patrons already established outside of London for providing wet nurses to infants despatched following admission to the Hospital. For example, with regard to Ackworth, the London Foundling Hospital had close associations with Yorkshire from as early as the 1740s, when an energetic inspector, Rev. Thomas Trant, brokered apprenticeships for boys sent from London in the Hemsworth area.[39] Taylor White, the charity's erstwhile treasurer from 1745 to 1772, whose portrait by the fashionable artist Francis Cotes hung in the council room of the Foundling Hospital, was an assize judge on the Northern Circuit whose contacts in Yorkshire also helped establish links in the north.[40] Many of the great landowners of Yorkshire such as Sir Rowland Winn of Nostell Priory were persuaded to become Governors and helped to raise subscriptions to fund the purchase of premises that became the Ackworth branch hospital, the largest of the six branch institutions. Jonas Hanway became involved in all aspects of the Hospital's activities during the General Reception, and proved himself to be an able administrator and advocate in favour of the charity, lobbying against those voices that were raised in protest at the high mortality rates among infants who were admitted indiscriminately. He looked into the food supplies for the Hospital, arrangements for smallpox inoculation, clothing, and the condition of the estates. His administrative capabilities proved invaluable.

To give some idea of the scale of the Foundling Hospital's activities, on the eve of the General Reception in June 1756 there were 612 children under the care of the Hospital, 189 in London, with a further 422 at nurse in the countryside. At the peak of the General Reception period, in December 1759, there were 6,293 children under the care of the Foundling Hospital Governors. By September 1760 the Hospital was organizing the placement of and payment for 5,814 babies put to nurse, with 270 infants and children housed in the London Hospital. The maximum number housed at the London Hospital at any one time was 407, in December 1764.[41]

The decision by parliament effectively to 'write a blank cheque' to the Foundling Hospital needs to be placed not only within the context of the outbreak of war, but also within a shifting dynamic between local parish authorities, philanthropic charitable organizations, and central government. Successive Westminster administrations launched new initiatives in the second half of the eighteenth century to address the strain that population increase, urbanization, crime, and poverty were placing upon the parish relief system. By the end of the seventeenth century, the Old Poor Laws, which had provided a safety net for the sick and destitute, were starting to creak under the strain of population increase. These laws dated back to the time of Elizabeth I, and were amended but not over-hauled significantly until 1834. They provided the mechanisms for distributing 'outdoor relief' at the parish level (doles of money to parishioners living in their own dwellings, rather than in institu-tions such as workhouses), raised by taxing more affluent ratepayers to parishioners experiencing hardship. To a person of modest means who might be vulnerable to poverty through illness, disabil-ity, or another change in circumstances, such as the death of the male breadwinner in a household, it was crucial to secure 'settlement' in the parish where they resided. The conditions for settlement were amended over time, secured by virtue of having been born in a parish, or by fulfilling the terms of an apprenticeship (normally seven years under the Elizabethan Statute of Artificers), or in some circumstances by proving a close family connection or marriage into a local family.[42] Settlement could also be secured by working as a servant or farm labourer for a year in a parish, but this applied only to unmarried people. If all else failed, a person could claim settlement in a parish if their father had been born there.[43]

Disputes over settlement were common, and parish authorities took steps to ensure that the risks of paupers marrying and having children they could not maintain, or producing illegitimate children 'chargeable upon the parish', were minimized. Tales of unmarried women in the agonies of labour carried to and fro across parish boundaries on their birthing stool, midwives harrying them all the while to disclose the name of the father, may have been largely apocryphal. In reality, poor people were at the mercy of a complex web of locally negotiated political wrangles over who was deemed 'deserving' and therefore worthy of parish relief, and who was not.[44] There is much evidence that even illiterate parishioners, or those who could scarcely read and write, whether male or female, were well versed in the legal entitlements that came with settlement and even the humblest citizen knew how to use the correctly deferential but assertive claim upon the petty officers of their parish when petitioning for poor relief, as their surviving letters testify.[45]

With more people claiming settlement rights and outdoor relief, pressure upon the Old Poor Law system was particularly marked in metropolitan parishes. The fastest-growing of these, St Martins'-in-the-Fields, had increased from a population of about 19,000 in 1660, to 86,000 by 1700, and 100,000 by 1720. To try and cope with this population rise, new parishes such as St Paul Covent Garden, St Anne Soho, and St James Piccadilly were formed from the original 'mother' church. Overpopulation still presented a huge logistical problem for the parish authorities. The surveyor John Strype reported that St Martin's 'remaineth a very great parish, and too populous for one Church to receive the Inhabitants'.[46] By the later eighteenth century, ratepayers complained that Poor Law petitioners were so numerous and so needy that the poor's traditional reliance upon parish settlement as a means of gaining access to outdoor relief was no longer feasible or affordable. Spending on parochial relief rose rapidly, from £1,529,780 in 1776 to £4,267,965 in 1783, outstripping both population growth and the rise in national income.[47] The vast sums ploughed into the Foundling Hospital by the Westminster parliament (about £30,000 a year between 1756 and 1771) were still relatively small in comparison to the £700,000 spent on prison hulks on the Thames in the quarter-century after 1776, or £1 million spent on transportation to Australia between

1787 and 1797.[48] The Foundling Hospital was not unique in its receipt of state funding, nor did it deter other state-subsidized social experiments, but as an experiment in state-subsidized philanthropy its influence on welfare provision for pauper infants and children was without precedent in England.[49]

Nearly 15,000 children were admitted during the General Reception up to March 1760, of whom a shockingly high number, over 10,400, died while in the care of the Hospital. During this period, the annual mortality rates amounted sometimes to over 90 per cent of those admitted. On one hand, critics lined up to condemn the General Reception for providing a 'legal licentious Asylum for *every* Bastard (of *every* Whore, and of *every* Whoremonger) under the Name of a *Foundling*, even where, not One of them All is a Foundling'.[50] Some argued that the Hospital was quickly becoming a drop-off point for parents to have the funerals of their dying offspring paid for at the public expense, that lawful marriages were being discouraged since the government had provided a solution for what to do with illegitimate babies, and even that unscrupulous carriers and wet nurses were profiteering from the high turnover of infants.[51]

The survival rates of the infants raised through the charity's activities at this time were indeed dismal, even considering high infant mortality in the eighteenth century, and the overall failure of London parishes to preserve the lives of pauper infants. The branch hospitals and their inspectors returned regular and dismal accounts to the London Governors, listing the names and numbers of children who had died, sometimes with details of the causes. These make for terrible reading. During the General Reception, ill and badly nourished infants and older children were admitted indiscriminately according to parliamentary instruction. Some did not survive their journey to be wet nursed in the countryside; others were syphilitic or sedated. Fleas, lice, ringworm, and other parasites, and scabies ('the itch') were endemic. A number of studies have looked into the Foundling Hospital's various experiments with prescribing breast milk, trial medicines, inoculations, and 'pap' foods (solids and liquids known to be harmful to babies in modern times) that were tried out on the sickly infants under their care.[52] A letter from Mrs Birch, an inspector who lived near Abingdon in Berkshire, written on 6 April 1760, gave an account of the combination of sudden and predictable infant and child deaths that were an all too frequent occurrence, particularly as a consequence of the General Reception:

> To the Secretary
>
> Sirs
>
> I enclose you the certificate of the death (burial) of John Penrose. [I] am sorry to tell you that I have lost a fine thriving child, Ann Morice, No. 15338, who lay ill but a few days and dyed lat Wednesday. The certificate of her burial I shall send you next Tuesday. Her disorder was a violent fever, I believe, occasioned by worms as she brought up one of 6 inches long.

The very next day, Mrs Birch wrote again, this time of James Mildmay,

> a very sickly, weak infant...now very ill. Blood and corruption [sic] is continually coming from the child's nose and mouth and all over its body is full of a livid colured eruption. I have put the child under a course of crabs' claw powder. If your physicians think of any thing else, be pleased to inform me.[53]

Even by the standards of the day, this was terrible suffering indeed. Similar catalogues of horror were posted to London from inspectors all over the country, many of whom exacted their responsibilities to document the children's illnesses and deaths with considerable scrupulousness. Between the first baby's arrival in 1741 and the end of the eighteenth century, 18,539 infants gained admission to the Foundling Hospital, of whom two thirds did not survive beyond infancy.[54] Infant mortality rates for those admitted to the London Foundling Hospital before 1756 were comparatively high: 40 to 55 per cent died within the first year of their admission, although this compares favourably with how many infants perished in workhouses at this time.[55] But infant and child mortality rates were skewed dramatically by the General Reception, raising a general outcry. Public donations slumped during the General Reception and its aftermath. When the state began to pay for a service that had previously been reliant upon philanthropy, private donors became less inclined to reach into their own pockets. The reasons for this are complex but not unfathomable. The scaling up of the Foundling Hospital's activities in many respects had dismal consequences. Though the Hospital was not the direct cause of the very high infant and child mortality in most cases (many of the sick children admitted indiscriminately were already unlikely to survive), it became associated with humanitarian failure. Perhaps as great a crime for parliament and the taxpayer, as this disastrous experiment unfolded, was the perceived inefficiency and wastefulness of the General Reception scheme.

The Foundling Hospital Governors began to be concerned for the charity's reputation and future survival. Jonas Hanway continued to be a vocal supporter, but even he began to question whether this was the best use of public money to the maximum benefit of the nation.

Hanway started to pursue an alternative plan for supplying the Navy with manpower. The Marine Society, founded in 1756, went on to become the most successful charitable organization to 'breed up a more numerous race of mariners' for the nation. He saw from the Foundling Hospital experiment that the laborious process of raising children from infancy was costly and time-consuming, requiring many years for a lad to mature before he could be of use to the Navy. But finding an alternative solution was a pressing matter: success in military campaigns, and prosperity in trade, rested upon Britain's ability to find a ready supply of manpower. As Hanway observed, captains of merchant ships carrying 'sugar, rice, tobacco, hemp, timber and iron' trading with the Baltic, Russia, and the New World all 'depend upon our having a *sufficient* number of *seamen*'.[56] Aside from the question of timing, which was problematic since most naval apprentices were aged seventeen or above, and few children went to sea below the age of twelve, there was no guarantee that a poor boy raised at great public expense would be sufficiently hardy for life at sea. Instead, the Marine Society adopted a different strategy to the Foundling Hospital: the charity would sponsor poor boys who had already reached an age where they could go straight into the Navy, providing them with sailors' clothing, supplied at the point of the ship's departure to prevent them absconding. This cost-effective solution was first tried by Lord Harry Powlett, who took poor boys from the London streets and paid for their clothes at his own expense to add to his crews. This practice was adopted by the Marine Society and, over the course of the Seven Years' War,

10,625 boys and men were supplied to the Navy in this way, about 5 per cent of the overall recruitment at a crucial time when fresh labour supply was needed to make up for a heavy toll of casualties.[57] In 1761, Spain and France forged an alliance, and the Cabinet in Westminster resolved to attack Havana, the epicentre of Spanish power in the Caribbean and a lucrative centre for trade. Navigating the perilous north coast of Cuba, British naval forces were able to land a surprise attack on Havana. The Spanish surrendered, but the campaign cost 9,000 British troops, with only 3,000 remaining to secure the captured territory.[58]

The Seven Years' War ended in 1763, the peace brokered by the Foundling Hospital's governor, the duke of Bedford. According to the terms negotiated with France, the character of the British Empire changed profoundly. No longer was it an 'empire of trade' composed mainly of an agglomeration of English-speaking Protestant communities on the Atlantic Seaboard in North America with mutual trading interests, but one forged through war, occupying lands and peoples with diverse languages and cultures. These included footholds in St Lucia in the West Indies, Senegal in West Africa, and unfortified trading posts in India such as Pondicherry, Chandernagar in Bengal, and Calcutta, which had previously been under French influence. Control of Havana and Manila was restored to Spain, in return for British sovereignty over Florida and Minorca. Growing in confidence and experienced in developing effective strategies for successful maritime warfare, the British Navy's main rival, the French, had been more or less obliterated.

Ultimately, parliament granted a total of £550,000 to the Foundling Hospital, the equivalent of over £30 million today. The subsidy ended in 1771 with the Foundling Hospital reverting to its former reliance upon charity. By then, infant admissions were in sharp decline. Only ninety-four children were at nurse in December 1771 and 410 children in total in the care of the Hospital by December 1773.[59] By the end of the eighteenth century, faced with falling donations, the Governors sought alternative means of raising funds. They invested shrewdly and became rentier landlords, allowing speculators to build on land owned by the charity in the Lamb's Conduit Fields area of Bloomsbury, and then collecting rents whilst maintaining ultimate ownership of the freehold.[60]

Jonas Hanway used what he had learned from his first-hand experience of being a governor of the Foundling Hospital and Marine Society to reform the treatment of pauper infants under the Poor Law system. During the early 1760s, he gathered as much information as he could about mortality rates among the infant poor within the Bills of Mortality, and published lists of the number of deaths within each parish and their causes. These covered ninety-seven parishes within the walls of the City of London, seventeen extramural parishes, twenty-seven in Middlesex and Surrey, and ten in the City of Westminster. It was a huge undertaking. Hanway devised a system for compelling parishes within the Bills of Mortality to publish an annual register indicating mortality rates of children and infants under four years old. This was given parliamentary backing, since it was cost-effective and shone a light on the very high levels of child and infant mortality that existed in some parishes. The register uncovered shocking statistics, such as the fact that in 1766, 80 per cent of children admitted to the parish workhouse of St George's Bloomsbury and St Giles-in-the-Fields died before reaching their first birthday.[61] The former parish was termed by Hanway 'the greatest sink of mortality in these kingdoms, if not on the face of the whole earth'. He demonstrated to parliament that the best option for preserving life was to send infants to wet nurses in rural parishes outside of London, rather than sending them to infamous 'parish nurses' appointed by officers in parishes such as St Giles-in-the-Fields, and workhouses.[62] Hanway had envisaged a much greater role for the Foundling Hospital in the implementation of the 1767 Act, which was known by his name, but this did not materialize. Instead of the Hospital acting as an intermediary between parishes and nurses, which was Hanway's preferred model, parliament took measures to ensure parishes would themselves remove their infant poor from cities, establish mechanisms for inspection, and provide financial incentives to nurses to ensure their charges thrived. These measures did a great deal towards reducing the mortality rates for parish infants in the course of the next decade. In 1778, a House of Commons committee found that in sixteen parishes covered by the Act, almost 80 per cent of children had survived. Hanway's dedicated service to humanitarian causes, and his patriotic contribution to serving the national interest, were recognized by the state, and when he died in 1786 his final resting place for services to the nation was in Westminster Abbey, one of only a very few philanthropists to be honoured in this way.[63]

The Foundling Hospital undoubtedly benefitted from having the support of Jonas Hanway, one of the most effective parliamentary lobbyists of the eighteenth century. The question remained of how the thousands of surviving children admitted to the Hospital during the General Reception would be educated and apprenticed. Those children who had survived infancy with a wet nurse and lived long enough to be returned to the Foundling Hospital or one of its six provincial branch institutions would need further preparation for the destiny which their social betters had planned for them.

CHAPTER 4

Foundling Education

F OR MANY FOUNDLING children, being fostered by a wet nurse for just a few short years was their only first-hand experience of family life. How this shaped their emotional and psychological development is the most obvious question we might ask today, but this is difficult to answer because of the lack of evidence written by the children themselves. But there is one account from this period, recorded by foundling George King, who documented his earliest memories in his own words (Figure 4.1). We may imagine him sitting down with a blank sheet of paper and starting to write with the momentous headline 'Diary of the Incidents of the Life of the Undermentioned for Forty one years'. And so he began to tell his life story: 'George King was born at Hemel Hempstead in the County of Herts on the 10th day of June, 1787 and nothing materially occurred till I arrived at the age of four years...six months'. The archives tell us that George had in fact

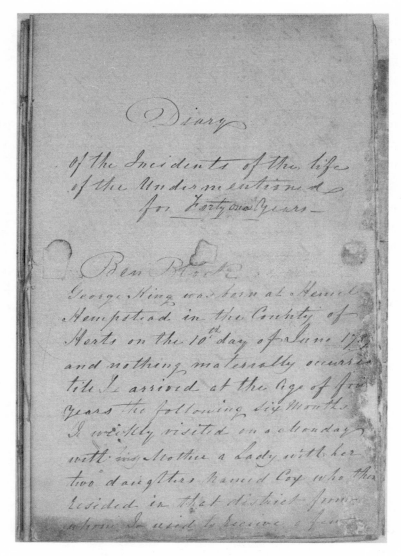

FIGURE 4.1 The first page of the autobiography of George King.

been admitted by ballot to the London Foundling Hospital on 10 November 1787.[1] Throughout his life, George would never have known the name of the woman who had given birth to him, but the Hospital's meticulous record keeping makes it possible for the prying eyes of posterity to know what he never did.[2] His birth mother's name was Mary Miller, and remarkably we are able to find out more about her since by the late 1780s the Foundling Hospital had a new policy that required women to give details of their circumstances when they came to surrender their babies. Mary Miller's petition survives (Figure 4.2), which she addressed 'To the Hon[our] able Gentlemen Governors of the Foundling Hospital', which in her own words:

> sheweth that your Petitioner is a very Great Object [of charity] having had the misfortune of having a Child with a young man who has Quitted her and Child leaving them in the most Extreme misery and not knowing where he is gone to as she has no Friend nor any way of maintaining herself nor Child. She humbly intreats Gentlemen that you would be graciously pleased to grant her the privilege of Drawing for the benefit of your Charitable Hospital which will be a Charity of greatest Merit being Conferred upon an Object in the greatest Need of Charity & who remains with all possible gratitude. Gentlemen, Your most Grateful Petitioner Mary Miller.[3]

There is no reason to suppose Mary did not pen the letter herself, since the handwriting is consistent with the signature. The style and content of the letter suggest indicates that she had a fairly good level of education for a woman of modest social status. The paper cover enveloping her petition records that the General

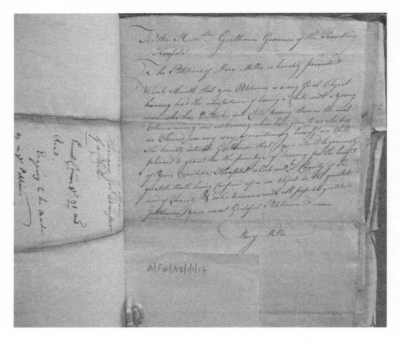

FIGURE 4.2 Petition of Mary Miller, George King's mother, whose name would have been unknown to her son.

Committee received her petition and considered it on 7 November. Her success in being entered three days later for the ballot to admit her baby was in part due to the support of a sponsor, Rev. Mr Harper, a clergyman who had 'recommended this Person as a proper object [of charity]'. Without further details it is impossible to be certain, but the evidence of her handwriting and the support of a clergyman suggests that Mary may have been a 'respectable' young woman who had been seduced, or allowed a relationship to be consummated on a promise of marriage, then deserted, circumstances which were accommodated by the Governors. Any hint that she was in the habit of pre-marital sex, or that she had a poor sexual reputation in her neighbourhood, and her petition would have been looked upon less favourably.

There is no way of knowing George's true birthday, but the Hospital's matron or clerk, or a wet nurse with long experience, guessed that he was five months old when his mother drew a white ball from the bag and he was taken away from her on 10 November 1787. He was one of nine babies admitted in the ballot, and like the others was immediately stripped of the clothing in which he had arrived, given a physical examination to check his health, and issued with a lead tag with his admission number. The necessary paperwork was completed. He was then baptised, bundled up with a package of baby clothes, and despatched to the countryside with a wet nurse.

In his autobiography, George stated that he was from Hemel Hempstead, but the actual location of his birth would also have been unknown to him. Again, the Foundling Hospital records yield up more of their secrets to explain his identification with this part of southern England. The wet nurse who suckled George was a woman named Ann Yeulet, and it was she, not George, who was from Hemel Hempstead. Her paid employment, to breastfeed and care for foundlings, was conducted under the scrutiny of the Foundling Hospital's local inspector, Lady Marchmont.[4] Ann would have been paid ten shillings every month, a generous sum compared with the wages of wet nurses employed locally by the parish to care for pauper infants, and a bonus of an additional month's wages if the child in her care lived for a year.

Happily, George was among those infants who survived their stay with a wet nurse during those early, perilous years of life. It is not surprising that he identified with Hemel Hempstead as 'my native place' since it was where he enjoyed a family life, nurtured by Ann, whom he referred to as his mother. His autobiography gives small and touching insights into the happy formative experiences that shaped him as a young child. His earliest memory was that at the age of four: 'I usually visited on a Monday with my Mother, a Lady with her two daughters named Cox' who used to give him sugar plums. This kindly neighbour also once gave him 'a small Wheel barrow' as a gift, 'for which I was thankful and first made use of it...to pick up a Horse dung which I thought myself very superb'. He also recalled going to a public house with his mother and receiving a fright from the assembled men, a rowdy group of farmers and soldiers. The surprise of seeing someone's head appearing above a settle chair 'as if [it] had been sawn or split asunder' (since he was too small to see the body that the head belonged to) set him crying for an hour. He also received a lesson in fairness when one of two boys who accompanied him to Hempstead Fair stole an orange from him. The kindlier of the two boys, whose name was Tom, made the thief return the fruit to its rightful owner and beat up the other lad for his crime.

George recalled many happy childhood memories that amused him in later life. His nurse was a good carer who evidently made him feel secure, placing his head upon her knees and carrying him to bed when he cried. The two other boys mentioned by George may have been the birth children belonging to the family in the household where he was raised. They gave him a nickname, 'Jack of Clubs', which, he reasoned, had been because he was 'nearly as thick as long'. George was evidently a stout, well-fed child who had treats and whose foster mother was proud enough of him to take him visiting in the neighbourhood. There was no mention of a father figure, and it is difficult to tell from this whether Ann Yeulet was a widow or whether her husband simply was absent in George's memory. That she was or had been married is certain. Unmarried mothers would not knowingly have been commissioned as wet nurses by the Foundling Hospital, in spite of the Governors' compassionate and enlightened attitudes for the time in relation to the illegitimacy of many of the infants admitted to their care.

For children raised at the expense of Foundling Hospital charity, their early years meant relative freedom among cottagers' families where some had been well treated, receiving the comforts of a maternal figure who took care of them. That George survived where so many others died was due in part to the care he received from his wet nurse Ann, but also to another twist of fate. The Foundling Hospital relied upon its network of genteel volunteers who acted as unpaid local inspectors, and the inspector in Hemel Hampstead, Lady Elizabeth Marchmont, was unusually diligent. She was the second wife of Hugh Hume Campbell, 3rd earl of Marchmont, a Scottish peer, politician, and bibliophile who divided his time between his estates in Berwickshire and his English country seat, Marchmont House in Hemel Hempstead.[5] Elizabeth *née* Crompton was the daughter of a bankrupt Cheapside linen draper, who in her teens had turned the earl's head at the theatre. Some twenty-three years her senior, Hugh was completely captivated by her beauty, and proposed to her almost immediately. The Marchmont marriage, though aristocratic, was negotiated in a language of love, passion, and sentiment that were of a piece with the popular idea of romantic love in the mid-Georgian era. During their brief courtship, Lord Marchmont had written her love letters that frankly expressed both his desire for her and his regard In one love letter the peer declared his passion: 'Lay your reason out of the question, don't say, *I ought to do so & so* to Lord Marchmont, but ask your heart, if there will be pleasure felt in…preferring him to every one of 'em'.[6] They were married, after just three weeks of courtship, in 1748.

Known to her husband as 'Betty', Elizabeth's relatively humble beginnings in an overcrowded London parish may have given her a lifelong interest in the plight of the metropolitan poor. She had only one child, a son, Alexander, Lord Polwarth, who died childless aged thirty-one, in 1781. Lady Marchmont's bereavement deepened her commitment to charitable work, and during the 1780s she threw herself into fulfilling her duties as an inspector for the Foundling Hospital. Writing in her own hand (with the aristocratic dignity of referring to herself in the third person), she corresponded frequently with the matron and secretary of the Foundling Hospital in London. She regularly asked for practical help, such as additional clothing for the children, and the advice of the Governors, showing she was keen to demonstrate that she was carrying out their instructions faithfully. She gave good references for the 'careful' nurses under her inspection, and passed on detailed information about the children, of whom there were up to fifteen 'under her Eye' (as she put it) at any one time. She expressed her sorrow when she had to report that one or more infants had died, and took it rather personally. She wrote on one occasion, at the time that George King would have been living with his foster family in Hemel Hempstead under her inspection:

Lady Marchmont is very sorry to send an account of the death of another foundling. There is a disorder among the children

about us, that has carried off several young Infants, but as every
care was taken of these children, she recommends the nurses
for others.[7]

The Georgians were no prudes. Perhaps spurred on by the example
of the pious and charitable aristocratic women who had sponsored the Foundling Hospital enterprise from the outset, Lady
Marchmont spent years of her respectable middle age helping to
sort out the plight of girls who had succumbed to seduction, and
their illegitimate offspring. She wrote in person to the secretary on
behalf of an unnamed local girl 'to know whether a Child can be
received into the Hospital, a poor young creature [having] had a
Child by a man who is run away'. Though her question was a proced-
ural one ('I shall be glad to know the proper way of proceeding'), the
Governors would have understood that Lady Marchmont's intervention was designed to exert her influence on the girl's behalf. Her
pride in her work, and in the young children in her care, shine
through her letters small. On 23 January 1791, foundling Mary Gibbs
was returned to London, brought up in Hemel Hempstead under
Lady Marchmont's watchful eye to be 'a very fine Girl' and to be
more educated than many poor boys at her age ('the Nurse has
taught her her Letters').[8]

In the light of Lady Marchmont's unusual diligence as a Hospital
inspector, there is another detail almost hidden in the archives that
enables us to piece together even more of her influence over the
lives of foundling infants in her care. A previously unseen letter
hidden in the General Correspondence indicates that it was she
who gave George King his name. Writing from Hemel Hempstead

on 9 November 1787, having received news that two babies were ready to be despatched to her nurses, Lady Marchmont wrote to the secretary, as was her custom:

> Sir,
>
> According to your desire I send two nurses Frances Rofe and Ann Yeulet. Please to name the Children George or Charlotte King, George or Charlotte Windsor & whenever more nurses are wanted I can send as many as you please for dry nurse Children.
>
> I am Sir
>
> Your Humble Servant,
E. Marchmont[9]

The register that recorded the despatch of infants to their nurses indicates that Lady Marchmont's wishes were carried out. At the same time and on the same day as George King (no. 18,053) was baptised in the Foundling Hospital Chapel, another baby received the name of George Windsor, and the next sequential number in the register (no. 18,054). Though other evidence is lacking, her choice of names is a hint that Lady Marchmont regarded her dedicated service not just as a form of Christian charity appropriate to her rank and gender as an aristocratic woman: it was a patriotic act of public service. In 1787, fears were deepening that the king's health was again deteriorating, and that he was showing signs of degenerating once again into 'madness'. The Marchmonts were well connected in the House of Lords, and war overshadowed international affairs, considering trouble was brewing in France and the loss of the American colonies was a recent, painful memory. Lady Elizabeth's patriotic naming of the two infant boys was a small gesture of solidarity with the reigning monarch in uncertain times.

The foundling children named George King and George Windsor survived the perilous early years of life in relative safety. On 28 October 1792, having reached the age of nearly five years, George Windsor was returned from Hemel Hempstead to the London Foundling Hospital. George King was also due to be returned, but Lady Marchmont reported that he was 'so ill of a fever that the apothecary thinks there wou'd be great danger in removing him [from Hemel Hempstead] at present'.[10]

But his reprieve was temporary. Unbeknown to young George at the time, his happy early childhood was about to be interrupted, and his life changed beyond measure. After just a few short years, those children who survived being raised by wet nurses were returned to London to be given a rudimentary education and training for work that was suitable to their station in life. The first that George knew of his departure from his carefree rural life, less than a month after he had recovered from his illness, was that he was taken 'from my native place in a Stage Coach for a passage to London with my mother to a School in Holborn'. Keen to emphasize in retrospect that this seemed to him to be a great adventure, he added that this was 'not without taking plenty of Ginger-bread where I had a regular surfeit on the passage'. That day, 11 November 1792, was the last time he would ever see Ann Yeulet, the woman he regarded as his mother. If George suffered lifelong trauma by being separated from his foster mother, he did not record his feelings in his autobiography. He was just five years old when it happened.

Some wet nurses may have been mercenary, and treated the babies in their care with indifference. But in other families, many foster mothers gave their charges maternal affection. There is evidence that many foundlings at the point of apprenticeship ran away from their masters and instead tried to return to their foster families in the country, or begged the Governors to be allowed to be apprenticed to them. Even in the early years of this system's operation, the clerk who witnessed the children being separated from their foster mothers noted that the women 'shewed the most lively sorrow in parting with them' and the children 'cried very much after their Mammys', anecdotal evidence that George was not alone in regarding his wet nurse as his mother.[11] Elsewhere in the Foundling Hospital archives there is evidence of some nurses caring deeply for the babies whom they were paid to look after and to suckle. On 23 January 1762, in the presence of six Hospital Governors including Jonas Hanway and Hans Sloane, a letter was read from Dr Collet to the secretary recommending:

Nurse Sarson who is come with the Child Elias Booth supposed to have the Stone [gallstones] as a tender Nurse fit to have the care of the Child if returned to Newbury and offering that she should stay in Town a few days to wait the Resolutions of the Physicians relative to the said Child.

At the next meeting, the same Nurse Sarson appeared before the committee herself 'and requested that she might be permitted to stay with Elisha Booth'. The committee resolved she should be allowed to stay another week so that 'he may be delivered to the said Nurse who seems to be tender of him'.[12] Real ties of affection and emotional bonding could take place between nurses and their foundling charges, and evidently George was one of the lucky ones. Some, such as nurse Hannah Reed from Farnham in Surrey, who had fostered foundlings William Freeman, William Luckes, and Thomas Arundell, later wrote to the Foundling Hospital Governors, asking to be remembered, with the humble request that they should 'please to give my Love to...my Childern [sic]'. Hannah had some skill with a pen and so others took the opportunity through her to pass on their love to their former charges ('Mary Budd will be glad to know how William Steel and Manney Thomas is').[13] There is no evidence that Ann Yeulet ever tried to be reunited with George King, whom she had nursed with such care, nor that he ever attempted to contact her again.

But some did try. Foundling Hospital Governors took a hard line when older children absconded from the Hospital and made their way back to their wet nurses, often at great distances from London, to the only family homes they had ever known. This was not an uncommon occurrence: a typical example was James Shrewsbury, apprenticed to Joseph Baxter of Vine Street, Christ Church Spitalfields, a wool comber, on 8 November 1769, who ran away shortly after he was put out as an apprentice, fleeing back to his wet nurse in Dorking.[14] James had spent the first five years of his life there, before being returned to the Foundling Hospital in June 1769. In this and similar cases, the General Committee instructed their local network of inspectors to ascertain the facts of the case and to order the foundling to be sent back immediately to his or her master, above all to preserve their own authority and credibility with employers and to maintain good social order.

Many children must have experienced the symptoms of trauma from the shock of being removed from their foster families. They were sent without warning to London and barracked in friendless living quarters with other children who cried themselves to sleep and wet their beds in distress. There is no reason to suppose that the effects of separation from families where they had spent their early years were different for eighteenth-century children from those experienced by children raised under a similar regime in the Foundling Hospital in modern times.[15] When Harold Tarrant was admitted in the early years of the twentieth century, babies were still being baptised on admission and given a new name, a medical examination, and were sent to the countryside to be nursed. Harry was returned to London by his foster family, and recalled 'there was lots of crying', although the children thought it was an adventure at first. He recalled, 'That [first] night when we went to bed we were told to kneel by our beds and say our prayers. There was no good-night hug or kiss and in the morning our dreams were not realised as we were still there.' In the daytime, Harry and his fellow orphans were not allowed to walk close to the Hospital walls, in case they came into contact with the corrupting influence of the outside world, or were tempted to run away. The children's hair was cut close, they were issued with uniforms, and they became institution-alized. From the perspective of a foundling in modern times, for Harry this was the moment when 'we lost our personality'.[16]

It is difficult to recover the direct experiences of poor children born in the eighteenth century since hardly any left their own accounts of their experiences. How they felt about wearing uniforms we can only imagine. Other sources of evidence suggest that at this time even the very poor, given the opportunity, wanted to express their individualism through their clothing.[17] It may be that a sense of pride could have been instilled in the children by wearing the Hospital's smart uniform designed by William Hogarth. The uniforms were made of sensible Yorkshire serge cloth in red and buff colours, the girls with 'cleanly' aprons and both boys and girls wearing white hats with red trims, their white neckerchiefs a mark of respectability. Certainly there was careful attention to the warmth of the children's clothing in winter. The quality of Foundling Hospital uniforms was beyond the means of many pauper families living in overcrowded London parishes at the time, but it also meant instant recognition that the wearer was a foundling, and made visible the stigma that came with being assumed to be 'bastards'.[18]

Once they were returned to London, the manner in which foundlings were raised was influenced by fashionable ideas about the proper way to educate children. These ideas were changing in the eighteenth century. In Western Europe, from medieval times through to the seventeenth century, the traditional Christian view held that children were inherently evil, born of the original sin that was present in the sexual union that was necessary for their conception. Evil was present even in newborns who were the legitimate offspring of a married couple and it was thought was the cause of children's bad behaviour. The best method of dealing with a child's disobedience was for parents to respond with correction and corporal punishment (hence the old English proverb 'spare the rod and spoil the child'), an idea 'deeply embedded in the traditions of Christian society'.[19] These ideas continued after the sixteenth-century Reformation in England: Puritan tracts focused on the necessity of beating children as 'physick to purge out much corruption that lurketh in children and as a salve to heal many wounds and sores made by their folly'. One author even claimed that buttocks were created by God so that they might cushion the child from injury whilst undergoing physical punishment.[20]

According to this world-view, illegitimate children were especially stigmatized. Their very existence was living proof of illicit and irregular sexual unions, and as a result of the circumstances of their birth such children were considered by many to be especially prone to sin, vice, and idleness. Some historians believe there was little change in discriminatory attitudes towards illegitimate children over the course of the centuries. More recently, new research has suggested that the Georgians came to see illegitimate children as objects of pity and compassion, rather than scorn. Fears about the ability of the British nation to defend itself in the face of military aggression from rival imperial powers, most especially France, on one hand presented an urgent need for manpower, but on the other raised concerns about the moral fabric of the nation. Critics of the Foundling Hospital warned of 'National Evils' and 'National Destruction' that would be unleashed by the charity becoming an established cause licensed and financially supported by the British government. Stern commentators argued that 'Destructive social Evils' and 'Illicit Carnal Incontinence' would produce generation after generation of illegitimate children predisposed to degeneracy, and the country would be ruined. The sexual morality that underpinned this condemnation, informed by Christian teaching and social custom, was overlaid with jingoistic support for the superiority of Britain in the struggle for European imperial supremacy. The supposedly French manner of dealing with urban poverty via foundling hospitals, some argued, would lead to a further increase in 'French disease', producing weak and sickly offspring unable to work and defend their country, enfeebled with syphilis and other venereal infections.[21]

Many Georgians had a different, rather more optimistic view of society and the nature of humanity, which presented a different set of principles regarding children's education. They argued that humankind was not inherently wicked, just misguided, and began to question whether children 'inherited the sins of their fathers'. Following the philosopher John Locke's influential work *Some Thoughts Concerning Education* (1693), the idea began to take hold that the child was from birth a *tabula rasa*, a completely clean slate, open to character formation through good education and moral instruction from parents and tutors. Locke's views were radical for their time, although not especially kind to modern eyes. He recommended toughening children up by such measures as deliberately making them wear thin shoes in cold, wet weather and not wrapping them up to keep warm, ideas that doubtless influenced the stoical attitudes expressed by the Foundling Hospital's physician, Dr Cadogan.[22] According to these new 'enlightened' attitudes, parents, doctors, and educators, not children, were to blame for moral failings in society. As the eighteenth century progressed, children came to be admired as closer to nature than adults, more open and free to express their inclinations and emotions, unfettered by habit and convention. Children had always played, but now their play was celebrated in childrearing guides and didactic literature, given licence, and regarded as an inherent right.

For the children of the working poor, these sentiments usually had little direct relevance in their daily lives. The Christian kindness and humanist values that inspired charitable giving to help ameliorate the suffering of orphaned and abandoned innocents did not erase the stigma that was attached to illegitimacy across the social spectrum. And yet, in the realm of education and philanthropic charity, the lives even of pauper children were touched by the effects of these changing ideas about childhood later captured in the French Enlightenment philosopher Jean-Jacques Rousseau's *Émile, or, On Education* (1762). Rich and influential patrons of children's charities enjoyed witnessing the improving effects of their social experiments with the latest childrearing philosophies. Like Rousseau, they argued that if brought up by vicious or neglectful parents, a child would turn out bad. The *philosophes* claimed that, all other conditions being equal, humanity tended towards good, and the best instructor for this was the natural world. Reason could conquer superstition and things could change and be made better, including society itself.

In an extreme example of the vogue for experimenting with Rousseau's ideas on childrearing, Thomas Day, an eccentric young law student, in conspiracy with a well-connected gentleman schoolfriend, Richard Lovell Edgeworth, duped the Foundling Hospital Governors into handing over two young girls, Ann Kingston and Dorcas Car. The Hospital records confirm that twelve-year-old Ann and eleven-year-old Dorcas were to enter into service in Edgeworth's household. One of the safeguards upon female foundlings' reputations, as recounted by the Hospital's treasurer in the year 1799, was that 'No girl is apprenticed to an unmarried man, nor to a married man, unless the wife has seen the girl, and has expressed her concurrence in the application'.[23] This may have sounded reassuring to the guardians of public morality, but did not prove a failsafe method in practice. Edgeworth, a respectable lawyer and a married man, used his marital status to secure the girls (although there is no evidence that his wife was required to provide evidence she consented to this arrangement). He then handed them over to his friend to raise them as he pleased, according to Rousseau's pronouncements, so that Day could pick one of the girls and make her his wife once she was of age. Neither of the children was aware that this was Day's intentions until many years later.

In the twenty-first century, Day would undoubtedly be accused of paedophilia. It appears from surviving correspondence that his motives were more pedagogical than sexual, though whether the archives would ever yield the full truth is unlikely. His entire project was deemed morally and ethically questionable by friends who were aware of his intentions. When Day tracked down the philosopher and author of *Émile* himself to tell him of his 'experiment', Rousseau was horrified and declared his intention was never that anyone should take his philosophical work literally. The girls themselves, renamed 'Sabrina' and 'Lucretia' by Day, were subject to all kinds of strange regimes, as well as unusual opportunities for travel, education, and mixing in polite circles, but left no account of their unorthodox upbringing in their own words. Neither of them fulfilled his ambition of becoming his wife one day, since they both exhibited the troubling quality of having minds and opinions of their own.[24]

It was from among these radical new ideas about the nature of the human condition, of which the philosophy of childrearing was an important component, that the discipline of political philosophy was born. An assortment of new philosophical experiments, called the Enlightenment in retrospect, came to dominate European thought. These ideas were also translated to the New World and ultimately influenced the constitutional foundation of modern America.[25] Charity was seen by devout Christians and sceptics alike as the logical response to suffering, arising from humanitarian concern, but also the demands of creating and sustaining an ordered society. Instead of accepting that things were as they were because God willed it so, men and women started to believe that they themselves could be the agents of change, remaking a better world. It also helps to explain the new interest in children and childrearing that emerged. It was not that earlier generations had been unloving towards their offspring. But, in the eighteenth century, the question of how to raise the next generation became a proper subject of inquiry in its own right, preoccupying moralists, philosophers, and the emerging nation state.[26] Even those who weighed these problems in strictly economic terms could see the need to supply an expanding global British Empire with an escalating standing army and navy hungry for soldiers and sailors. No longer was it possible to ignore the social problems attendant on the rise of London, a teeming metropolis full of indigent poor with numberless infants. These questions were of more than theoretical concern: they became the most pressing social problem of the Georgian era, and the Foundling Hospital was the pre-eminent institution that enabled a vast experiment to be conducted in children's education.

The Governors of the Foundling Hospital were influenced by Enlightenment ideas regarding the moral education of children, and innovated according to medical fashions of the day, in terms of the dietary regimes and medical treatments that were tried out on children in their care. Dr Richard Mead, a pioneer of vaccination against smallpox and governor of the charity, implemented the wholescale vaccination of foundling children. Their days started at 6am (or later in winter) with the older ones helping the younger ones to dress, and they busied themselves with chores, such as drawing water and tidying and cleaning their wards. Breakfast was followed by lessons all morning, with dinner at one o'clock. There were more lessons in the afternoon, and playtime was allowed for part of the day, particularly for the younger children. Work was incorporated into the daily routine, with Saturdays taken as a half-day (and Sunday observed as a Sabbath rest day).[27]

As with pauper children in workhouses, the education of foundlings was a matter of raising children whose lives were pre-ordained to follow certain lowly occupations in unskilled or semi-skilled employment. It was decidedly not, of course, about discovering their potential and encouraging them to better themselves, in spite of their humble origins. The foundlings slept and ate decent but simple food communally, and became accustomed to the institutionalized and impersonal regimes overseen by nurses, schoolmasters, and chaplains. Their basic schooling was in alphabet rote learning (to enable them to get by with basic literacy sufficient to learn and understand Bible lessons), physical discipline, manual work, and handicrafts that befitted paupers of obscure origins. One account written anonymously in 1749 in answer to public curiosity about how the children were being raised gave the following assessment: 'Their Work consists in such bodily Labour as is suitable to their Age and Strength, and may best fit them for the Sea Service'. Their education also gave them the requisite skills 'for Agriculture', such as 'Digging, Houghin, Plouwing, Hedging, cleaving Wood, carrying Burdens'. This early narrative displayed some prejudices that were later abandoned or modified. One such opinion was that 'Manufactures in general seem improper for the Employment of the Boys, being likely to incline them to a Way of Life not intended for them'. Less controversial were repetitive, 'simple and laborious' tasks, such as 'spinning and twisting Thread and small Ropes'.[28]

The original ethos of the Foundling Hospital was to raise girls and boys to live industrious lives according to their station, as expressed by Jonas Hanway's opinion that 'to suffer so many *children to be bred to beggary*, as if it were a *regular trade and occupation*, in a country renowned for laws, industry, skill, and opulence, is a circumstance credible only from its being *seen*, and of all faults in political economy, perhaps the greatest'.[29] The Act for Confirming and Enlarging the powers Granted by his Majesty to the Governors and Guardians of the [Foundling] Hospital (1740) specifically enlarged their absolute authority to despatch children to suitable occupations:

> That it shall and may be lawful for the said Corporation...to detain and employ in any Sort of Labour or Manufacture, or in the Sea Service, and all and every such Child or Children by them so maintained and educated [boys until the age of twenty-four, girls until twenty-one or marriage] or to bind any such child or Children Apprentice or Apprentices to any Person or Persons who shall be willing to take the same or to place them out as Servants, or as Mariners, to any Husbandmen, Master or Captain of a Ship, or other Person whatsoever.[30]

The frontispiece to the 1759 imprint of the *Account of the Hospital for the Maintenance and Education of Exposed and Deserted Young Children* (of which there were four separate publications under the same title

THE FOUNDLINGS.

Engraved by H. Setchell, from the Original Drawing by Hogarth.

Jones & Cº Temple of the Muses Finsbury Square London.

FIGURE 4.3   Foundling children are shown at the point that they are returned to the Hospital from their wet nurses in the countryside. They hold the work tools that were thought appropriate for boys and girls, a prediction of their 'industrious' lives ahead. Frontispiece by William Hogarth, Anon., *Account of the Hospital for the Maintenance and Education of Exposed and Deserted Young Children* (1759).

between 1749 and 1807) (Figure 4.3) made a graphic connection between the useful employment of foundling children in a variety of occupations, specifically for the purposes of empire building and the prosperity of Britannia. The boys were depicted with the tools for useful trades: a plumb line ('plummet') and measuring rule for building trades, a trowel for gardening (or, symbolically, farming), and a card for combing wool. Other boys wear sailors' jackets and trousers. The girls were shown perfecting their skills for diligent domestic labour, with spinning wheel, needlework sampler, and broom at the ready.[31] On the far right-hand corner of this image, a child kisses his nurse goodbye, thereby assuring the more sensitive that their mission had not been without feeling and attention to children's emotional development. But it was a parting nonetheless, featured as a goodbye to motherly affection at a socially sanctioned but tender age. The presence of a British fleet in the distance was a reminder of the nation's pressing need for more labour. Hogarth depicts the rational utility of the Foundling Hospital's mission in 'decent' order (in contrast to the scandalous wastefulness of the chaotic abandonment of infants shown in the wayside) and with attention to Christianity (the prophet-like central figure resembling Moses was supposed to be Thomas Coram himself).

The purpose of the Foundling Hospital, reiterated with new force during the General Reception when expense was at the public purse, was to preserve life, to 'render [the children's] ... lives useful' and promote industry and piety, to 'recover connexions with parents or blood kin' where possible (although as has already been noted, this proved a vain hope in most cases), and finally to 'exonerate the public, as speedily as is consistent with the preservation of each particular child'.[32] Educating children in their basic letters, and in gender-appropriate skills for their humble social rank, was part of the Governors' mission. In 1757, following concerns about their charges' lack of schooling, the Governors had employed Robert Atchison, a reforming schoolmaster, who (unusually at the time) taught boys rudimentary writing skills as well as reading, and better levels of numeracy than they would have received in the parish system. His legacy was considerable. By 1800, nearly 100 per cent of foundling boys could sign their names.[33] Some knowledge of arithmetic was also valuable for apprenticeship to employment requiring more high-level skills, such as dealing in weights, measures, and account keeping.[34]

George King was one of those whose lives, and career prospects, were transformed by this small educational opportunity unavailable to the vast majority of poor children raised beyond the gates of the Foundling Hospital. In his autobiography, he called the Hospital his 'school', and wanted particularly to record that he was placed 'under the care of Mr Robert Atchison the Schoolmaster and a worthy gentleman he was'. Following the devastating separation from his foster mother, George evidently found himself a mentor and protector in his teacher. He recalled, 'I took a liking to learn my lessons for which I frequently got small presents from my Schoolmaster'. Significantly, he found himself a male role model at about the same time that he was 'breeched', which would have taken place around the age of seven, receiving his first pair of knee-length trousers that symbolized the moment when a boy entered the world of men. Perhaps because he showed unusual diligence and a desire to learn, George was 'put to Writing'. His studiousness evidently paid off. Some years later, in 1798, at the age of about eleven, he recalled, 'I copied a Writing from my Schoolmaster addressed to the Treasurer of the School for which I received one Shilling'. Not all boys showed George's aptitude, nor benefitted from the schoolmaster's particular attention. In his case, the acquisition of better literacy skills, notably the ability to be a precise and clear copyist with a good hand, made the difference between a life of obscure drudgery and a decent living, with the ability to leave for posterity a record of his autobiography.[35]

There were considered to be different vocations for boys and girls, reflecting what was deemed appropriate spheres for men and women of low birth. For poor boys raised in the Foundling Hospital (unlike those raised in workhouses), physical strength, discipline, and a certain institutionalized mentality were fostered by the repetition of military drill and marching upon the parade ground outside of the Hospital's main court. In keeping with the Hospital's mission to raise good citizens for the nation, imperialist ideas about the desirability of sea service or the army were imparted early. We know that George King witnessed this first hand for himself from his recollection that the Hospital grounds were used by the Bloomsbury and Inns of Court militia for drill practice.[36] One of the most memorable episodes of his young life was witnessing a parade inspection by George III. The king had temporarily recovered his health, and visited the Foundling Hospital in June 1800 following a general review in Hyde Park of 40,000 troops belonging to volunteer regiments. He recalled that after the corps was inspected on the parade ground: '[His Majesty] was shewn into the Chapel where two Chairs was [sic] placed by the Aisle...the Organ commenced with the Coronation Anthem and after God Save the King the Boys and Girls that sung were two Hundred'. To mark this special occasion, the children were given 'plumb Cake' ('a great treat') and more thrilling still, George recalled that the soldiers left behind them upon the parade ground a number of spent cartridges containing traces of gunpowder. This was a cause of great excitement for George and the other boys. He alone was bold enough to hazard an experiment—writing his initials in gunpowder and setting them alight. 'In an Instant', he recalled, 'the whole went off and I had the Satisfaction to have my eye brows completely

shaved', an accident that caused him always to be careful of handling gunpowder. The sense of camaraderie among the foundling
boys emerges from this unfortunate incident. The fact that George
was something of a hero among his friends for his bravery (he completed the exercise 'my Companions looking on') was an indication
of the derring-do that led him on to great adventures in later life.
His first experiment with gunpowder certainly scared him witless
('for a minute I did not know whether I was alive or dead'). It also
hinted that he formed a close bond with other boys of a similar age
who mattered greatly to him. 'All things went on gaily while I was at
School' was his cheerful final reflection on the subject.[37] If there
was bullying, he did not mention it. Here and elsewhere in his autobiography, George recorded that he forged a close bond with his
best friend, Henry Rivington, evidence of an affectionate fraternal
relationship between the pair that animates the dry historical record of Henry, which simply lists him as 'foundling no. 18,050'.
George recalled in later life how, since he quit the Hospital before
Henry, he would return for visits, taking 'as many apples and oranges
as my little stock would afford sampling the choicest for my poor
Rivington'.[38]

George King's account of his education at the Foundling Hospital,
with an attentive, kindly schoolmaster, fondly recalled boyhood
scrapes, and best friends, surely has an element of rose-tinted
hindsight. There are no other first-hand accounts written by boys
of George King's generation that would enable us to test his version
of events, and none at all by girls that would give us their perspectives on their childhood experiences, but memoirs from more modern times are a caution against too much of a happy picture. Former
foundling Harry Tarrent, writing his account of his upbringing in

the Foundling Hospital retrospectively at the age of ninety-two, gave his impressions of a childhood deprived of affection and family belonging, and reflected 'it is not a life I would have wished upon anybody else'.[39]

There was little choice for eighteenth-century foundlings as they grew up about how they would make a living. Aptitude mattered less than the dictates of would-be employers. Mending nets, picking hemp rope, and other repetitive tasks instilled in boys the idea that they were hard-working members of the 'industrious' poor. Masculine qualities were instilled by such labour: silk manufacture was deemed 'too effeminate for the larger Boys' and it was resolved that they should instead 'be employed in the open Air, and enured [sic] to the changes of Weather'.[40] For girls, a lifetime of drudgery and servitude lay ahead, although in this they were no different from members of their own sex and rank who were raised beyond the Hospital walls. They were given lessons in housewifery ('Needlework, Knitting and Spinning, in the Kitchen, Laundry, and Household-work, in order to make them useful Servants'), and the bourgeois emphasis upon female chastity was repeated to them often.[41] Their lowly social rank was reinforced even by the kind of needlework that the girls were taught—usually rough and practical mending rather than fine embroidery, making it less likely that they would find themselves gainful employment with a level of skill beyond the most menial tasks. The idea that the girls could turn out to be no better than their mothers was an underlying anxiety on the part of the Hospital's Governors and polite visitors. The importance of maintaining virtue and modesty, appropriate to their humble rank as well as their subordinate sex, was impressed forcefully upon foundling girls. These themes were inculcated by the adult women who staffed the Hospital, including the matron and nurses, and were often repeated in their religious instruction by their schoolmistresses and the Hospital chaplain. Segregation by gender of dormitories, schoolrooms, and even play areas was thought to be the most decent way of raising the girls and boys under the Hospital's care. The watchful supervision of three schoolmistresses ensured order was kept in the three groups into which the girls were divided as they were instructed in needlework and reading (but not writing). As appropriate for their future occupations as domestic servants and wives, they assisted in household work increasingly as they got older, with hands-on experience in the Hospital's kitchens, doing laundry and mending garments.[42] Recent research has also highlighted the sheer volume of work undertaken by Foundling Hospital girls in making clothes for the infants under the institution's care, and the cost saving that this represented. Just twenty-five foundling girls produced over 6,400 garments in a year, including linen shirts and caps, and neck-cloths, long stays, aprons, clouts (nappies), and sleeves made from various other textiles, an average of over 250 items each.[43] The hardworking poor girls raised within the Foundling Hospital's walls were schooled to have expectations no better than their counterparts raised outside of the charity's care in London parishes. But in other respects they fared better: they were protected, sleeping in single-sex wards, overseen by a female matron, and instructed in letters, well fed, and clothed warmly. Both boys and girls, however, risked the hazards of contagious diseases that spread rapidly through institutional living. The most common cause of death was dysentery, spread by contaminated water, milk, or solid food, but scabies, fevers, and smallpox also presented major threats to the children's health, especially during winter.[44]

Some boys and girls were returned from country nurses to be raised at one of the six provincial branches of the London Foundling Hospital set up during the General Reception to cope with the volume of children taken in during the period of direct funding by parliament. The idea was that they would be treated in a similar fashion to those in London, with the same ethos of hard work, discipline, and minimal education. Each branch had its own secretary who co-ordinated a network of local inspectors overseeing wet and dry nurses in the area, and wrote regularly to London to request instructions on all matters relating to the running of the branch institutions, from the appointment of staff to the keeping of accounts, and the reception and disbursal of children. It was a significant part of the charity's ethos to make visible the industriousness of their small charges, whether raised in London or in the branch hospitals. Sir Thomas Bernard, the London Foundling Hospital treasurer, stated proudly that for girls aged between eleven and fourteen years raised in London, 'the average annual produce of [their] ... work [is] £2 13 0 for each girl' (that is, £2 and 13 shillings, about a quarter of the annual wage of a female domestic servant).[45]

The children of the Ackworth branch of the Foundling Hospital had a distinctive pattern of work: they were employed in making uniforms out of the local worsted cloth for themselves and for the foundling children in London, capitalizing on their proximity to new cloth manufacturing industries in the West Riding of Yorkshire.[46] Children at Ackworth engaged in the production of cloth from start to finish—they carded, combed, spun, and wove cloth made from wool and flax.[47] The London Governors found it difficult to maintain educational standards in the branch hospitals, where the lessons available to children varied, and where the length of stay could be shorter at different times of the year, depending upon the demand for employment in local areas. The Ackworth Hospital was criticized after the London Governors discovered that only two out of eight boys returned to London from Yorkshire could read. The Ackworth secretary, Dr Lee, protested, pointing out that 'this hospital has been more a place to put out children, than to instruct them in reading', although the girls, more than the boys, had received the instruction of a schoolmaster since they spent longer in the Hospital before being apprenticed.[48]

Visitors to the London Foundling Hospital paid to watch the foundlings at work every day of the week apart from Sundays, and benefactors who gave money to support the charity could receive the gratification of knowing their investment was helping to produce industrious citizens. The usefulness of the children's education was also advertised to genteel visitors by means of a shop stocked with handicraft goods made by the children, an essential part of a visit to the Hospital by the fashionable visitor engaged in the exercise of sensibility and compassion.[49] The Foundling Hospital enterprise was as much about economic rationalism within the context of British colonial ambition and Enlightenment rationality as it was about Christian charity. Spasmodic concern over whether children were receiving adequate instruction in the gospels led to the issuing of Bibles and public catechizing of the children in the Hospital chapel, where they recited by heart the main creeds of the Christian faith.[50]

The only other option that was considered for foundlings' education was a proposal to set up a music school, which would have offered an alternative career to boys and girls who showed a talent for singing or instrument playing. The idea was supported by the famous musicologist Dr Charles Burney, and the virtuoso violinist Giardini, who was a governor of the Hospital and had helped stage concerts in the chapel. They presented a plan that would generate further donations and provide employment for the children, but the idea was quickly crushed by the Governors as an unnecessary expense that would encourage dissatisfaction among the children about their station in life.[51] Those who opposed this proposal cited the terms of employment set out by the Act of Parliament, since 'music was not either a labour or a manufacture'.[52] Tragically, only foundlings who had no alternative form of employment were allowed to pursue any musical inclinations. In 1753, an exception was made for blind foundling Tom Grenville, who at the age of seven was allowed to learn to play the harpsichord, and proved to be so talented that he later went on to play the chapel organ.[53] The idea that education 'above their station' might be provided to some foundlings would have been intolerable to many eighteenth-century people. As Jonas Hanway commented, addressing the charitable members of the prosperous middling and upper sorts of people:

> Whilst we exercise these duties of *humanity*, we shall teach the *common people*, that due obedience to *superiors*, in defence of the *public good*, is the only solid ground on which they can hope to be *free* or *happy*![54]

Foundling children received this message from many sources, not just the Governors, schoolteachers, and nursing staff. The benefactors of the Hospital, and paying visitors, could witness for themselves the neat array of foundlings in their uniforms, scrubbed up on a

Sunday and singing hymns in the chapel. Some of these were written especially for the Foundling Hospital, and reminded the children of their origins and obligations. The short and to-the-point Foundling Hymn, drawing upon the 27th Psalm, emphasized the children's abandonment, reliance upon charity, and God's providence in saving them from certain death:

I
Our Light, our Saviour is the Lord,
For nothing need we care;
The mighty Lord is our Support,
What have we then to fear?

II
When Parents, deaf to Nature's Voice,
Their helpless Charge forsook;
Then Nature's God, who heard our Cries,
Compassion on us took.

III
Continue still to hear our Voice,
When unto Thee we cry;
And still the Infant's Praise receive,
And still their Wants supply.[55]

The foundling who took to heart the words of such hymns every Sunday could have been in no doubt about his or her absolute abandonment and their utter reliance upon God's benevolence. It may be that the dour sentiments of the hymns mattered less than the collective experience of communal singing for the children. Perhaps their performances before people of fashion made them feel special, and provided a welcome break from their daily routines.

Certainly George King remembered hymn singing fondly in his autobiography, and he recalled with pleasure how he used to go back voluntarily to the Hospital on Sundays to attend evening worship in the chapel once he had left.[56]

Once the children had reached the age for apprenticeship, the Governors of the London Foundling Hospital were charged with seeking suitable employment for them as they entered adolescence. Since the days of Elizabeth I, it was customary for London youths between the ages of fifteen and seventeen to be bound over by their families as apprentices, and slightly younger (aged thirteen or fourteen) in towns outside of London. Families paid a premium for their children, usually but not exclusively their sons rather than their daughters, to learn a trade over a period of seven years. The value of the premium reflected the prestige of the trade into which they would enter, and the status and wealth that would likely follow from earning a living in that occupation.[57] Poor children raised at the expense of the parish in a workhouse, and foundling children, were similarly bound over as apprentices, but usually at a younger age.

Apprenticeship had moral and practical dimensions: as historian Jane Humphries has observed, it 'saved the children of the poor from social exclusion and, by providing them with basic maintenance and some general training, enabled them to become productive adults'.[58] There was undoubtedly an element of social engineering attached to the system of indentured labour that became customary in Shakespeare's day. The poor apprenticed their children at a younger age than the better-off, and the kinds of occupations that were within their reach were much more limited, since premiums for them to learn more lucrative trades were too costly. The system was designed to cut down on vagrancy and unemployment, the biggest social problems in Elizabethan England. Justices of the peace could enforce this means of employing young people from families 'overburdened with children' who might otherwise be chargeable to the parish, and premiums were raised by overseers of the poor from ratepayers' taxes. Until the end of the eighteenth century, this proved to be the most effective means of ensuring young people married late and had fewer children.

For children admitted to the Foundling Hospital in 1756, the average age of apprenticeship was eleven, which was slightly lower than in the years leading up to the General Reception period. Those foundling apprentices sent out to work during the 1760s and 1770s seem piteously young to the modern eye, but by contemporary standards they were only slightly younger than many children despatched by their parents to learn a trade, and were normally older than, or at least the same age as, pauper apprentices sent out to work by parish authorities.[59] A traveller throughout England at this time would have seen children toiling in fields, as well as in towns and cities. The family budgets of agricultural workers employed on low wages between 1787 and 1816 suggest that agricultural labourers generally put their children to work at the age of eleven, while factory workers' children began to earn their living at just under ten years.[60] Some workhouse children at this time were sent out to work as young as four. Similar cases of foundlings being apprenticed as young as three to five years old remained exceptional and were only granted by special dispensation of the Governors.[61]

Responsibility for securing apprenticeships and issuing all indentures (the legally binding documents with the master or mistress taking the child as an apprentice) was co-ordinated by the secretary of the London Foundling Hospital, acting upon the instruction of the Governors. Further afield where this responsibility was delegated, the six provincial branches were obliged to make inquiries as to the good character of potential masters or mistresses and return signed testimonials to London from respected members of local parishes. The General Committee minutes indicate that this was a routine part of the Governors' and inspectors' business. In January 1756 the Governors present at the general committee noted that 'in the present Year... there are 32 Children, who are of Age to be placed out Apprentice'. The steward was charged with compiling a list of children and making suitable inquiries to find masters and mistresses via local networks of inspectors, a practice which widened to a nationwide search in the years following the General Reception.[62]

The most common method for finding a master or mistress who would take a foundling as their apprentice was by inspectors inquiring by word of mouth in a neighbourhood. The details of anyone who came forward were then reported in writing by the inspectors to the Hospital Governors. John Hewitt the Elder of Meeting House Yard in the Parish of St Mary, Whitechapel, a weaver, was said to be 'willing to take [James] Scribe as his Apprentice'. The report was read on 25 July 1770 at the General Committee and the steward was despatched to enquire after the character of Hewitt.[63] Written confirmation was needed from a reputable neighbour of the prospective master or mistress regarding their suitability, particularly that they had sufficient means to maintain a foundling apprentice and were of upright character and reputation. The steward reported to the General Committee on 2 April 1788 that another prospective master, Mr Badland, a shoemaker of St Clement Danes, was by reputation in his neighbourhood, and according to the Hospital's inspector, 'a very industrious indefatigable Man thoroughly conversant in his business and a man of some property, his house is full of Journeymen that he employs'. The apprenticeship indenture for the boy George Grafton to this master was recorded in the apprenticeship register as being issued on 14 May 1788, indicating an indenture could be issued quickly once a reference had been received.[64] The efficiency and speed of the Foundling Hospital's methodical system for apprenticing boys and girls were shown in the case of the master Captain Luke Rippon 'as soon as Possible' as he was going to sea 'immediately' and needed two boys for sea service.[65] Standard practice was for two copies of the indenture to be signed, and these were then sent to receive the Hospital's seal One copy was returned to the master, and the other retained by the London Foundling Hospital, even if the apprentice was employed at a distance from the metropolis (in a few cases, this involved one or more foundlings being sent immediately overseas).

Modest premiums were usually offered by the Foundling Hospital Governors to employers who took a foundling apprentice at £5 per annum. This relatively small sum was to deter the 'wrong' kind of master from taking on an apprentice (that is, someone seeking to profit from the premium that came with taking a child). The parish workhouse of St Martin's-in-the-Fields offered a paltry premium of only £2 per apprentice, which similarly acted as a deterrent to would-be profiteers. Campbell's 1747 book, the *London Tradesman*, suggested that £5 was at the bottom range of premiums, and that it represented a standard amount for entry into many artisan trades.[66] Exceptionally much higher premiums could be paid to apprentice foundlings to masters in lucrative occupations. The example of foundling George Grafton was one such case, a privately sponsored child with an aristocratic name who was despatched with a £21 premium. The additional sum had been invested in his upbringing by an unknown patron, on the grounds that the shoemaking business 'was of such a nature that no Man that was properly instructed it need be out of employ a day in the Year'. Such children inspired speculation that they were the illegitimate offspring of aristocratic liaisons, particularly if they appeared well dressed upon admission to the Foundling Hospital and had better prospects than other children upon leaving the Hospital's care.[67] So we find nine-year-old Felix Coram, apprenticed on 13 December 1769, to John Kittle, a glovemaker at St Dunstan in the East, recorded as 'Private Child: No Fee' when he went out into the world, an apprenticeship to a relatively high-status 'genteel' trade. Glovemakers dealt in fine fabrics and their customers were prosperous citizens and gentry, which meant that this kind of trade was normally beyond the orbit of former foundlings. In this instance, the cost was met by a private sponsor and incurred no expense to the Hospital.[68] This feature of Foundling Hospital apprenticeships was unusual and distinctive to the charity, with no parallel in the parish system for apprenticing children who had been raised in workhouses.

Each foundling was despatched with 'decent' clothing for their employment and instructions on how to behave themselves as good workers and citizens. Early in 1764, John Pearse, a 'poulterer' (who made his livelihood from selling chickens), braved attendance at a General Committee meeting of the Hospital Governors, bringing his wife along with him. They proposed before the assembled dignitaries that they should take seven-year-old Hannah Turner as their apprentice for 'household business' provided that she came with a fee of £5 and that she proved able to read, say her catechism and prayers, and 'work at her needle'. Another condition was that she should be supplied by the Hospital with decent and durable new clothes, as was customary upon apprenticeship, which was a substantial expense for poorer members of society. For little Hannah as for the other girls, this consisted of a coat, two petticoats, three shifts (undergarments), three capes for daytime wear, four for nightwear, two bibs and apron (essential for household work), two pairs of stockings, two pairs of shoes, and a hat. Together with the regulation issue of a Bible and Book of Common Prayer, the total cost came to just over £1 and 15 shillings for girls. There was a similar allowance for suitable clothing, a Bible, and prayer book for boys.[69] In addition, each child received printed instructions on the necessity of upright Christian living, good conduct, and obedience towards their masters.[70] Since married women were unable to sign indentures themselves, women employers represented among the apprenticeship records would have been either unmarried or widows. This must have been the case for mistress Rebecca Webb, a 'Barber and Peruke [wig] maker' by trade, who took thirteen-year-old Prescot Embrey to be her apprentice.[71]

Some of the families that had fostered children from the Foundling Hospital saw an opportunity to have the children returned to them on a permanent basis through apprenticeship. The emotional attachment between foundling children and the families in which they had been wet nursed and fostered seeps through the official documents and minutes that recorded the apprenticeship decisions of the Foundling Hospital's governing committees. So, for example, we find the sub-committee receiving the following letter in January 1762:

> Mr Whatley communicated to this Committee a Letter from Mrs Searle of Bishops Hall in the parish of Lambourn Essex Inspectress of the Children of the Hospital there acquainting him that John Richardson of the Parish of Stapleford in Essex proposed to take as an Apprentice a Boy named Abraham Western No. 5035 Nursed by the Wife of the said Richardson. Mrs Searle writes to Mr Whatley [Secretary of the Foundling Hospital] that she realy [sic] believes those Persons can maintain the Child. They rent a Farm of about £30 a Year and are sober and industrious. The Man is Church Clerk of a Parish adjacent to Mrs Searle. He proposes to give the Boy a Trade & to send him to a Free School in a Parish belonging to Lord Fortescue.

In this case, the Hospital Governors looked favourably upon the proposal: 'It is the opinion of this Committee that the said Child should be Apprenticed to the said Richardson & it is referred to the General Committee to give orders accordingly.' In the apprenticeship register, the entry for foundling Abraham Western confirms that this boy was indeed apprenticed to John Richardson of the Parish of Stapleford Abbots in Essex on 27 January 1762. The official indenture record alone gives no indication of the ties of affection between foundling Abraham, his former wet nurse, and her husband that led to his apprenticeship with them at the unusually young age of five. For this family, and for little Abraham, this must have been the happiest possible outcome.[72]

There are other examples of foundlings being apprenticed to the families in which they had been fostered. In June 1762,

Mr Hanway and Mr Whatley of the sub-committee of the Foundling
Hospital 'Read a Letter from Mrs Searle of Bishops Hall near
Lambourn in regard to two Persons who desire to take two
Children Apprentices'. The first of these petitioners was John
Mott, aged twenty-nine, who:

> appear'd before this Committee and alledges that he keeps a lit-
> tle farm of £13 a Year and gains 8 or 10s a week and as a
> Husbandman and has only one Child of his own and has had
> none for 5 Years and desires to take No. 3334 Eliz. Fish as an
> Apprentice, his Wife Martha who has nursed several Foundlings
> being present and requesting the same and both appear as very
> decent and sober persons.

The second petitioner was 'Laurence Viney aged 32' who:

> has a small Farm and gains 8 or 10s a week as a husbandman
> and desires to take [foundling no.] 3486 Sarah Moore as an
> Apprentice, his Wife Elizabeth also appearing and confirming
> the same and expresses a great desire to take this Child, tho' she
> has three others not grown up, alledging that she has full a great
> tenderness for her as she has for her own Children, and this man
> and his Wife also appear as very decent sober persons, which
> corresponds with the Character given of these 4 Men and
> Women by Mrs Searle.

The Governors and inspectors were cautious, almost cynical it
seems, in their scepticism about foster families' claims to having
a 'tenderness' for a particular foundling child. It is no coincidence that they inquired closely about whether a family was by
reputation both 'sober' and industrious. The apprenticeship sys-

tem, if abused, could be the means for an unscrupulous master or mistress to obtain money through the premium that came with the child. Apprenticeship properly understood was the means by which a young person received instruction in a trade, but an exploitative master or mistress could regard an apprentice as no more than a source of unpaid labour. On 28 August 1762, 'Joseph East of the Parish of Iver in Bucks of the Protestant Religion' appeared before the General Committee and 'desired Carolina Man who was nursed by his Wife as an Apprentice'. Joseph declared 'that he had but one Child unprovided for, and was in a way of Life as a Husbandman of providing for the said Child, and that he would consider Carolina Man as his own'. The committee 'Ordered That Mrs Clarke of Swakely be desired to acquaint the Committee of Joseph East and his Wife are Protestants and sober and industrious persons & take good care of their own Children'. A hard-headed calculation was made by the Governors as to whether families' claims to respectability could be proven in writing from neighbourhood testimonies, and whether they had sufficient income to maintain a foundling apprentice. Only then would the indentures be issued, as was the eventual outcome for foundling Carolina Man.

In general, the Foundling Hospital authorities did not look favourably upon bypassing the normal process by which wet nurses gave up their infants at the correct age deemed by the Hospital, never to return. At the point of apprenticeship, the children were sent away from the care of the Hospital into the outside world only by the authority of the General Committee. Any alternative arrangement threatened disorder and the setting of difficult precedents. During the 1760s, when they were under pressure to despatch a large number of General Reception children, the sub-committee received a letter from the Rev. Dr Altham, one of the Hospital's most dedicated inspectors and patrons in Essex. The clergyman had taken a particular liking to a child named Alice Gardner under his inspection. Rev. Altham suggested that he could 'keep Alice Gardener to Nurse at 18 [shillings] a week for 2 Years, beyond the usual term, and then to take her himself as an Apprentice'. This would have involved bypassing the usual system whereby Alice would be returned to London at the age of five or six, when a child was normally sent away from her wet nurse and foster family. This placed the sub-committee in a difficult position, since they had to make a recommendation to the Governors about how to proceed. After a lengthy deliberation, they recorded their response to this proposed scheme:

> Resolved. That it is the opinion of this Committee that the Child will be properly disposed of, but that it may possibly lay the foundation of other Demands of the same nature, which however may be a less Evil than withholding Children from the sober and industrious poor in the Country when they contract a strong affection for them.[73]

The Governors wrestled with the ethics of turning down petitioners of low social status who 'contracted a strong affection' for their charges, which was evidently a not infrequent occurrence. In the event, the committee turned down Rev. Dr Altham's request and Alice was sent to the home of a respectable spinster of the parish in Chingford. Emotional ties between foundlings and their foster carers were real, and went beyond a slightly diffident idea of Christian benevolence among the Governors that kept the children at arm's length. Such ties were sometimes acknowledged, but often they were overridden as a regrettable inconvenience to the smooth running of the apprenticeship system.

Up until now, where the children were sent and how they were employed has remained something that historians have speculated about but not looked at in detail. Where the foundlings were sent and how they were employed casts a new and unique perspective on the monumental changes that were taking place during the early decades of the English Industrial Revolution. If we take a closer look at what actually happened, to the foundling boys at least, it was not what Thomas Coram, nor the original Governors and patrons of the Foundling Hospital charity, nor the British parliament who had part-funded this costly enterprise, had planned at all.

CHAPTER 5

Finding Work

IN HIS AUTOBIOGRAPHY, George King wrote in detail about the fateful day, 25 September 1800, when he was bound as an apprentice out of the Foundling Hospital for ever. He recorded that he was sent to 'Mr. John Browne, Grocer and Confectioner residing at No. 10 Fish Street Hill...to learn the art of Confectionery'. Unusually, he gave some insight into his emotions on the day he left the Hospital, 'the day appointed for quitting the School arrived, and the thought of parting from my playfellows and especially from Rivington overcame me for a time'. Here, the kindly Mr Atchison was once again his saviour: 'at two o'clock I proceeded with my good friend the Schoolmaster to my new abode'. The man and boy would have exited through the imposing gates of the Foundling Hospital and out into the bustling streets, which would have got busier as they proceeded south towards the River Thames and towards the Monument to the Great Fire of London, near St Paul's Cathedral.

Almost directly opposite the Monument was the shop belonging to his new master, Mr Browne. Things very quickly began to look up for thirteen-year-old George. As the shop door opened and he stepped over the threshold, he was presented with every child's dream: 'I cast my eyes around and was delightfully surprised at seeing so many Hogsheads of Sugar and boxes of Raisins which I anticipated I should soon have my fill'. He shook hands with his new master and was given a lecture on good conduct by his mentor, the schoolmaster from the Foundling Hospital, who then departed—the third major parting in George's young life from someone who had cared for him.

George found himself in a bustling multi-storey household containing the Browne family, a foreman, servants, and other apprentices. In addition to the front-of-house shop, there was a back office or counting room, and a confectionery room where the barley sugar was boiled and the oranges and lemons were candied. In a separate kitchen, George was to eat his dinner daily at 3pm. Without any time to lose, he was set to work making 'Raspberry cakes with a Tin Mould and a knife'. He did not get to visit the Foundling Hospital again to see his school friends for another two months.[1]

His life now entered a new phase, with the demands of a master and hierarchies between family, staff, and servants to negotiate, since he was now part of a household 'family' that shared bed and board, as well as a common enterprise in business. George did not earn wages, but his master was obliged by the terms of his indenture to provide him with the necessaries of life, including food, lodging, and other 'decencies'. In return, George undertook to behave diligently as an apprentice and apply himself to learning his master's trade, not to get drunk and cause fights, and to remain celibate until he finished the term of the apprenticeship at the age of twenty-one. His friend Henry Rivington, by George's account, was apprenticed to a pocket book manufacturer in Red Lion Street, Clerkenwell, so they were able to see one another on Sundays. George's memory of what happened is confirmed in the archive of the Foundling Hospital, which records that Henry Rivington was apprenticed in June 1801 to Mr James Upton, of Red Lion Street in the parish of St James Clerkenwell, a pocket book maker.[2]

The fate planned for George King and Henry Rivington was to find useful employment in retailing and small manufacturing trades. This would have met with favour from the Governors and patrons of the Foundling Hospital charity. Their enterprise was to turn pauper children into self-sufficient and respectable citizens who would find a parish settlement through the fulfilment of their apprenticeship term. But, as we shall soon see, things did not turn out as planned for these boyhood friends.

George and Henry's employment as apprentices to London tradesmen was a typical pattern for boys engaged in learning a trade that extended back to the 1600s, but which was assuming a distinctive character by the end of the 1700s. London was a centre of consumption, associated with luxury, pleasure, and vice, but it was also a hive of production. Across the city and into the East End and Isle of Dogs, the streets echoed with the sounds of people engaged in making goods, the smells of cooking and brewing, and the drilling of carpenters, hammers, saws, and shouting as builders, labourers, and craftsmen went about their trades. Provisioning a city of nearly 1 million citizens required a ready supply of food and efficient organization of markets and transport links from the surrounding countryside.[3] Thousands were employed in producing sufficient clothing and shoes to meet the needs of a vast and expanding population in the period before mass production of ready-made clothing; curing, cutting, and stitching horse leather, and working in metal to produce all manner of goods, from pins to belt buckles.[4] Growing demand for the 'necessaries' of life, such as food and basic clothing, underpinned the buoyant economy of Georgian England. But there was also a growing demand for luxury. London workshops engaged in a huge variety of industries, from the delicate craft of making high-end Spitalfields silk and lace, to the mass production of everyday items. Innovation was the order of the day, with English manufacturers experimenting to produce their own versions of popular imported goods such as bone china, made in Bow, in London's East End, in imitation of Chinese porcelain. Imported comestibles such as sugar, citrus fruits, and tea were becoming increasingly affordable to a growing tier of society who would come to be known as the middle classes. These included professional households headed by clergymen, doctors, and army and navy officers, and prosperous tradespeople and their families.[5] Amid rising consumer spending, small businesses and manufactories thrived, such as the confectionery shop where George King was employed, and the pocket book maker who engaged his best friend Henry Rivington.

The importance of George and Henry serving out their allotted time diligently as apprentices is difficult to fathom in modern times. Without serving the full term of an apprenticeship, a young man could not set up shop in his own right, nor join one of the city guilds that regulated business and conferred privileges upon trades-men and merchants as citizens of London. There was a hierarchy among trades that corresponded roughly to the level of manual labour required, cost and 'cleanliness' of the goods that were handled, and complexity of skills needed (requiring different levels of literacy, numeracy, and manual strength). Unskilled tradesmen and labourers in the dirtiest occupations, such as the night-soil men who carted away human excrement, were among the lowliest occupations. The next lower-ranking tradesmen were coopers (makers of barrels), butchers, barbers, chandlers, cordwainers (who worked in leather), and tanners. There was often an overlap between the manufacturing and retailing of goods among the 'middling sort' who dealt in 'cleaner' goods. This included George's master, Mr Browne the maker and seller of confectionery, and, Henry's master Mr Upton the pocket book maker, who sold the products they manufactured in their own workshops. Further up the hierarchy were vintners, haberdashers, and goldsmiths, who dealt in high-value luxury goods and wrangled in high-end warehouse showrooms over credit with genteel customers or who at least had genteel aspirations. Merchants and dealers in silks, fur, precious metals, and rare wines catered for the richest in society—royalty, nobility, and upper gentry—and had access to the largest amounts of credit that kept their businesses afloat. These wealthy merchants often had social and political ambitions to match the kudos and scale of their enterprises. They contributed as 'citizens of London' to bankrolling the national debt, held high office in the City of London, and exercised benevolence to prestigious charitable institutions.[6]

London provided numerous and well-publicized examples of tradesmen who made their fortunes, including apprentices who married their dead masters' widows. But social ambition to 'rise' in the world through hard work and merit was tempered by other factors: the need for capital to set up shop or establish a credit network that was essential to the purchase of raw materials in trade, the protectionism of the guild system, and the fact that the more prestigious occupations tended to 'keep it in the family', with the sons of higher-ranking city merchants marrying 'up' into the gentry, or at least into families of a similar social standing.[7] By the end of the eighteenth century, patterns of employment were changing. Historians have long believed that the apprenticeship system itself was in decline at this time, just as the power of the guilds was also waning in the face of growing industrialization. But recently some historians have looked again at whether this was indeed the case, particularly for pauper children, who continued to be bound over by their parish or charitable institutions after the Poor Law reforms of 1834. One recent study has shown that many poor children continued to be bound over by parishes and charities to masters in England's port towns until the 1870s.[8]

In the shifting social and economic conditions of the late 1700s, when it came to sending children out to work, the Foundling Hospital Governors adopted a similar system in many respects to the Poor Law commissioners and other charitable organizations at the time, but with some notable differences. The social influence and connections of the Governors of the major London charities, including the Foundling Hospital, placed pauper children within a network of patronage and support that was different from the parish system. The Marine Society, for example, had Governors who were successful in finding placements for the sons of men employed in sea service, while Christ's Hospital apprenticed the children of fathers employed in traditional London guilds in semi-skilled and skilled trades, dealing and manufacturing. The strong ties between the Foundling Hospital and the Marine Society via Jonas Hanway meant that some attempt was made to put foundling boys to sea. The results were not always satisfactory, although contact between the two institutions remained cordial and close. In 1791, Mr Newby of the Marine Society sent one unnamed boy back to Mr Kirby of the Foundling Hospital with his compliments, but informed him that the bearer of his note could not be admitted by the Marine Society because he 'has got the itch'.[9] Just how many foundling boys went to sea is a question to which we shall soon return.

The placing of children as apprentices was an enormous bureaucratic task for the Foundling Hospital administrators. Details of each foundling apprenticeship were entered in a detailed register kept more or less sequentially by date. This was kept meticulously by successive clerks employed by the Hospital. It documented each child's admission date to the Foundling Hospital, the name and identifying serial number of each foundling, on what date they were apprenticed, their masters' and mistresses' occupations and parish of residence, the term of their apprenticeship, and the premiums with which they were bound.[10] An early entry mentions John Abercorn, the thirty-sixth foundling admitted to the Hospital, in April 1741. John was apprenticed at the age of ten in January 1752 to William Greenwood Esq. of Devon, to remain there until the age of twenty-one, 'from w[hi]ch. time the Gov[erno]rs. release him from all future Service'. The first girl mentioned in the register is Mary Georgia, apprenticed to John Osmond, a silk dyer of Leadenhall Street, London, at the age of eleven.[11] Tantalizingly, these are often the only details that are recorded of what happened to children once they left the Foundling Hospital's care. Some of the six provincial branches of the Foundling Hospital set up during the general admission period also kept their own apprenticeship registers, although these were not as comprehensive, and overlapped (as far as it is possible to tell) with the main record keeping in London.[12]

It is possible to recover some details in this 411-page apprenticeship register of the fate of around 6,000 children who survived being raised under the care of the Foundling Hospital long enough to be apprenticed for the first time, before many of them disappeared for good from the historical record. In the early to mid-1760s, the Hospital had to find between 40 and 100 apprenticeships each year for children reaching an age to be sent out into the wider world. The scale increased dramatically during the 1760s, when children taken in during the General Reception reached an age to be apprenticed: around 500 children were apprenticed in 1767, and nearly 1,200 children in 1768. The peak year for placing children in employment was 1769, when an extraordinary 1,430 children were apprenticed in one year alone.[13]

The history of child labour is difficult for privileged Westerners living in the developed world to comprehend, and yet it formed a crucial, if often invisible, part of the creation of England as a modern industrial society. As two leading historians on the subject, Sara Horrell and Jane Humphries, have commented, the history of children's work, like the history of women's employment, remains 'under-recorded, inconsistently measured, and buried in the family economy'.[14] In recent years the classic interpretation of the rise of the Industrial Revolution during the half-century from 1770 onwards has been revised. The concept of the English Industrial Revolution as passed on to generations of schoolchildren in history lessons conjures the idea of 'dark satanic mills', the advent of coalmining and factory work, and the creation of great industrial cities in the Midlands and north of England. It was in this era that Birmingham became the 'workshop of the world', and Sheffield the centre of steel and other metal-work production. Other archetypal centres of industry were the potteries of Staffordshire, the cotton mills of Bradford, Leeds, and Manchester, and the glass industries of Wearside. Coal ships plied the maritime trade between Newcastle and London. Energy from coal provided essential fuel for steam-powered technologies that revolutionized mass production. Improvements to transportation systems created a national and international network of maritime coastal shipping, while the efficient inland movement of coal, raw materials, and manufactured goods was made possible by new canals and a national network of turnpike roads.[15]

None of these stereotypes about the Industrial Revolution is actually incorrect, but more recent interpretations have suggested that some profound transformations were already taking place in England's economy even before the eighteenth century. It is only by understanding these changes that we can really grasp why the question of child labour in general, and poor children's labour in particular, including that of foundlings came to be so vital to the national interest.

Throughout European history, the vast majority of men and women had toiled on the land, but from around the end of the 1600s in England a mass shift from working in agriculture to working in industry had begun. Recent research has overturned previous assumptions that this process only began in earnest during the Industrial Revolution. Historians now estimate that just half the population of England was employed on the land during the reign of Queen Anne at the start of the eighteenth century, and that this fell still further to about 36 per cent of the adult working population by 1817.[16] By comparison, as late as 1871, over half the male workforce in France was still engaged in agriculture, and 61 per cent of men in Italy.[17] An 'industrious' revolution was at the heart of these changes across northern Europe and the New World, most notably in England.[18] For most of the eighteenth century, the economy was buoyant and male wages were high, although the price of goods fluctuated according to harvest yields and whether the nation was at war or peace with her neighbours.[19]

In London, the business of producing goods became more specialized. Markets became more diverse, with greater customer choice for home-produced and imported goods, available from specialist retailers who clustered in different parts of the City and West End. In the English counties, towns and cities could not match the size or scale of London markets, but different geographical areas became known for certain kinds of manufacture, such as button making in Yorkshire and ribbon and lace making in the West Country. Some rural areas became depopulated as young people migrated to find work in nearby industrial areas. Certain groups that had been a feature of English society for centuries, such as yeomen farmers, disappeared in the eighteenth century as farms were consolidated into larger units. Women gradually withdrew from agricultural work, with heavier tools and eventually machinery used with greater efficiency that required the strength of men to operate.[20]

These changes were gradual and took many decades, but during the eighteenth century the character of rural and urban England changed profoundly. Agricultural reforms to farming techniques, including the enclosure of common land used traditionally to graze livestock, meant that crop yields could increase with fewer labourers. Employment in factories, particularly in the textile mills of Lancashire and west Yorkshire, provided wage incentives for a new generation, who could now bypass the years of unpaid labour that were conventionally taken up with learning a trade by means of an apprenticeship. For a long time, and in many locations, factories and their 'pre-industrial' small-scale prototypes existed alongside one another. 'The spinner's wheel, the weaver's loom, the cordwainer's bench, the nail-maker's forge, and the seamstress' humble pins and needles' were not replaced immediately. Merchant-manufacturers relied upon hired wage labour to turn raw materials into such items as ready-made clothes, hosiery, boots, and shoes. Many hundreds of people found employment in this way well into the nineteenth century: the cotton manufacturers Dixons of Carlisle employed 3,500 handloom weavers in the 1830s in the border counties of England and Scotland; a decade later, a firm of hosiers in Belper provided orders for 4,000 knitting frames making stockings across Derbyshire, Nottinghamshire, and Leicestershire.[21] Not all industrial activity happened in factories, but the pay for small-scale 'outworking', as it was called, could be very low, the rates only suitable for women and children. Manufacturing processes were broken down to make them more efficient through division of labour and specialization: the famous example used in *The Wealth of Nations* (1776) by Adam Smith was pin manufacture. Instead of one person making a pin from start to finish, the manufacturing process now entailed specialization in just one component of the process, from the making of each pin head to the drawing of wire for pin shafts.[22] As it happened, the moral attitudes of the Foundling

Hospital Governors superseded economic incentives to employ foundling girls in this particular manufacturing industry. Foundling girls were debarred from pin manufacturing, since it was deemed by the Governors to be 'a very poor employment' with a prospect of girls earning just 7 or 8 shillings a week once their apprenticeship had been served 'working from 5 o'clock in the morning 'till 9 or 10 at night'.[23] Since the manufacturing process had become so simplified, broken down into (as Adam Smith observed) '8 or 9 different branches...no art is required...any body almost can work in it'. There was high unemployment as a consequence, since the girls had few skills to offer employers. The steward of the Foundling Hospital went to inspect a pin factory for himself, and reported to the Governors that any girl sent to work there would not have the opportunity of 'acquiring proper habits and notions of cleanliness or any other requisite of a Female'. The steward observed that there was no segregation of men and women employed in this kind of manufacturing (which involved 'the promiscuous mixture of both Men and Women of the lowest class'). He alleged that many of the girls employed in pin factories 'turn out prostitutes afterwards', not implausibly given their precarious livelihood and few other options. His account was sufficient to ensure that foundling girls did not take part in this particular example of the Smithian revolution in manufacturing.

More labour was needed to undertake the arduous, repetitive jobs that, thanks to new technologies, did not always require the strength of a fully grown man. Since it was costly to employ adult men, whose labour in any case was in short supply, the participation of children, and women, in the paid workforce became essential to factory-based employment and to the 'putting out' system. And opportunities to find extra workers among women and children were there. Late Georgian society was extraordinarily youthful, the exact opposite of today's aging populations in the developed world. During the 1700s, the number of young people in Britain as a percentage of the overall population was on the increase.[24] By 1826, when the population was at its most youthful, almost 40 per cent of people were under the age of fifteen.[25] The national economy came to rely on the labour of the young, just as individual households came to depend more on the contribution of young adults and children to the family income.

Children despatched by the Governors of the Foundling Hospital and its branch institutions were 'unfree', like parish apprentices sent out from workhouses, and had little or no autonomy to decide their chosen destination and type of employment. Pauper apprentices were at the bottom of the employment ladder, with boys placed as labourers in unskilled employment and girls in domestic service. In this respect, foundling apprentices were usually no different from other poor children. Lacking friends in the world, their expectations depended upon them being able to negotiate the competing demands of their masters, the expectations of the Governors and benefactors at whose expense they had been raised, and the officials of the parish where they were apprenticed.

As with all pauper apprentices, children from the Foundling Hospital could gain or earn a parish settlement by domestic service or agricultural labour for a full year while unmarried, or by completing an indentured apprenticeship and then living in the parish for more than forty days.[26] Parish settlement was a deeply cherished right, valued by the poorest members of society. Settlement conferred legal rights as well as a sense of identity and belonging within a community. Perhaps most importantly, it meant that a poor person was entitled to relief in the form of practical help in hard times, whether caused by illness, disability, or other unexpected catastrophes. Unfree poor boys from parish workhouses or charities employed without choice in unskilled work and poor girls in domestic service were in 'a far more dependent and, obviously, exploited position', as historian Patrick Wallis has commented, than 'free' apprentices who were indentured with higher premiums and instructed in skilled or semi-skilled occupations.[27] Foundling children had the additional disadvantage that they only qualified for settlement by working, since the place of their birth was unknown. Orphaned and abandoned boys like George King and Henry Rivington were different from their workhouse counterparts, however, in the respect that they benefitted from a slightly better education at the Foundling Hospital that taught literacy to a higher level (including rudimentary writing skills) and numeracy. In the lifetime of George King and Henry Rivington, this was largely due to the Governors' employment of the reforming schoolmaster Mr Atchison, the same schoolmaster who had taken a particular interest in George's education. By 1800, nearly 100 per cent of foundling boys could sign their names, compared to just 60 per cent of semi-skilled tradesmen and 35 to 40 per cent of labourers and servants, although these figures varied between London and the rest of England.[28] For girls, basic literacy to enable them to read scripture, rote learning of catechisms, and housewifery were the only skills deemed necessary in preparation for their life of servitude beyond the Hospital.

Placing foundling apprentices depended partly upon where there was demand for child labour, but also upon the networks of local contacts established by the Foundling Hospital Governors. Inspectors were under considerable pressure to despatch large numbers from the general admission period in the late 1760s, just as parliamentary subsidies for the Foundling Hospital, including special grants to support child apprenticeships, were running out.[29] Out of a total of 5,885 first apprenticeship records in the Foundling Hospital apprenticeship register, 682 contain incomplete information since they have no record of the master's or mistress's occupation.[30] The vast majority of these were in England: only seventeen apprenticeships were in Wales and Scotland, fifteen were in Jersey, and one foundling was sent immediately to Newfoundland.

Many foundlings were reapprenticed and sent to other employers, including some overseas, and others never completed their term of indenture because they died or became ill, their masters went bankrupt, or either party deserted. Very little of this information was recorded systematically. It is mainly information about first apprenticeships that we are left with to piece together in order to provide a 'snapshot' of where foundling children were sent to work. If we exclude those records where information was blank or incomplete (leaving a total of 5,170 first apprenticeship records), the evidence from the apprenticeship register shows that the greatest number of children (1,960 altogether) were sent out to work close to the Foundling Hospital, in London and Middlesex.

In spite of occasional gaps in the register, close inspection reveals that it is the most complete source of information about where foundlings were sent when they left the Hospital, and how they were employed. Their labour contributed to a wide variety of industries, trades, and manufactures, with girls and boys employed differently. Boy workers in London tended to be employed in skilled trades such as tailoring, or boot and shoe production, and manufacturing in a variety of workshops. Two hundred and forty foundlings were apprenticed to employers engaged in footwear manufacture, of whom 70 per cent were boys. A further 230 foundlings were apprenticed to employers in iron manufacturing, of whom 66 per cent were boys; 144 in machine and tool making, of whom 82 per cent were boys; and 171 engaged in 'dirty' industries using leather, bone, and other materials associated with 'noxious' processes, of whom 78 per cent were boys. Certain kinds of manufacture were seen as 'male domains' even though less physical strength was necessary in certain kinds of production through the introduction of new technologies, which increased from the 1760s.

The employment of male children in workshops and handicrafts was higher in London than in other parts of England and Wales, whereas factory employment was much higher for male and female children outside of London.[31] So we find that 146 foundlings apprenticed in London or Middlesex (36 per cent of all children sent to work in those locations) were employed by masters or mistresses engaged in a range of occupations, from tailoring, to makers of breeches, stays, mantuas, hats, gloves, and stockings. Outside of London, the regional specialization of clothing manufacture was mirrored in the employment of foundlings, for example, to button manufacturers in the West Riding of Yorkshire.[32] One hundred and seventy-one foundlings were apprenticed in the county of Staffordshire, which was one of the top three counties outside of London and Middlesex for foundling employment (after Yorkshire, which took 1,895 children, and Surrey, which took 266). Of the foundlings sent to Staffordshire, 155 went to work in industrial manufacturing. Known for its burgeoning potteries, and metal-working industries producing items such as buckles for clothing and shoes, this part of the West Midlands was within striking distance of the Shrewsbury branch of the Foundling Hospital. An astonishing number of foundling children, forty-eight aged between ten and twelve years, the vast majority of them boys, went to work in Wolverhampton, Walsall, and the surrounding area, employed in making buckles, or 'chapes' (buckle components). These particular boys were not sent in 'batches' to large-scale factories with one employer, as might be expected during the Industrial Revolution, but in ones and twos, to as many different workshops with different masters. Others were despatched in a similar way to locksmiths and tool and instrument makers in the same county; a dozen foundling boys were sent to work in toy manufacturing. Metal working in small-scale manufacturing workshops in the Midlands was just one important outlet for employing male foundlings during the 1760s, at a time when demand for boys' labour was met with a supply of children who had reached just the right age a decade or so after the General Admission.

Demand for foundling girls' labour was also coming from new kinds of industry that were springing up in the home counties, the Midlands, and the north. In Surrey, proximity to London meant that the range of foundling employment was very diverse, reflecting the need to supply all kinds of clothing, footwear, and luxury accessories (from hosiery to gloves and feather making) to consumers in the capital. There was also evidence that girls' labour was in demand for 'batch' employment to calico printing. Calico was a brightly coloured and fashionable Indian cotton textile that could be imported ready-made, or printed on arrival in Britain. One such business was owned by John Arbuthnot, a calico printer from Mitcham in

Surrey, who took eighteen foundling girls to work in his factory in two batches (August 1760 and August 1761). These girls were remarkably young, many of them only eight or nine years old. Arbuthnot had persuaded the Foundling Hospital's authorities to engage in a different kind of apprenticeship to factory work *en masse*, at a time when the Governors were under pressure to find work for a large number of children. The experiment proved disastrous: the girls complained that they were given insufficient clothing, and Arbuthnot was later accused of physically and sexually abusing the girls in his employment.[33] Another business in Surrey, run by master embroiderer Felix Ehrliholtzer, was less catastrophic in terms of the children's welfare. He took seven nine-year-old girls between 1766 and 1767 to work in his embroidery business, producing finer needlework than was usually anticipated for girls who had been educated at the Foundling Hospital. He soon moved his business to Plaistow and was allowed to employ a further two boys and nine girls, having been inspected by Jonas Hanway in person. The master proved that he was a good employer who treated the children well.[34]

Though some girls provided sought-after labour in newly prosperous textile industries, the fate of the majority of foundling girls was rather more predictable. Domestic service was the largest single occupational grouping for girls, especially in London, up until the mid-nineteenth century.[35] The foundling apprenticeship register tells us that, where this information was recorded, 1,416 foundlings were employed in 'household business', presumably in domestic service. Of these, 1,275 were girls, and just 141 were boys. A distinctive feature of the pattern of employment of children as servants is the despatch of 441 foundlings to the houses of 'Distinguished, titled gentlemen', encompassing 'gentleman', 'baronet', 'esquire' from as far afield as Devon, Lincolnshire, Kent, and Shropshire, and 408 to the homes of professional employers. Employing a foundling was seen as another way for a patron to show their charitable support for the Hospital, one step up from making a donation since it entailed taking a child or adolescent into the private domain of their household. One of the very first infants admitted to the Foundling Hospital, in March 1741, was given the name John Bowles. John was one of only six of the thirty infants taken in as part of the first admissions who lived long enough to be apprenticed. He was bound apprentice in August 1751 to Stephen Beckingham Esq. and went to work on his estate at Bourne Place, near Canterbury. By taking a foundling into his own home, this leading member of the gentry in Kent extended his benevolence and association with the charity.[36]

It is striking how many foundlings were put to work in the north of England. After London and Middlesex, the next highest number by county, 1,895 foundlings, was apprenticed in Yorkshire, where 707 children were employed in agriculture, 793 in manufacture and trade, and 395 in selling, dealing, and other occupations. Of the six branch hospitals set up to cope with the high number of foundlings taken in during the General Admission period, Ackworth in Yorkshire was by far the most successful at placing large numbers of foundling apprentices. The Foundling Hospital had close associations with Yorkshire from as early as the 1740s, when an energetic inspector, Rev. Thomas Trant, brokered apprenticeships for boys sent from London in the Hemsworth area.[37] Later, many of the great landowners of Yorkshire such as Sir Rowland Winn of Nostell Priory were persuaded to become Governors and helped to raise subscriptions to fund the purchase of premises that became the Ackworth branch hospital. The success of Ackworth in placing a high volume of apprentices was the result of a combination of forces: the patronage of local elites, a network of energetic inspectors, and a dynamic labour market. This was stimulated by the booming industrial economy of the West and East Ridings, which after Lancashire and Surrey were the fastest-growing English counties in the second half of the eighteenth century.[38] While many foundlings were sent to work in factories, many others were put to 'traditional' small-scale manufacturing. Many others were sent to backfill labour shortages in rural areas where young people had left in the hope of better wages in industrial towns.

Outside of London, agriculture, livestock, and fisheries formed the largest source of jobs for adolescent boys, accounting for more than a third of the national labour force aged ten to fourteen.[39] In the North Riding of Yorkshire, agricultural labour was urgently needed: the area had lost over 18,000 residents in the half-century before 1801, in contrast to an increase of nearly 22,000 in the East Riding and 95,547 in the West Riding, owing to rapid industrialization.[40] Sending London's unwanted children via the Foundling Hospital to work across English counties, but most especially in parishes across Yorkshire, must have backfilled some of the shortfall of ready labour for agriculture and domestic service. The reasons for labour shortages were local and particular, but young people born in rural parishes at this time were migrating to London, thriving port towns, and northern manufacturing centres to find work. Large-scale transatlantic migration from the North and East Riding of Yorkshire was another drain upon local populations from the late-1760s, with families driven by a combination of poverty and the lure of a better life in the New World where non-conformist Christian religion was the norm rather than the exception, offering the utopian hope of a Godly, more egalitarian society.[41]

Local inspectors in Yorkshire brokered apprenticeships across many parishes, which ensured that poor children were sent where their labour was in demand, thereby avoiding complaints that parishes were being 'overburdened' or that local employees were being done out of jobs. Of the 672 foundlings who were employed in their first apprenticeship in agriculture in Yorkshire, 186 parishes took between one and five foundlings apiece, twenty took six to ten foundlings, six parishes took eleven to fifteen foundlings, and just four parishes took more than fifteen: Alne in the North Riding (sixteen), Newton Upon Ouse (eighteen), Topcliffe (nineteen), and the City of York (twenty-eight). Foundlings were distributed evenly across 216 parishes in total, with the number of foundlings per parish almost equalling the number of employers. Before 1834, the vast majority of Yorkshire parishes took between one and three foundlings each, with the greatest concentration of numbers being in the decade after the General Reception. A smaller number of parishes took between eleven and fifteen foundlings each; for example, Escrick (eleven foundlings, shared between ten masters), Featherstone (eleven foundlings, going to nine different masters), Kirkleatham (eleven foundlings, distributed to nine masters). Many foundlings were sent to work for 'improving' farmers known for experimenting with more efficient farming techniques and creating model estates at the time, such as Christopher Turner of Kirkleatham, a governor of the Ackworth Hospital, who requested thirty boys to be apprenticed to his tenant farmers.[42]

Since we lack first-hand accounts written by the foundling apprentices themselves from this period, we must look elsewhere for evidence of what their lives were like when they were put out to work. We know that from the first ever national census in England in 1801, up until the mid-nineteenth century, young, unskilled men worked most commonly as farm boys, crow scarers, livestock minders, and ploughboys.[43] First-hand recorded information about the experiences of rural apprentices is scant, such as the life experience of foundling John Collier, apprenticed at the age of nine in June 1767 to a farmer by the name of Thomas Stephenson of Howden in the East Riding 'to be employed in Husbandry'.[44] Though there are no diaries as yet discovered written by eighteenth-century foundlings employed on the land, there are other sources of evidence that provide some insight into the kind of life experienced by poor boys sent out to toil the fields. William Gifford, born in 1756, was an exact contemporary of many of the General Reception foundlings. He lost his father at the age of eight, a drinker with a 'ruined constitution', and his mother, 'exhausted with grief and anxiety', when he was thirteen. As an orphan with few prospects, he was sent to work ploughing fields but rebelled against the 'drudgery of husbandry' and ended up going to sea: his younger brother was raised in the workhouse and was sent at the age of seven as a parish apprentice to a husbandman 'with whom he endured incredible hardships which I had not in my power to alleviate'.[45] William Lawrence, born later in 1791, was better off than foundling apprentices (who did not receive wages) since as a 'free' child employed working on the land he was able to earn 2d. a day to scare birds and 6d. a day as a ploughboy. His slightly better working conditions as a builder's apprentice did not prevent him from being regularly beaten with a horsewhip.[46]

By contrast with the success of Ackworth in finding work for foundling apprentices, advertisements placed at Westerham and

Sevenoaks markets in Kent informing potential masters that parliament had given 'Small Sum by way of Fees to promote the putting out of Foundling Children Apprenticed' evidently failed to attract prospective masters or mistresses in any great number, although it was later noted by the sub-committee in London that 'very few persons Apply for Children at this Hospital therefore this Committee have no chance of Apprenticing of the oldest Boys'.[47] Unlike the West and East Riding, Kent did not have manufacturing industries on any scale, and actually experienced a dip in population during the 1770s. Westerham was at the additional disadvantage of having had its funds embezzled by the overseeing governor, the notorious John Wilkes MP.[48]

It has sometimes been assumed that the majority of foundlings went to work in industrial towns and cities, with factory work absorbing a 'rising tide' of children from the Foundling Hospital.[49] There was indeed a brief four-year period between 1767 and 1771 when a significant number (nearly 300 children aged on average between nine and ten years old) were sent out from the Foundling Hospital to be employed in textile industries. Nearly half of all first apprenticeships issued (affecting 1,562 boys and 1,076 girls) were to various kinds of manufacturing and trade. Of these, over a third of the children were set to work in clothing and textile manufacture.[50] This pattern was mirrored all over Europe, where orphans were to be found similarly employed in centres of textile production, such as the silk industries in Italy.[51]

The availability of foundling children's labour was an attractive prospect to merchant-manufacturers and company owners setting up new factories in England during the 1760s, at a critical early stage of the Industrial Revolution.[52] For employers, children who had been raised by charities such as the Foundling Hospital were an additional source of labour to child apprentices supplied from workhouses. Pauper apprentices, whether from the workhouse or a charitable institution, were bound over to their masters by the terms of their indenture. Provided their masters supplied board, lodging, food, and clothing, they were not obliged to pay them wages during their apprenticeship. The question of what would happen to paupers once the term of their indenture was up provoked local concerns. The Foundling Hospital Governors took advice from a lawyer named Galliard of Lincoln's Inn in September 1768, regarding an anonymous gentleman, referred to as 'A'—the owner of 'a large manufactory in the Country in the which [sic] he will Employ a considerable number of people and especially young Female Children'. His proposal was to take girls from the Foundling Hospital and 'other public Charities and to bind them Apprentices'. The factory owner faced local opposition, however, in case 'they become chargeable to the parish'. He wanted to know whether his local parish could force him to pay a security to indemnify them in case his female labour force became chargeable to the local ratepayers. This would happen if they obtained a settlement and his business failed, or if they became ill, or produced illegitimate babies. The legal advice he received was that he 'may take as many Apprentices as he pleases without the consent of the parish officers or giving any indemnity whatsoever'.[53] There was nothing to stop factory owners employing children, and girls' labour was especially desirable since they were cheap and thought to be nimble workers.

'Batch' employment of up to a dozen children to one factory employer was an apparently logical solution to the surplus supply of apprentice-age foundlings ready to work at a time when the age of child workers generally was falling, and there was greater participation of children in the national labour force.[54]

From the 1760s, under pressure to despatch children admitted during the General Reception, Foundling Hospital Governors routinely accepted petitions from industrialists to take batches of apprentices. Some northern manufacturers saw the availability of foundlings in bulk to be an attractive prospect, and at Ackworth advertisements were issued to factory owners in the local press. On 5 February 1770, the *Leeds Intelligencer* contained an advertisement placed by the Governors of the Foundling Hospital at Ackworth to the effect that apprentice fees would be given with girls from the Hospital 'in Proportion to their Age, Strength and other Abilities', and that prospective employers could apply on the first Monday in every month 'and at no other Time'. No persons could apply 'who are not of known Ability' to one of the Governors, and they were advised to bring certificates with them signed by a minister of the church to confirm their good reputation. The reason given for this was to prevent fraudulent applications and to safeguard the welfare of the children. A form of wording was published to make it easier for clergymen to write such endorsements without too much trouble:

> These are to certify, That—of—in the parish of—in the county of—has his legal Settlement in—aforesaid is of the Protestant Religion, a Housekeeper, of good Character, and proper Abilities to take an Apprentice and instruct—in the Business of—[date].[55]

Elsewhere and on other occasions, prospective employers made direct petition to the London Governors asking to receive children to come and work for them.[56] Provided that they could produce testimonies of their good reputation, and that they were married men if they were seeking to employ girls, it was shockingly easy to the modern eye to obtain a foundling apprentice.[57]

In 1760, industrial magnate Sir James Lowther requested a batch of thirteen boys from Ackworth, some for employment as 'banksmen' in open-cast mining. He later took twenty boys and twenty-three girls for his carpet manufactory, reflecting labour shortages in rural Westmorland, which in the half-century before 1800 lost nearly 12,000 inhabitants.[58] In some industries, foundling labour was a critical part of a speculative business without a ready supply of adult labour, or where child labour could be deployed to save wage costs. Another case was of a Staffordshire 'wood screw manufacturer', Job Wyatt. In 1760, a Royal Letters Patent had been granted 'to Mess. Wyatts, of Burton upon Trent, for a new-invented Machine to make Screws of Iron, commonly called Wood Screws'.[59] The Wyatt brothers, Job and William, bought a watermill at Tatenhill and converted it to a screw factory in about 1776 at a cost of £1,100. The factory produced 700 gross of screws of all sizes every week and, since Tatenhill had a population of only 2,000 people even by 1831, it is likely that from the outset the Wyatt business was heavily reliant on foundling labour. The repetitive work of operating Wyatt's patented machine was light enough for girls to perform, since he took eleven foundling girls aged nine to ten years in February 1767 for his factory. This was followed by a further ten girls of the same age the following year (April 1768). By 1770, their access to Foundling Hospital child labour had dried up, the peak of general admission children having been despatched, and the Governors were appalled to discover that Wyatt had been an abusive employer. This was only one of several factors contributing to the decline of this particular enterprise: within ten years the Wyatts had sold the business at a loss.[60] Although we do not know what happened to Wyatt's girl apprentices in the longer term, scandalous cases of mass neglect by a single industrial employer help to explain why the Hospital's Governors proved increasingly reluctant to allow batch apprenticeship. Another factor was simply that the large number of children taken on during the General Reception had been despatched by 1771.[61]

Considering the original enterprise of the Foundling Hospital's founder and Governors, and many of their patrons, was to provide manpower for soldiering and sea service, it is perhaps surprising that relatively few foundling apprenticeships were issued to merchants, mariners, or captains. One hundred and fifteen boys were sent to first employment in various kinds of maritime and inland transportation, with a wide geographical distribution across sea ports and dockland areas, from Whitby, Scarborough, and Northumberland in the north to Rotherhithe, Wapping, and Ramsgate in the south. The experience of foundling John East, sent to sea, was the kind of useful labour envisaged by the Foundling Hospital's founder and benefactors, although as we have now seen, his experience was far from typical considering how few foundlings, boys especially, went to sea compared to those who were sent to rural areas to toil on the land. Apprenticed at the age of ten to James Manbey of Hermitage St, Wapping, a merchant who promised him a living to the age of twenty-four, John was promised an additional £5 a year for the last three years if he served out his time.[62] More usually, particularly after the foundation of the Marine Society, putting boys to sea became more of a punishment for miscreants than a source of regular employment for former foundlings. In 1762, Francis Pearson, a husbandman and gardener of Pontefract in Yorkshire, wrote to the sub-committee of the London Foundling Hospital asking for permission to turn over his apprentice, Augustus St Quentin, to the sea service or husbandry, 'Observing that the boy is very perverse but has no objection to the Sea'.[63]

The apprenticeship records give us a new picture of where children were sent when they left the Foundling Hospital, and how they were employed. This offers a remarkable glimpse of the profound changes that were taking place within a relatively short space of time to the character and shape of English society and economy in the face of rapid urbanization and industrial growth. In the late 1750s, the Westminster parliament had directly sponsored the Foundling Hospital's charitable enterprise at the time of the Seven Years' War, ploughing in vast sums of money with the express intention of building up Britain's military forces at a time of national crisis. However, it took approximately a decade for those boys and girls admitted at taxpayers' expense to reach an age where they could be apprenticed, and by the late 1760s, the country was at peace. Instead, foundling children were sent wherever there were labour shortages: to toil in rural Yorkshire where many of the young people had moved away, and to work in all kinds of manufacturing, especially but not exclusively in London. The vast majority of foundling girls were sent to the daily grind of domestic service, as anticipated by the Foundling Hospital's patrons and Governors.

Northern textile factories took in a significant number of boys and girls, eager to capitalize on the availability of child labour from charities, as from parish workhouses.[64] Experiments in this kind of employment, as we shall soon see, often had disastrous consequences for the children's welfare.

Without this overview of how and where foundling children were employed, it would be impossible to judge whether what happened to George King and his best friend Henry Rivington was typical. As it turns out, they could as easily have ended up scaring crows or picking up stones in the windswept fields of north Yorkshire as making barley sugar and pocket books in London. They escaped being sent to toil in the fields, or to endure the hard labour of factory employment, and their prospects for learning an honest trade looked promising. Much depended upon their conduct, and the disposition of their masters, as to what would happen next. There were numerous examples of foundlings running away, then being reapprenticed and returned, willingly or unwillingly, to the Foundling Hospital. Some proved 'saucy' and disobedient, others suffered cruelly at the hands of brutal masters or mistresses, while others worked hard and served their full time, going on to lead honest lives and earning their living decently. But George's fate, strangely, was more in keeping with the original intentions of Captain Thomas Coram and the Foundling Hospital that had raised him.

George King's first few months working as an apprentice passed without incident. Given the temptations of the sweet shop, there was especial vigilance on the part of the foreman against pilfering by the apprentices. George's conscience told him not to steal, but he was young and found that it was difficult to resist dipping into the store of treats that surrounded him as he worked. He was soon given an early lesson in how easily he could be caught if he took advantage of his position. One day, two city marshals appeared without warning, charged in the days before modern policing with investigating allegations of misconduct on behalf of the magistrates of the city. George and the other 'male Servants' in the household were told one by one to empty the locked boxes kept in their bedrooms. A neighbour had reported seeing a young man leave the shop regularly on a Sunday with a barely concealed parcel, presumably of stolen goods. This time George was lucky. The marshals found nothing when they searched the box in his bedroom, but he confessed 'the pleasure I felt when I arrived in the Kitchen is indescribable...I soon emptied my pockets with that fruit that caused me so much uneasiness and ever after while there I was there I shunned that practice'.[65]

George passed his early teenage years happily enough, largely avoiding the temptations of city life. He and his best friend Rivington enjoyed the occasional visit to Bagnigge Wells, a 'poor man's' version of the fashionable pleasure gardens at Ranelagh and Vauxhall. According to George, they indulged in harmless recreations, although the place had a reputation as a den for thieves and prostitutes. Little did they know that their fortunes were about to change, and that George would soon become embroiled in a dispute with an older apprentice that was to change the course of his life forever.

But first, it is worth pausing to consider what we can know about the experiences of the other foundling children who were his near and exact contemporaries. Unlike George, who had an unusual level of literacy among his peers, none left their own detailed autobiographies. But the official documents that do survive provide a testimony to the spirit, resilience, and sometimes outright rebelliousness of eighteenth-century orphaned children. They also contain the often hidden histories of brutality and hardship that these children suffered in an age otherwise renowned as one of progress, profit, and Enlightenment.

CHAPTER 6

Industry and Idleness

I N 1747, JUST one year after completing *Moses Brought before Pharaoh's Daughter*, the epic biblical painting that touched public sentiment about the fate of foundling children, William Hogarth began a major series of prints on the theme of *Industry and Idleness* (Figure 6.1). The series depicts the lives of two fictional characters, Goodchild and Idle, apprentice weavers whose names betrayed their destinies. Hogarth's express intention was to instruct young apprentices, and their masters, about the importance of hard work, sobriety, and good conduct (the prints contained 'Awful Warnings' which were 'calculated', as he put it, 'for the use & instruction of ... young people'). The industrious Goodchild 'performs the duty of a Christian' and is shown reading in church alongside a pious beauty who will become his future wife (his master's daughter) once he successfully completes his seven-year apprenticeship. By contrast, the layabout Tom Idle loses his position and is sent to sea for his rebellious

FIGURE 6.1 Apprentice weavers Idle and Goodchild are given similar opportunities to learn an honest trade, but signs of their future destinies are already present, with scriptural warnings that their lots will be different in life. William Hogarth, *Industry and Idleness*, 1747. Engraving (265 mm × 348 mm).

behaviour. An ominous sign is that he drops his apprenticeship indenture (the precious document that will safeguard his future in an honest trade) into the sea. In the latter part of the series, Idle returns after a number of years. His fortunes go from bad to worse. With few options left to him, he becomes a highwayman, living in squalid destitution in a crumbling attic with a syphilitic prostitute who betrays him to the authorities. While Goodchild's fate is to ride in the Lord Mayor's carriage, Idle is destined for the long drop at Tyburn, meeting an ignominious end as the centrepiece of a public execution.[1]

The piquancy of this narrative lies in Hogarth's comparison between two young men who receive a similar start in life, but who choose to take different paths that shape their destiny, one towards professional success and personal happiness, the other to utter ruin. At the heart of the morality tale of *Industry and Idleness* was the Protestant conviction that hard work and dutiful service would bring rewards, illuminated in scriptural quotation at the foot of each print in case the message was insufficiently clear to the viewer. On the first illustration, there are two quotations from the Book of Proverbs; subscribed under the shady figure of Idle (gazing at the ceiling instead of at his loom). It reads 'The Drunkard shall come to poverty', whereas under the radiant Goodchild, intent at his work, the message is 'The hand of the diligent maketh rich'. It was an enduringly damaging fiction for Hogarth to give the impression that the destinies of young apprentices, including those pauper apprentices sent out into a hostile world by the Foundling Hospital, were entirely in their own hands. From birth, the weight of social censure, limited education, and narrow horizons of opportunity were afforded to those foundling children who survived being raised institutionally. Upon leaving the Hospital as an apprentice, a girl or boy on the verge of adolescence could choose the path of virtue, or of vice. Some of the Foundling Hospital children took the path favoured by Goodchild, and others followed Idle's disastrous course of life, although whether either of these options was fully within their control was a complexity which Hogarth did not, perhaps could not, illustrate.

It was no coincidence that Hogarth chose to depict Goodchild and Idle as weavers' apprentices to illustrate their contrasting fortunes. Weavers' livelihoods were notoriously precarious, with entire industries at the mercy of changing fashions. In the late-eighteenth century, the kind of small-scale, domestic production on hand-looms undertaken by Goodchild and Idle was still employing large numbers of apprentices. This kind of industry would soon come to be seen as the flashpoint of early nineteenth-century industrial disputes and 'Luddite' protests, as handloom weaving was gradually superseded across England by mechanized factory production.[2]

During the late-eighteenth century, 163 foundling children were sent on the first apprenticeships to work for weavers engaged in small-scale enterprises. In the late 1760s, twenty-nine foundlings were sent to Kidderminster, which had become famous as a centre of carpet manufacture. This industry grew out of the Midlands wool trade, and flourished once the technology for carpet weaving was imported to the area from Belgium in 1749. By 1807, 1,000 giant Brussels carpet looms were turning out fine Kidderminster carpets to furnish the demands of luxurious furnishings for pros-perous households across Britain.[3] The fact that the foundling children were employed in this part of Worcestershire to as many different masters is just one indication that these were not appren-ticeships to large-scale machine manufacturing, which did not arrive in Kidderminster until 1825.[4] Another forty foundlings stayed within the London area, working in the parish of St Matthew, Bethnal Green, which together with neighbouring Spitalfields had been the centre for all kinds of fine textile manufacture since the arrival of Huguenot refugees at the end of the seventeenth century. Much of the silk and brocade worn by people of fashion in Georgian society, if not imported from France, was made in East End workshops that also served as family dwellings.[5] The unpredictable prosperity of handloom weavers such as these was illustrated in the real-life example of foundling James Scribe, whose master was a weaver but whose fortunes declined. James's master abandoned him, a fate which only came to light when a neighbour, John Hewitt the Elder of Whitechapel, came forward offering to take on the young man as his own apprentice. The Foundling Hospital General Committee were favourably disposed to this reapprenticeship and the steward was charged with enquiring after Hewitt's character.[6]

Any foundling apprentice who discovered their master's business was in decline was in a precarious position. If he or she stayed, their livelihood could sink alongside their employer's, but if they sought reapprenticeship it could lead to bad feeling, even violence. Ann Boteler found herself in such a predicament when her master, a fiddle maker, went bankrupt and ended up in the King's Bench Prison. His wife had taken a public house, and Ann was released from her indenture by the parish, but she also sought permission from the Foundling Hospital Governors to find alternative employment.[7] Running away could lead to imprisonment if caught, since it broke the terms of the apprentice's indenture. It was in just such a predicament that young Francis Desse found himself. He was apprenticed out of the Foundling Hospital at the age of ten in 1783 to Thomas Haywood, a shagreen case maker of St Bride's. Several years later, Haywood's business was in decline, but the master evidently had a short temper, and started to abuse his apprentice when he said he might look for another position, 'giving him the worst of language and telling him he himself had no occasion for Him'. Discovering Francis's plan to join another master in the same occupation, Haywood had him summarily arrested by a constable and taken before the Aldermen of the City of London at Guildhall, who had jurisdiction over punishing runaway apprentices. The boy languished in Bridewell Prison, sentenced to hard labour and kept in solitary confinement while he awaited the Governors' merciful intervention in his unfortunate case.[8] It was a testimony to Francis's character (and to the influence of the Foundling Hospital Governors) that the Hospital schoolmaster paid a visit to a contrite Mr Hayward, who agreed to 'freely resign him', adding deferentially, 'he will attend the Committee if they think proper'.

For every example of a headstrong or idle apprentice who vexed the authorities, there were others whose apprenticeship was terminated for reasons of chance misfortune that could befall them or their employers. A schoolmaster living in St Martin's Street, Leicester Square, thought it prudent to inform the Governors that one of his neighbours, an apothecary named Davies, had dropped dead. The welfare of Robert Porteous, his foundling apprentice, was a cause of some concern, and it was discovered that Davies's widow had sent the boy to sea, 'contrary to his inclination'.[9]

The Hospital Governors took a firm line on the importance not just of industry, but on what they decided was the right kind of industry according to the low social status of foundlings raised in their care, and generally not according to the 'inclinations' of the children. Their intervention in the lives of former charges of the Hospital continued during their apprenticeships. Thirteen-year-old Edith Marshall, whom the Governors had apprenticed to a shoemaker, was caught red-handed by the steward of the Hospital returning from an errand with 'a pewter Measure in her hand' after being sent out to distribute drams of gin with another girl from their residence, which was found to be 'a very small Public house and Gin shop...in a mean Neighbourhood viz. Bedlam Court in Old Bedlam'. Though Edith may not have been unhappy or mistreated, her morals were deemed to be at risk through such employment and she was hastily removed.

Some foundling apprentices were summoned to the Hospital to account for alleged bad behaviour before the Governors. This did not happen much in relation to the total number of children apprenticed, but amounted to two or three hearings before the General Committee per month. Some masters complained to the Foundling Hospital directly about the children they had received into their households as apprentices. The causes of their complaints were numerous but tended to follow certain themes. William Badgley of High Holborn 'Complains the Girl is an Idle girl'. Thomas Ballard was slow to learn the business of a cooper, his master Benjamin Masser's occupation, and instead was sent to sea as a landsman.[10] In the petition of Samuel and Elizabeth East of Lincoln's Inn Fields to have their apprentice, Ann Whitworth, taken back to the Foundling Hospital, they cited her 'disobedience' as the main reason, but added 'her Eyes are too weak to practice the...Business of a Mantua Maker', which was supposed to have been her chief employment.[11] References to children's 'infirmities' or 'idiocy', which, when discovered, prevented them from working, were a cause of complaint to the Foundling Hospital by employers of foundling apprentices, as though the Foundling Hospital had issued them with 'damaged goods'. The wife of Charles Cole, a silk dyer of the Old Exchange, attended the General Committee to try and persuade them to take back their apprentice, Laetitia Keene, who was 'said...to be in a declining way'.[12]

If release from an indenture could be obtained from a magistrate for an apprentice's bad behaviour, or if a foundling proved to be unable to work due to sickness or disability, the Foundling Hospital

Governors tried to find alternative arrangements. This could involve reapprenticeship or temporary doles of money or clothing for young men and women who were not fully self-sufficient. There was a 'revolving door' phenomenon of children who were returned to the Hospital for a variety of reasons. John Barton's name was noted in the black book of punishments with misdemeanours on five separate occasions between October 1844 and August 1846.[13] Hannah Draper was exceptionally unlucky: her first master Edward Burnell, an ironmonger of Holborn, went bankrupt. Not wishing to live in the house of the 'kept mistress' of her dead master, she went to work at the house of a parish clerk in St Mary Axe in Leadenhall Street, but left after six months, 'the work being too much for her'. She proceeded to work in three further households in the Cheapside/St Martin's area for less than a year each time as a servant and childminder. She suffered recurrent illness and spent a year in St Thomas's Hospital, leaving her in a debilitated state and earning a precarious living by her needle. Hannah re-emerged back in the historical record when she petitioned to the Hospital's Governors for relief.[14] Sarah Dixon, apprenticed at just under the age of twelve in January 1785 to a Mrs Hutchins who ran a boarding school in Highgate, where she was a servant, was reapprenticed and issued with new indentures just over two years later to James Robottom, an engraver who lived in Clerkenwell. Her master attended the sub-committee in person to complain about Sarah's behaviour.[15] Likewise, foundling Sophia Lee had the disruptive experience of being reapprenticed three times, first as a gentleman's household servant in Westminster, then across the English Channel to a shopkeeper in Guernsey, then once more after being returned to London, to a

'Meal Man', Mr Scott, who attended in person 'to complain of her behaviour'.[16]

The General Committee was aware that allegations against foundling apprentices could be false, and took pains to uncover the truth about a complaint on either side of the master/apprentice relationship. Foundling Maria-Ann Thompson testified to the General Committee that her master, Thomas Ratcliffe, a hairdresser residing at a fashionable address in Cheyne Walk, Chelsea, and his wife, were of 'very good Character...& says it is a very good place'. Her testimony differed from that of another foundling, Harriet Wilkins, who had also been apprenticed to the Ratcliffes; unlike Maria-Ann, Harriet did not get on with her employers, and was removed shortly after Mr Ratcliffe complained of her behaviour. Maria-Ann's testimony sealed Harriet's fate, since it was Harriet, not her employers, who were proved to be at fault.[17] The Governors sometimes despatched the steward to make inquiries, often via the network of local Foundling Hospital inspectors, to delve into complex allegations. This often entailed interviewing multiple witnesses to inquire after the circumstances surrounding a complaint. Sophia Lee appeared in person before the General Committee to 'complain of the ill usage of Master and Mistress', which complaint, the Governors noted, 'is corroborated by the testimony of Hon. Miss Manners if required who lives in the house as well as other witnesses'. The titled status of Sophia's character witness would have impressed the assembled dignitaries. A week later, Mr and Mrs Scott attended in person 'when it was agreed they were to apply to Miss Manners to keep the Girl till she could get a Place'.[18]

In the traditional narrative about the role of child workers during the first period of the Industrial Revolution in England, children are often portrayed as passive victims of cruelty and neglect, subject to endless depredations and given little protection before the advent of legislation to improve their working conditions. More recently, a different picture has emerged of attempts by children and young adults to exert a degree of control and choice (or 'agency') over their lives, albeit in some of the most straitened conditions.[19] This is not to downplay the terrible material circumstances in which many impoverished children found themselves, nor the physical hardships they suffered. Children's skeletons from parishes where factory work was common provide evidence of children's stunted growth, bone deterioration, rickets, and traces of inherited degenerative diseases that came with hard labour, inadequate diet, poor medical care, and other problems associated with intergenerational poverty.[20] Even with these social and educational disadvantages and health problems, many foundling children devised their own strategies for survival, including forms of resistance to the idea that they should be passive, obedient, and subservient to their social superiors. Richard Bickerton was reprimanded for being 'Insolent [and] overbearing and dissatisfied with his situation'.[21] Domestic servant and foundling Hannah Jackson was so 'extreamly obstinate' that she was taken to 'the Locking House' in November 1787 after refusing to submit to answering questions from the sub-committee about her behaviour towards her master, a watch case maker of Clerkenwell.[22]

Insubordination from the lowest ranks of society had worried authorities for many centuries, but the problems associated with vagrancy that had troubled the Elizabethan ruling elites, and which had led to the introduction of the Old Poor Laws, were overtaken by other concerns. By the late-seventeenth century, population growth and labour migration were not meeting the demand for workers in an era of economic expansion. The shortage of free labour meant that young men and women could demand higher wages and choose where to work, refusing to complete their indentured apprenticeship when there were plentiful opportunities to earn their own wages instead.[23] The phenomenon of young people demanding to choose their own work and seeking the opportunity for paid employment rather than an unpaid apprenticeship was therefore not new. But by the late Georgian period, rapid industrialization brought even more opportunities for paid work that offered strong incentives for the young to abandon unpaid apprenticeships. Without much corroborating evidence, it is hard to tell how many foundlings rebelled against being bound over to a master for no wages, and no choice according to their inclination. It was relatively easy for male foundlings to run away, since there were many more opportunities for them to find employment, but for girls as well as boys there were alternative, if illegal, options too. Matilda Bell, admitted to the Hospital in April 1769 and apprenticed aged ten in September 1769, was raised to undertake 'plain worke at her Needle' and was said to have been indulged 'with the Tenderness of a Child more than an Apprentice' by her employer John Brecknock at High Ongar. Nonetheless, Matilda stated her intention to 'get her Liberty' and become her own mistress, for reportedly 'she Wants to go to Servis & have Wages & Move from place to place at her pleasure'. The right to make the most fundamental decisions for ourselves, about where to live and how to earn a living, is often taken for granted in the modern world, but for poor men and women in pre-modern times it required considerable courage to challenge both legal constraints and social customs as Matilda did.[24]

It was expected more of adolescent boys than girls that they would cause trouble. A long tradition of drunken disobedience, violence, and mob behaviour was part of the rite of passage associated with male youth culture and apprenticeship, especially in London.[25] Pauper and charity apprentices, since they were fatherless, were regarded as particularly vulnerable to being led astray if they associated with other apprentices, or older men who proved to be poor role models. John Yates was apprenticed at the age of eleven to John Damon of Weymouth in Dorset, captain of a merchant ship engaged in the perilous business of trade in unsettled times at the end of the 1700s, when Britain started to engage in a series of wars with the French. Captain Damon reported to the Foundling Hospital Governors that he had set sail five weeks earlier from the London docks only to turn the boy off the ship in Normandy.[26] Upon further inquiry the captain was brought before the Governors to account for himself, but gave a different reason for his actions: 'his Men…had corrupted the Boy and learnt him bad habits'. According to the captain, young John had robbed him and then 'ran away at Rouen on Shore'. Another witness was brought: a Mr Blood from Jamaica Row in Rotherhithe, a fellow sailor who had sailed on the same ship and who testified that the captain had 'always used the Boy well' and that his account of the facts was true.

Another foundling who caused the Governors a headache was Charles Bloxham, apprenticed to William Mashiter, a shoemaker of St Clement Danes, in April 1785. The Hospital sent out the steward to inquire why Bloxham had been reapprenticed without their express permission to a Mr Preidel, and was informed that Mr Mashiter 'got him into Preidel's service because it was a light easy place consisting of no more in [the] family than his Master and Mistress, Maidservant & himself'. Bloxham had been given the opportunity of learning how to make shoes, a lucrative business for which apprenticeship foundling George Grafton's sponsor had paid a high premium. But in this case young Charles 'exprest a disinclination to the Shoemaking business and said he never would attempt to learn it'. His new master, Preidel, also discharged him, however, 'because he latterly did not regard his commands nor ever went about executing them without grumbling'. The steward reported that Preidel had kept the youth 'much longer than he would have done to oblige Mr Mashiter', but after several warnings Charles 'grew so bad at last he could keep him no longer'. The sub-committee resolved on 6 October 1787 that there was 'nothing to be done for Bloxham'. The apprenticeship register provides some further intriguing information: Charles Bloxham was already sixteen years old when he was apprenticed to Mashiter the shoemaker, unusually old. This was because he was already on his second apprenticeship, having failed to serve out his time with his first master, John Furman, a stationer of Inner Temple, to whom he had been bound in 1777.

Evidently personal choice could play a role in how foundlings settled upon their future life, but only if they were willing to defy their employers, local magistrates, and the Foundling Hospital Governors.[27] If all else failed, running away was an option open to able-bodied foundling apprentices, although it is hard for the modern eye to appreciate the seriousness of this course of action. Without legitimate apprenticeship, there was no prospect of earning an honest living or gaining a parish settlement in the longer term. On an unspecified date in 1770, James Shrewsbury, apprenticed to Joseph Baxter of Vine Street, Christ Church, Spitalfields, a wool comber, 'Ran Away from his Master on Thursday last' and the master reported that he 'would be glad to know how he is to proceed in respect of Obtaining of him again'. A note was added that the secretary would inquire whether James had run away to his nurse, which was a common problem.[28]

Foundlings could also sometimes abuse the kindness of their masters, although we do not always have the full picture of circumstances described by the master in each case since the apprentice did not often leave a record of their side of the story. Foundling Robert Maxwell absconded from his master, Thomas Watson Whittle, a stocking manufacturer in Bow, east London, with whom he had lived for over six years, in January 1791. Thomas felt it was his duty to inform the Governors that the boy could not be found: 'I am the more concerned for the fate of the little fellow on my wives Acc[oun]t she being as well as myself very fond of him'. In fact, the 'little fellow' was over sixteen years old when he ran away, and seems regularly to have tried the Whittles' patience ('we were always more desirous to blame ourselves than him', recorded the master, adding that he had only used a 'little correction' sometimes in order to mend Robert's ways).[29] Rev. Mr Leach from near Rochester in Kent wrote in a somewhat shaky, perhaps elderly, hand in July 1790 to the Governors regarding George Ward, an apprentice who ran away from his master, another Rochester clergyman, and was sent by the local justice of the peace to a house of correction on account of his bad behaviour. The correspondent explained:

I thought as he was a good looking Lad to have made something of Him, on which he was bound to me by the Hospital till he was one and twenty. I have taken great pains to make him usefull but my complaint against him is this. I can never get [him] out of his Bed till eight o' clock in the Morning, he will do as he pleases he is addicted to Gambling, neglects his business and will go out to Cricketings whenever he pleases tho absolutely forbidden by me, I have never exercise'd my authority over him by Beating of him and he tells me I have no such power over him, be this as it may, I have threatened him often and vehemently but never struck him.

The seemingly kind clergyman noted, 'I have been much advis'd to send him to sea' but thought it proper to ask the Governors first to see if they approved, noting 'a Voyage at Sea might be of service to him'. The air of desperation was also conveyed by the correspondent's request that the Governors should 'inform me *soon*' of their receipt of his letter.[30]

Following the path of virtue and hard work could be eased sometimes if a foundling's employer proved to be kind and fair, and if they themselves showed an aptitude for the trade to which they were assigned. In the year 1800, the Foundling Hospital started up a new system by which foundling apprentices would be given 5 guineas for seeing their training through to completion, payable once the General Committee had received written confirmation from a local worthy that the apprentice had served out their time diligently to their employer's satisfaction. The references received by the Hospital Governors played into the rhetoric of identifying which of their charges had become fully trained and socialized members of the 'deserving' poor—hardworking, observant Christians and obedient to their masters or mistresses. The Vicar of Tamworth wrote to the Governors on 2 October 1800 to confirm that Peter Wright, 'a Gentleman of real worth and respectability', a resident of his parish with whom he was well acquainted, was very pleased with his apprentice Sarah Short and had continued to take her on as a hired domestic servant following the completion of her apprenticeship. The clergyman confirmed that Sarah was 'a very deserving person and one worthy of any Gratuity or Recompence you may be pleased to allow her'.[31] He was writing from Staffordshire, but other records indicated he was formerly of Pall Mall in London, where he had earned a living as a milliner. Sarah went to work for him in 1794 at the age of fourteen. She completed her apprenticeship on 7 July 1800, and had received from him in addition to some new clothes a guinea out of his own pocket. He commended her 'good behaviour' and added that she 'has Regularly attended divine service all her time, & of late the sacrament of the Lord's Supper'. All Foundling Hospital babies were baptised as infants into membership of the Church of England, but Sarah's participation in communion indicates that she must also voluntarily have been confirmed as an Anglican, something which would have met with the approval of both her employer and the Hospital Governors. A further letter written by Mr Wright conveyed Sarah's thanks to the Governors for their 'very Liberal and Beneficent gratuity to her'. He passed on that she particularly wanted to thank 'her Great and Good Benefactors for so great a mark of their Goodness to her & that she will now Pray for Gods Blessing on those who so liberally Provide for the destitute'. Sarah's master added at the end of the letter, 'I beg to repeat my thanks for the part *you* have taken in this Business in which I am found by Sarah Short'. Evidently, both master and servant girl had been a blessing to one another.[32]

The adjectives used to describe foundlings who had earned their gratuities according to their employers are indicative of the qualities that apprentice masters and mistresses demanded of girls and boys whom they took on as apprentices. Mary Bishop had been sent all the way to Wales to serve out her time in service, and was confirmed by her master as having 'conducted herself with propriety and attention to the Rules given her'.[33] Elizabeth Clarke was 'very industrious and attentive in all things to her Mistress', Mary MacKenzie, who wrote a character reference documenting her 'great satisfaction' so that Elizabeth could claim her gratuity, countersigned in a careful hand by Elizabeth herself.[34] Charlotte Dowding had behaved with 'Honesty and sobriety with civil attention to her Employers' in a 'respectable family'. Charlotte's difficulty, however, was that her original employer, a baker, had died, and she had served out her time in another household. Her new master was of an 'indolent disposition' according to the author of the letter, the sister of the deceased baker, Mr Sibley, and could not be bothered to attend the General Committee at the designated time to confirm Charlotte's years of hard work and good character.[35]

Boys were also praised for good conduct, though using slightly different language than that used to describe girls, and with an emphasis on other qualities appropriate to the rank and gender of both employer and apprentice. This was particularly the case if a master were writing about a male apprentice. The master John Cleghorn, was a man of business, and penned a briskly rigorous note in praise of his apprentice John Cox, to the Governors of the Foundling

Hospital from Old Street Square. He declared John Cox had 'demeaned himself Soberly the whole time exerting himself according to his abilities in my Business'. Cleghorn added, 'I think he will not disgrace the excellent Institution by which he has been protected up to Manhood'.[36] George King's mentor, the Foundling Hospital schoolmaster Robert Atchison, was evidently keen to give credit where it was due, and added his own testimony regarding John Coulson and another boy, Hussey Fleet, whom he had presented to the Governors in 1797 and 1795, respectively. Both had served Mr Cleghorn, 'and by their good conduct and superior abilities in their profession are a credit to this institution'. The schoolmaster added, 'they are both married and live in a very decent manner'.[37]

Reward followed if children grew up to perform the work that had been assigned to them and in obedience to the authorities who had control over their lives. These included the Governors of the Hospital, their masters or mistresses, church authorities who sanctioned 'Godly' observance, magistrates who enforced the formal laws that governed apprenticeships, and neighbours, who informally policed the conduct of those who were young and poor. The inclinations and characters of the children themselves, their individualism, and their identity were given little priority when decisions were made about their future lives. Of course, it was the supposed malleability of foundlings that some masters and employers found appealing: the possibility of training and moulding a compliant orphan child into a hardworking young adult to suit their own ends, for business and domestic service, without the possibility of blood relatives or friends of their apprentice intervening. In one very unusual case, that of John Morton, this normally unspoken aspect of foundling apprenticeship was brought to light. Foundling John was a hardworking lad, apprenticed at the age of eleven to a silversmith, Thomas Wright, in the parish of St Giles, London, who proved to be of a 'mild, docile disposition and ready capacity', which was in keeping with the character described when Wright took him on in December 1787. John was doing well at a trade that promised a good living if he was able to complete his term as an apprentice. However, soon after he was sent to work with Wright an inquiry was made at the Hospital by 'a Lady, a Friend of ... John Morton's Mother', who claimed that she would take the boy in and take care of him 'till able to provide for himself'. Since English law regarded married women as 'covered', their identity subsumed under the authority of their husband's, this lady asked that John should be 'turned over to her Husband, who was Captain of a Ship in the American trade and who proposed to take him to sea'.[38] The Foundling Hospital Governors, the unnamed lady who claimed John, and John's master Mr Wright then entered into a negotiation about what was in the boy's best interests. The silversmith recognized that it could be an advantage for John to discover 'his Mother's Friends' and to hand him over to their care. As John's master, he had a right to enforce the terms of the apprenticeship, but he said that he would not do anything that would be to the boy's detriment ('he will not at any time have it said that he was the Boy's hindrance'). However, the master also observed that 'he could not conceive how ... taking [John] from a good Trade he was about to learn and sending him to Sea' would be in his best interests.

Mr Wright evidently had a strong liking for his apprentice ('he has a very good opinion of the lad') and lobbied hard to keep him. He argued that John was not physically strong, and a sailor's life demanded a tough constitution and ability to withstand harsh discipline. 'Sea service', the master opined, 'was a refuge only for profligate and abandon'd Youth and a School of Vice and immorality.' It would be a great pity 'that a Lad of good disposition and who had not been brought up in the Streets but had had the advantage of only no more than the early religious impressions which are given them in this Hospital, should be place out in such a way of Life, as to render the first of no avail'. In a plea that sounds remarkably modern in its request for confidentiality, and which besets many adoption arrangements today, the master requested 'the Steward to acquaint the Governors that he begs they do not make known the place of his abode, in order that no persons but them or their Officers may have access to the Lad'. As it turned out, the silversmith had already trained many other apprentices 'who would have given him much less trouble than he has experienced from them if they had had no Relations or Friends to resort to upon any little disagreement'.

Their lack of friends or relations made the prospect of a foundling apprentice particularly appealing to some prospective masters, something which was jeopardized in the case of John Morton since this particular foundling turned out to have friends, including blood relatives, after all (the 'expectation of his Apprentice's implicit submission will be entirely frustrated if he is let to imagine he has any Friend besides his master, more than the Governors').[39] Some foundling boys did have better prospects than other pauper or charity apprentices. If they worked hard and found the trade suited them, some went on to become silversmiths, vintners, and shoemakers. This may have been because, like foundling George Grafton, they were 'private' children whose anonymous sponsors paid an extra amount for them to be apprenticed with a higher premium, but as the case of

John Morton has shown, it may also have been because foundlings were seen as particularly docile or innocent, and free from the meddling of family and friends who might question a master's authority. At the time, if anyone sought the opinion of John Morton himself, they did not record it. Frustratingly, the archives are silent about John's fate.

Fortunately, we do know a great deal more about George King's experiences as an apprentice from his autobiography. He recorded his inner struggle to remain honest as an apprentice to Mr John Browne, the grocer and confectioner of Fish Hill Street who was his master. Following his near-miss with the city marshals, who caught other apprentices red-handed stealing from their master, he usually resisted succumbing to the temptation of working in a sweet-maker's shop.[40] In 1802, aged about fifteen and just as he entered puberty ('I was springing up in height'), he found he had a liking for the business and wished to pursue it further. He was bound for seven years to one of the City of London Guilds, the Coopers Company, to which his master belonged. Had he been a parish apprentice, this would have been a very unusual opportunity, but being a charity apprentice from the Foundling Hospital gave him a degree of opportunity not enjoyed by the poorest of the poor.[41] Soon he found himself in conflict, however, with the eldest of Mr Browne's apprentices, whom George recalled 'used often to give me a blow'. Provoked one day by constant teasing by another apprentice, George took a pan reserved for boiling barley sugar and threw a gallon of scalding water over his tormentor, burning him severely. He was caned by his master and locked up 'in prison seven days and nights upon bread and water'. Though he promised never again to lash out and to mend his ways, George found the bullies continued to make his life difficult.

By 1804, George had set up a regular course of life visiting his friend Rivington until Henry's master turned bankrupt and the lad left to join the army. Echoing his attempt to maintain a virtuous course of life, George recalled that as a youth he still attended the Foundling Hospital chapel regularly ('I...used to sing with the boys, as I knew the hymns and psalms generally sung from each Sunday in the year'). He still felt a pull to the institution that had raised him. He spent the sabbath with friends he had made there, and returned to eat with fellow foundlings at the time in the week when other apprentices visited their families.

But George's attempts at staying out of trouble ended in vain. In the heat of summer he ended up in a pitched battle with another apprentice ('a regular turn-to which lasted about twenty minutes'). He was about to be hauled in front of the city chamberlain by his master at Guildhall, where most likely he was facing a custodial sentence in the notorious Bridewell Prison. But, on the very day before sentencing, he happened to bump into James Gardner (described by George as an 'old schoolfriend') whom he had known at the Foundling Hospital. James told the impressionable younger lad about his recent adventures on a merchant ship newly arrived from Archangel. George resolved to pack up his things and run away to sea.[42] Having made this resolution, he went with James to drink porter at the sailor's lodgings in Lambs Conduit Street, almost within sight of the Foundling Hospital. No doubt feeling very grown up, George recalled 'for the first time I commenced smoking a pipe of tobacco which...made me very sick'. He later recalled his inner life that night, saying goodbye in his mind to Mr Browne's household as he secretly packed his few belongings in a handkerchief ('I went to bed sorrowful').

The next morning, George stealthily made his escape, weaving his way from Monument to St Paul's, where he pawned his belongings to a Jewish trader for 16 shillings. He met up with his accomplice James Gardner, and the pair made their way to Seven Dials, where George traded his clothes for 'Purser Slops in a Man or War', a blue jacket and pair of common blue trousers that were to be his 'warfairing suit'. He was now ready for his adventure at sea to begin.

The young men journeyed south on foot and soon parted on Blackfriars Bridge, since James had to remain in town to settle some business. George's first task was to walk 30 miles to Chatham on his own, where he believed he would meet up again with his friend. The weather was fine and his spirits were high, although his conscience weighed heavily upon him about his manner of deserting his master. His clothing marked him out for conversation with other sailors, and he met men along the way who guided him and shared scratch meals. Finally, he arrived at Chatham exhausted, and took refuge at an inn where he had arranged to meet the London stage coach. There was no sign of his friend.

The bad conscience that accompanied George as he planned his escape, and actually absconded, was for a reason. His institutional upbringing had instilled in him in many different ways, via chapel hymns, prayers, catechizing, and schoolroom instruction, the idea that he was an unworthy recipient of charitable benevolence from his social betters. His life was marked by the stain of illegitimacy. His best hope was that he would grow up to be a member of the 'deserving' poor, and that if he worked hard he would earn an honest living in trade. Though we do not know for sure the cause of his bullying by other apprentices, it is highly likely that he was marked out from his peers by the public knowledge of his status as a Foundling Hospital apprentice. The consequences of breaking the terms of an indenture were intentionally harsh, with magistrates empowered to enforce the return of apprentices who attempted to escape their masters. Towards the end of the eighteenth century, more impoverished young people of limited prospects, both women and men, were testing the limits of the authorities to be able to enforce the strict terms of their indenture. Though factory employment was known to be harsh, offering hard labour conditions, they offered new opportunities to work for wages in hand. More young people embraced free labour systems where they chose their occupation, and began to marry younger and have more children. The smaller families of the Georgian age gave way to the large families we associate with the Victorians, compounding still further the problems of urban poverty but helping to feed the industrial economy hungry for a ready supply of workers.

For George, and those other young people of limited means and prospects who chose to rebel and enter a new world, there was no going back. Having run away from his legitimate master, his fate was soon sealed. At the inn in Chatham he overslept, and fell in with a press gang, who plied him with grog and tore up his precious indentures for the Coopers Company. The destruction of these documents effectively erased his opportunity for earning an honest living and settlement in a London parish. His career on land was effectively destroyed, and George would now have to make his way at sea. He was impressed as a sailor onboard His Majesty's Ship

Polyphemus, just fitted out in the Medway and commanded by Admiral Sir John Lawford.

By September 1804, George had experienced his first taste of life onboard ship. He soon recovered from his initial sea sickness, bade farewell to Dover as the shoreline disappeared from view ('I could not help admiring the chalky cliffs'), and his crew set sail. As fortune would have it, the *Polyphemus*, bearing seventeen-year-old ordinary seaman George King below decks, was to join with other ships of the line under the command of Admiral Lord Nelson soon destined for the blockade of Cádiz that marked the outbreak of renewed hostilities between Great Britain and the combined armed forces of France and Spain, under the command of Napoleon Bonaparte.

By running away from his master, George escaped the taunts and beatings by other young male apprentices and instead subjected himself to the hardships of life at sea, of which there were to be many. Other foundling apprentices stayed in their lawful places, obliged to follow the calling that the Foundling Hospital had destined for them. They would find it harder to escape the cruelty and at times shocking brutality of life as an unfree child worker in Georgian England.

CHAPTER 7

Cruelty and Kindness

S OME OF THE hardest historical material to read in the
Foundling Hospital archive because of its disturbing content
are those records which make only too evident the living and
working conditions of children when they first went out into the
world from the Foundling Hospital. The children, many of whom
were no more than ten or eleven years old, were at the mercy of
their masters and mistresses. With few friends and no family on
whom they could call, theirs was a precarious existence indeed. In
an era when children often received physical punishment, community scrutiny rather than social services were the main means of
policing orderly and kind relations between minors and their
parents or guardians, as well as employers. In some respects foundlings had a 'safety net' that mirrored the one that in theory protected other pauper apprentices sent out under the traditional parish
system. The network of Foundling Hospital inspectors, which

branched out to those provincial institutions established during the General Reception, was supposed to provide a safeguard to ensure that foundlings would not be treated cruelly, exploited, or abused. Following changes to the law during the eighteenth century, it was magistrates who normally received complaints by apprentices that they were being ill-treated by their masters, and who were empowered to break the terms of an indenture on the grounds of cruelty and neglect. Abuse was sometimes exposed by the diligence of Foundling Hospital inspectors, reports of neighbours, and in some instances the direct intervention of constables and magistrates and the public scandal of press publicity. In some cases of abuse, the system worked: in many others, it did not.

Even today, the challenges facing children who speak out about abuse of all kinds—whether physical, sexual, or psychological (or a combination of all three)—are only too clear in Western societies coming to terms with institution-wide 'hidden' histories, and where children's voices have been altogether trivialized or ignored. So it is intriguing to find that where Foundling Hospital inspectors carried out their duties with diligence (and this was by no means universal) and where magistrates listened sympathetically to foundling apprentices who complained about their treatment, children and adolescents were not only sometimes heard and believed; they could be removed from abusive situations. The test for this was not whether a modicum of physical correction, hard work, and privation was experienced by the foundling apprentice, for these were hard times for poor working children. Instead, certain criteria were used to decide whether masters and mistresses had behaved cruelly. These included whether living conditions were sufficient to keep the apprentice 'decently'—meaning adequately clothed and fed—according to the terms of the apprenticeship indenture. This stated that in addition to learning a trade the apprentice should be given 'Meat, Drink, Apparel, Washing and Lodging, and all other Necessaries according to the Custom of the City of London'. Physical punishment was common, but communities judged whether corrections meted out to child apprentices were harsh according to the communal standards of the day, and what was deemed normal according to specific circumstances, such as the social rank of the household and the gender of the child. The parallel was with other household members living under the rule of a patriarchal male head, including wives and other servants, not just apprentices. Corporal punishment, it was thought, should be used in moderation and only in extreme circumstances, and then without the one issuing a beating losing their 'reason' or gaining pleasure from it.[1] It should leave no lasting physical signs (such as bruises or scars) and there should be no other causes of suspicion, such as ragged, 'indecent', and inadequate clothing, signs of unusual dirtiness, or malnutrition. The household should not be known for drunkenness or disorder, and should not be associated with people of 'bad character'. Very rarely, the imputation of sexual abuse came to light, and perhaps surprisingly such cases were acknowledged in the eighteenth century with a frankness that is remarkable in the light of modern attempts to airbrush such stories from public view.

Community policing and the testimony of neighbours could lead to a tip-off for a Foundling Hospital inspector that all was not right, or even a direct report to the Foundling Hospital Governors. It is noticeable that the majority but not all of such reports were sent from within a twenty-mile radius of the London Foundling Hospital, suggesting that cases of abuse further afield were hard to detect. One such case was of Joan Cabot, apprenticed to Mrs Sidney Jackson in the parish of Christ Church Spitalfields, a 'Black and White Milliner'. In 1770, the General Committee was informed that her neighbour, Mrs Pollard, another woman in trade 'at the [sign of the] Pewter Pot Whites Row' had complained 'that this Woman Starves and Ill treats the Girl'.[2] In another case from the same year, a Mr Weals of no. 8 Goldsmith Street, Gough Square, notified the General Committee that he would attend to report that 'Jane Duck... apprenticed to William Adams of Execution Dock, Wapping, Surgeon and Apothecary, who is sailed in Business and his Wife uses the Girl in a Most barbarous manner; he likewise has a Boy of this Hospital which is not with him'.[3] The justices of the peace for the county of Middlesex took a sworn statement from Andrew Gray, a staymaker, who lodged at the house of Alexandra Young in Golden Lane, testifying to an incident that had occurred the previous week in which he had over-heard Mrs Young order her apprentice, Honor Lucas, to go into the cellar to fetch some sand, which she did 'with great Reluctance'. He heard Mrs Young tell her husband 'to Observe the Sulkey behaviour of his apprentice', after which Mr Young 'put himself into a passion and struck her once upon the face with his open hand', upon which 'she came forward against him and she told this Deponant that he struck her several times'. Next morning, Honor refused to come to breakfast and showed her resistance to further abuse by crying out so that her neighbours would be alerted. The neighbour also observed that, in spite of the beatings, 'the said Apprentice has not been debarr'd from Bread Butter or Chees and Small beer'.[4] The Youngs were beating, not starving, Honor Lucas into submission.

The perpetrator of violence could be anyone in the household: the master, his wife, or other servants or employees against male or female children. On 8 November 1787, foundling apprentice William Gray came to the Hospital to complain 'that his Master suffered his Journeymen to beat him in an unmerciful manner, that he desired they would and that he frequently beat him severely himself, tho' not so bad as his men did'. William displayed the marks of their violence: just the night before he had been knocked down by the journeymen and cut his head, and the only clothes he was allowed were those he was standing in when he appeared before the General Committee.[5] Christian Wilson, a girl apprenticed at just under ten years old to a shoemaker's household to be 'employed in Mantuamaking and household business', came forward at the age of eighteen to complain 'that her Mistress had beat & ill treated her, for straying 2 hours upon an errand she had sent her to gather some Rents at another house which she Lett into lodgings & bringing but 6 pence &c'. The girl wanted to show that her alleged crimes were trivial: she had been beaten on another occasion 'for taking some butter without leave to mix with some turnips'. She took refuge at the Foundling Hospital where she hid from her employers, 'being afraid of being beat again when she went home', and on this occasion the steward 'sent a Letter ... requiring her Master and Mistress to appear at the Committee ... to answer the complaints'.[6]

Christian Wilson's case illustrates the precarious experience of many of the poorest people in London, and how few options there were, especially for young women. Girls in service sometimes had employers who were barely surviving themselves, in spite of the Foundling Hospital's efforts at only placing children in established households. In the face of sickness, disability, bankruptcy, or death of an employer, female servants could slip from scraping a living as domestic skivvies or washerwomen into prostitution and crime. Apart from the Hospital Governors, their only source of support would be if they could prove that they had lived and worked as a servant for a year or more in a parish, thereby gaining settlement and entitlement to doles of money as 'outdoor relief' or, in extreme circumstances of last resort, admission to a workhouse. In these notorious institutions, men were segregated from women and children, and barrack-like communal dormitories provided ripe breeding ground for the spread of contagious disease. Even the very young and very old were not allowed to be 'idle', and were set to work at monotonous tasks such as picking oakum (unravelling coarse rope by hand to collect fibres that were then mixed with tar to make ships watertight) or breaking stones. Some historians have questioned whether conditions in Georgian workhouses were as universally harsh as the notorious Victorian workhouses of Dickensian ignominy, but there is much evidence that the poor themselves regarded these institutions as shameful places of last resort.[7]

One former foundling who narrowly escaped the workhouse because of the intervention of the Foundling Hospital Governors was Catherine Horton. Catherine served out over a year of her apprenticeship to James Flatt of Clapton, a coachman. In 1775, she left Flatt's employment 'on account of ill usage', and the Parish of Hackney turned her over to another master, a box maker in Cripplegate, until 1778. Though there must be some caution about linking more than one person with the same name, a Catherine Horton aged twenty-one in 1778 (which would fit her admission date to the Foundling Hospital, in July 1757) was ordered to be removed from the parish of St Giles, Cripplegate, which may have been when her itinerant life began, scraping a living by moving between public houses.[8] The Foundling Hospital only learned of her fate in May 1788 when they received a report that she 'has expended the wages she earned before', at which point she was given 8 shillings in relief by the charity that had raised her. Catherine's experiences demonstrate how difficult it was to negotiate between uncertain entitlement under the parish system and charitable institutions for London's poor, and how easy it was to slip into utter destitution.[9]

Like many pauper children, those who had been raised in the Foundling Hospital were expected to pursue a life of drudgery without complaint, and could be treated with casual brutality and rough justice. Some letters to the Foundling Hospital suggest that foundling children felt a lifelong safety net that originated from the sense of being under the patronage of the powerful Governors of the institution in which they had been raised. When foundling apprentice Francis Desse was thrown into Bridewell Prison by his vengeful master for saying that he wished to terminate his indenture, he obtained the skills of a fluent letter writer to petition the Governors for his release: '[Francis] thinks it a Duty he owes to the Governors of that Hospital to mention to your Worships that He is not confined among the abandoned Class of Persons but in one of the solitary Cells'. It was important for Francis that he, unlike some of the London poor, was not utterly abandoned, but had the patronage of the Governors upon which he hoped he could call in a time of crisis. He wanted to show the Governors that he would do them credit and would be able to maintain a degree of respectability in solitary confinement 'away from the Association of Thieves &c. &c'.[10]

Any pauper who could prove they qualified for settlement in a parish could claim assistance—usually in the form of doles of money by writing to the local Poor Law officials. Since the early days of the Foundling Hospital, anxious ratepayers had received guarantees that foundlings would not qualify for settlement in neighbouring parishes simply by virtue of having been raised there: similar guarantees were issued from branch hospitals across the country. Once they were out in the world, those foundlings who had not qualified for parish settlement could be found petitioning the only source of help they knew: the Hospital Governors. These letters constitute some of the few traces of foundling voices from the eighteenth century, offering insights into the lives of female foundlings in particular which are otherwise lost to the historical record:

> Most Worthy Gentlemen,
>
> I hope you will Pardon the boldness of a poor Unfortunate Woman formerly an Orphan in the House who has Sufferd Numerous Hardships and is greatly Distress'd hopes the Gentlemen will take her Case into Consideration that she may be enabled to go to Place as she has a Place in view but for the want of Necessary Apparel [spelling corrected] Cannot do it, she has Suffer'd greatly oweing to Sickness, she Humbly prays that the Worthy Gentlemen will pardon the Petition of their Distress'd Orphan H Harriet Searle [Seal] No. 12, 233.

A note at the foot of Harriet's letter indicated that she was 'Apprenticed 3 May 1769 to John Gourley of Round Court Strand to be employ'd as a Mantua-maker', although there was no means of telling whether she had served out her time.[11] Harriet's married name was Munden, and she wrote again, indicating that her fortunes had not improved, although she got married: she had 'not a Friend to apply to and am now quite Distress'd my Husband is gone abroad being Press'd having been at Sea before'. This rare fragment of a letter written by a female foundling in the 1790s gives some insight into the hardships caused among the labouring poor at the time of the Napoleonic Wars, when impressment was the main way of procuring sailors for the Royal Navy. Harriet reported that she was 'distitute of Cloaths to go to get a service or any way to provide for myself hope you will be so kind as Stand my Friend this time and never hope to Trouble you again without which I am quite a lost Creature'. A note at the foot of Harriet's letter verified that she was going to live in lodgings at Soho Square, and that the committee raised half a guinea for her relief.[12]

The Hospital Governors were petitioned for assistance if a foundling apprentice was unable to work owing to sickness or disability. When it was their charges who wrote to them, typically the Governors responded with a collection for a particular former foundling in distress in response to requests for urgent help. The girl Magdalen Hall was provided with relief amounting to 9s 6d, and was given 5s from this immediately, the remainder left with the steward for safekeeping and noted carefully. In her case, the relationship with her master had not broken down, but his employment as a schoolmaster left him with a precarious living that jeopardized his ability to provide for her.[13]

The patience of the Governors was tested when masters or mistresses returned to the Foundling Hospital to complain if their apprentice fell ill or proved unsuitable for work. The wife of Charles Cole, a silk dyer at the Old Exchange, attended the General Committee to let them know that their apprentice, Laetitia Keene, who had been with them since April 1787, 'has been taken ill & is said ... to be in a declining way'. Country air was advised, but Mrs Cole thought a preferable (and perhaps cheaper) solution would be for Laetitia to return to the Hospital to be nursed, offering to pay for her maintenance while she was there.[14] Less than a year after being apprenticed to a peruke (wig) maker and hairdresser in Holborn, eleven-year-old David Garrick's master brought him in, and the Governors had him examined by the Hospital's apothecary and surgeon, who treated him for disease. Perhaps there was a sense of continuing obligation on the part of the Governors owing to the fact that this was less than a year since the boy had been apprenticed, although the lack of dates on all documents makes it difficult to tell whether this was generally the case.[15]

We cannot know for certain what proportion of foundlings suffered abuse, nor how many apprentices did not serve out their term, and for what reasons. Only fifty-five apprentices are recorded as having died in the apprenticeship register, although this was most likely a substantial under-recording. These are skewed towards those in London and Middlesex parishes, with just over two-thirds of these entries reporting local deaths less than 10 miles away from the Foundling Hospital. Those children suffering disease and dying in hospitals such as St George's, or private residences near the Foundling Hospital in Bloomsbury, were reported more regularly: only a small number further afield were noted, perhaps because of the unusual circumstances of their deaths. Nine male foundlings reportedly 'drown'd' after having been apprenticed to sea service from coastal port towns, but two apprentices met their end during the term of their indenture from as far away as Jamaica and Guinea. Another apprentice died tragically having been 'Run over by a broad wheel Wagon and killed on the spot'.[16]

In 1747, a law was passed enabling any allegedly abused apprentices to complain to two magistrates if the premium paid to their masters for their training was less than £5. If their complaint was upheld, then they were released from their indentures, although the master could keep the premium paid with them, which was a gift to unscrupulous masters seeking to be rid of an apprentice on spurious grounds. From 1757, indentures were replaced by a stamped deed, often a printed document restating mutual obligations (although these were still commonly referred to as indentures). Though many foundling apprentices were despatched with a £5 premium (below the threshold that would have allowed them to use this form of redress if they were abused in some way by their masters), further legislation after 1760 increased the eligibility of all apprentices bound for less than £10 to complain to magistrates of ill treatment, with the introduction of a £2 penalty for masters against whom a complaint was upheld.[17]

As a result of these changes in legislation, many more stories emerge of foundling apprentices making complaints against their employers. Some of these cases were heard by the famous reformer and justice of the peace for the county of Middlesex, Sir John Fielding, the blind half-brother of the novelist Henry Fielding (whose novel *The History of Tom Jones, a Foundling* had been such a success). Sir John's interest in ameliorating the conditions of the London poor was witnessed in the part he played in helping to found an asylum for orphaned girls in Lambeth. He also demonstrated considerable sympathy to the cases of abuse reported by foundling apprentices. One such case was that of foundling apprentice Sarah Cadwick who gave detailed evidence in front of Fielding and his fellow justice of the peace, Sir Sampson Wright, that her master Roger White, a 'White Smith', had 'assaulted and cruelly beat' her, having 'neglected to find and provide for her sufficient Meat Drink and other Necessaries and hath otherwise ill treated her'. Sarah's experience as a young girl apprenticed at the age of ten to White's household in York to undertake domestic service was not untypical in its chaotic character, although unusually detailed in its thorough examination by the two magistrates. Sarah's master, Roger White, had 'always been a lodger', the court noted, and had been a 'common Soldier/Light Horseman', and he himself had failed to complete his own apprenticeship as a whitesmith when he absconded to become a soldier. As it turned out, the Foundling Hospital's safeguards failed in this case. White procured a false character witness from a sea captain so that Sarah's services could be obtained for his wife, 'who wanted a Girl to do her drudgery for her'. Mrs White turned out to be of 'Light character' (her sexual reputation maligned) for having been 'frequently visited by other Men who have been of service to her husband' in his absence. Roger White was himself described as 'profligate', fleeing to London to escape his creditors and tailed by his family and the rest of his household including Sarah. They were given a series of temporary lodgings, from a cellar near Seven Dials, to Tower Hill, and finally Drury Lane, as White moved to find work. In order to escape the cruelty of her first master, who forced her to go begging on the streets to help him clear his debts, Sarah deserted the White household and obtained a discharge from two magistrates from her apprenticeship before she qualified for settlement, since she had not spent more than forty days in any one parish. Since then, the precariousness of her situation was evident: 'she hath never lived as an hired yearly Servant one whole year together. Or been bound an Apprentice. Or done any other than Act or Thing whereby to gain a legal Settlement in any

Parish or Place.' Instead, she moved between various public houses, working as a servant for between two and nine months in a variety of positions, from a wine merchant's house in Islington to a bricklayer's and another establishment 'where Clothes were taken in to wash'. Sarah's lot was the embodiment of the 'economy of makeshift' that characterized the lives of poor women. She moved so frequently that when cross-examined about the chronology of each position she answered that 'she cannot recollect'. A copy of the lengthy evidence presented at the hearing, and the ruling, dated 1 October 1777, was filed at the Foundling Hospital, to provide documentary evidence for the Governors of Sarah's liberty from obligation to any other master or mistress should the opportunity for reapprenticeship arise.[18]

Another dimension to the scrutiny given to the treatment of foundling children as apprentices lay in the particular circumstances of the later eighteenth century, which witnessed the rise of the popular press. The idea of public opinion was forged through the circulation of newsprint in London and across the British Isles. By the second half of the eighteenth century, there was a growing sense among the rich and powerful that their lives were under scrutiny via the fourth estate, and though a very small proportion of the population had the vote (just under 5 per cent by 1800), a much wider reading public, both men and women of the middling and lower sorts, gained access to news and information on matters of high politics and general interest. Anonymous political commentators under the guise of, e.g., 'Observator', 'Junius', used a cloak of anonymity to expose corruption and criticize those in authority, particularly politicians and the king's advisors.

For as long as the Foundling Hospital had existed as a charity, the Governors were used to coming under widespread scrutiny and attack in the public prints. Their enterprise had been supported from the public purse during the period of general admission. Many critics were looking to make political capital of any cases which seemed to prove they were right to claim that foundlings would never make decent, hardworking citizens. Moreover, the conduct of the Governors themselves was called to account, with suspicion of embezzlement and neglect of duty. The editor of *The World*, a title specializing in miscellaneous national and international news culled from diverse sources, published one such letter from the anonymous commentator 'Observator' regarding the case heard at Guildhall involving ten-year-old James Squires, apprenticed to an apothecary in Cheapside. James' cruel punishment for minor and allegedly unfounded misdemeanours was described in sensational and graphic terms to shock the *World*'s readers into demanding 'some of the Governors of the Hospital [to] ... interfere on the part of this distressed Foundling, and save him from inevitable ruin'. Squire had been sent to Bridewell Prison, 'stripped naked from the waist upwards and ... whipped till his back was bloody', then had to endure a month's hard labour 'for some trifling offence'. The author of this account appealed to the idea of the helpless foundling imbued in public imagination following the success of Henry Fielding's novel *Tom Jones* and the plethora of literary spin-offs. So, the eye-catching large print title of the feature about James Squire was 'The Distressed Foundling. A True Story'. James was featured as a 'helpless orphan', 'left destitute of friends, or even a place to lay down in', 'forced to wander about the streets day and night, living upon what he could beg of the public' and reimprisoned as a vagrant, where he languished awaiting transportation before being 'accidentally discovered'.[19] An anonymous member of the public

sent the secretary of the Hospital a copy of the paper to ensure
that inquiries would be made, appealing to the 'humanity' of the
Governors in this case. Upon inquiry, the Governors secured written
confirmation from the Lord Mayor that James Squire had in fact been
guilty of 'divers Misdemeanours' including stealing from his master,
an apothecary named James Upton of Cheapside. In an illuminating
example of a tradesman and ordinary citizen taking seriously the
power of the press to impugn reputations, within a week of the sensational story being made public he wrote his own account of the
apprentice's crimes to the editor of *The World*. They had, claimed
Upton, 'unjustly charged' him of cruelty ('the grossest defect of
common Humanity and Charity, the two best principles of Human
Nature'). The press had made 'a false, malignant, and infamous statement, plainly intended to stab the character of an individual, hitherto
unimpeachable', and this under the 'flimsy pretext of Philanthropy'.[20]

Some of the most scandalous cases of abuse to be exposed by
Foundling Hospital inspectors, which made it into the press if they
resulted in criminal action against masters, related to girls despatched
to work in factories. Richard Blackburn, 'a very Considerable Silk
Manufacturer' in Stockport, Cheshire, needed 'a greater number
of hands of all ages than can be procured in the neighbourhood'
and sought to employ 'as many as would enable him to proceed in
a more Extensive way'. He faced opposition from local magistrates,
who sought guarantees that pauper children employed in large
numbers would not become chargeable to the parish. Having
secured the necessary assurances, Blackburn took on eleven foundling girls between the ages of ten and fourteen, reapprenticed to
him on the same day (23 November 1773) following the death of
their previous master Thomas Tatlock, who like Blackburn was

described as a 'Silk Throwster'.[21] This kind of employment could have catastrophic consequences for the children's welfare, as revealed by factory visits by Foundling Hospital inspectors. The apprenticeship register records that seven of the girls originally apprenticed to Tatlock died, an under-recording of the actual number of fatalities. The London Governors paid particular attention to the living conditions of the surviving girls who were sent to work for Richard Blackburn, and even received a letter from the girls directly which accounted for their favourable treatment by him, including the appointment of a friendly governess, and their lasting affection for the children whom they left behind in London:

> To foundling Hospedel   Stockport July 13th 1780
>
> This Comms Whith all our Dutes to you all hoping thease Lines whill find you all in good halth as it Leaves us all at Present bless god for it our Governess is the bearer of this Letter . . . being the best frend whe have found since we Left you. [We] have a verey good Please [place] on Every account whe have had new Cloathing Everey [year] and that which is verey genteel better than most Peepel of our Rank.

The unnamed young woman who wrote this letter, who would have perhaps been in her early twenties, added 'Loves to the Children' who were at the Hospital. The letter was not signed, but someone else wrote at the foot of the page that 'most of the Girls has served their time and stays with their Master', further testimony that the young women wanted to stay in Blackburn's employment for wages once their period of apprenticeship had ended.[22]

One of the most notorious cases of abuse and neglect was by Martin Browne, a clothier from Holbeck Lodge, Leeds, who requested fifty girls from Ackworth in 1764 to work in his factory.[23] Browne's grandiose plan had been to construct a new building, 'The Industrious Foundling Hall', 117 feet long by 26 feet wide, and employ fifty girls of seven years old to work making 'Cloath like the French Cloath for the East India or Turkey Trade', fine woollen textile manufacturing which he planned would rival the French monopoly on imported cloth. The industrialist attempted to bypass the Ackworth branch of the Foundling Hospital, where Dr Lee was asking too many questions about the project. He also attempted to extract the maximum payment from the London Governors since he had heard that the government was considering subsidizing foundling apprentices. In the event, parliament granted a further £2,000 for apprenticeship fees, and Browne demanded that he be paid backdated fees for taking so many.[24] The Governors capitulated and agreed to pay 'nursing money' for a year since the children he had taken were younger than the normal age for foundling apprentices. However, news was soon received by Jonas Hanway in London that twenty-four of Browne's apprentices had died of 'Putrid Fever'; another twenty children were in a 'perilous condition'; and upward of thirty more needed to regain their health from overwork and starvation. A visit by one of the Ackworth inspectors revealed a 'Putrid Stench from the Little House' [latrine], just one indicator of neglect and poor living conditions.[25] The children 'slept on corded beds with thin mattresses laid over them' which he observed 'must be very unfit to refresh those weary limbs that have kept the whole day to hard Labour'. Browne's grand scheme had been exposed as a scandal. In order to bail out his business, he had taken on contract work, engaging the small children in worsted spinning, a heavy and hard labour requiring them to be on their feet all day, which caused pain in their legs, hips, thighs, and knees. Browne was summoned by the Ackworth committee to account for himself, but was less than contrite: he shamelessly claimed that the children liked the beds he had supplied 'better than the boards' and he did not see anything wrong with their food or clothing. The case was brought before a magistrates court in Leeds, attended by the mayor and Alderman, but the authorities did not discharge the children from their indentures, finding Browne had no case to answer and perhaps mindful that the children could become chargeable to ratepayers in Holbeck. The London Governors did not prosecute Browne, perhaps in an attempt to minimize further adverse publicity, but they instead raised a charity subscription for the surviving girls, and new places were found for them.[26]

Not all cases of abuse related to foundling girls, and not all were confined to 'batch' apprenticeships. One particularly touching case was recalled by the Hospital secretary of foundling Samuel Storey, who attended the General Committee 'to make complaint of the treatment towards him by his Master'. He was questioned by the Governors and 'said he had insufficient to eat and to drink', but had a decent bed and was not overworked, although 'when he neglected to Work his master slapped him' and, Samuel added, 'I Have forgot all my prayers'.[27]

The segregation of boys and girls and male and female employees at the Hospital may have afforded pauper girls better protection from sexual exploitation than those of a similar age who more or less fended for themselves beyond the Hospital walls. The potential for sexual abuse was not confined to adult men preying upon young girls, but if there were cases of foundling boys suffering in this way, then their experiences were never recorded. The secretary Morris

Lievesley recalled that when the foundling girl Catherine Beecher, employed as a Hospital servant, was sent 'for some Herbs in the Garden' she was raped 'by William Lodge the Undergardener', having been 'taken into the Tool House and by him she had a Child'. Lievesley mused that this was 'The only instance of this kind of Mischief believed to have occurred within the Walls of the Hospital'. The shared single-sex children's dormitories and culture of surveillance at the Hospital might just have meant that this was true, but we should certainly treat his claim with scepticism.[28]

The sexual abuse of young girls outside of the Hospital was not uncommon, and several instances of this were noted by the secretary, perhaps because of the exceptionally young age of the girls concerned. 'A Girl thirteen and a half years of age applied in March 1843 for the admission of her Child aged 3 Months', recalled Morris Lievesley, which he calculated must have meant that she had been pregnant 'at the tender age of twelve and a half years'.[29] Such cases only came to light if they led to pregnancy, meaning pre-pubescent girls' abuse was less detectable. Lievesley also reported the case of a fifteen-year-old girl who claimed her father was the seducer and father of her child, which she brought to the Foundling Hospital. She and her sister had been the objects of their father's 'revolting passion', having separated from their mother, in a case which was treated sympathetically at the Hospital. The secretary reported with approval that the sisters had 'by their own industry and under providence not only been able to maintain themselves respectably in business but to contribute to the support of their kind mother'.[30]

Cases of sexual abuse by masters did come to light according to children's testimonies and were reported to the Governors. Sarah

Drew, one of the girls apprenticed to Job Wyatt, the wood screw manufacturer at Tatenhall in Staffordshire, reported that Wyatt 'had attempted to debauch her at Eleven Years of Age and completed it afterwards and continued the same ill Usage till Xmas last & beat her if she refus'd to submit to his Will'. Sarah had been told that Wyatt 'had also debauch'd several other Apprentices amongst whom were Mary Johnson Mary Rise and Ann Beauchamp who often talk'd of it to her'. The Governors saw to it that the girls were removed from Wyatt and their indentures discharged under the authority of local magistrates, and new places were found for them.[31] The lack of further legal action or punishment for abusive employers like Wyatt is shocking to the modern eye. The temptation may be to blame the *laissez-faire* attitudes of eighteenth-century governing elites and to claim that nothing so brutal could happen today. But the lack of legal redress for the poor, especially abused children and women, is something that persists to this day, particularly in the light of growing awareness of modern-day slavery and institutionalized abuse in Britain.[32]

In late-eighteenth-century society, there may actually have been a greater willingness on the part of neighbours to intervene in cases of abuse than in later periods, since during the Victorian era the home came to be seen as something private and sealed off from public scrutiny, particularly among the middle classes.[33] One former foundling and servant girl, Mary Largent, attended the General Committee to complain of 'uncommon severity' and beating by her mistress's second husband, John Warrington Rogers, whom her mistress 'did not blame for his severity but would rather abet and encourage him', using 'unjustifiable weapons' for 'trifling offences', including two walking sticks 'of considerable thickness' which he broke in the process of administering the beatings.[34] Mary's case was strengthened by the fact that she listed a number of neighbours including a 'Dr Cornish' who would verify the truth of her claim, and some disturbing details that suggested Rogers was 'wanton' in his administering of corporal punishment.[35] It was understood in the eighteenth century that some people gained sexual pleasure from flagellation, and the details that Mary passed on suggest that she, her neighbours, and the authorities would have understood the implication.[36] Rogers's actions were perverse and deliberate: he forced her head between his knees while he was administering beatings and kept her at home until bruises had healed so 'that they were not so visible', watching her to make sure she did not complain to the neighbours. Mary's spirit was not broken, even in the face of such tyranny. She bravely made her escape one day by climbing over the iron railings surrounding her master's house and fleeing south over Westminster Bridge, where she eventually secured the help of a kindly carriage driver and some 'reputable people' who had known her former master. The matron and apothecary of the Foundling Hospital examined her within the week and found under her clothing that 'the greatest part of her Body Arms and Head still...of a livid colour, tho' 6 days had lapsed' since her last beating.

Other documents reveal that Mary's widowed mistress had married John Warrington Rogers, a wealthy solicitor, who lived at the smart address of 22 Manchester Buildings, Westminster. A man of property and considerable status, Rogers's mortification that the Governors had received a report of Mary's mistreatment at his hands and intended to pursue not just the cancellation of her indenture but a prosecution against him is indicated in a lengthy and grovelling letter he wrote to the Governors, addressing their 'Glorious Institution', which is preserved in the Foundling Hospital archive. Mary's examination in November 1786 had led to Rogers's summons before the General Committee to account for himself, but he failed to turn up. He justified himself by saying 'a personal Information I received at the Hospital, [informed me] That writing wo'd be less trouble to you and have the desired Effect—Else I sho'd with great pleasure have waited on you to have the further Honour of stating the facts of their Case as they arose'. The lawyer realized, too late, that he had made a mistake in snubbing the aristocratic Governors of the Foundling Hospital, his more powerful social superiors. He protested that he had merely been following 'the Diction of my Duty [sic]' in correcting Mary and now he was being 'blamed, prosecuted and exposed for a fault which I might under the same alarming Circumstances have inflicted upon a Child of my own'. Rogers seems to have been on a personal crusade to stamp out what he saw as the 'fatal Consequences' of sin, 'by this means this City wo'd be less crouded with distressed Objects, misery wo'd become a greater Stranger—And your great and unspeakable Bounty less abused'. He was now himself labouring under 'unmerited severity' by the Governors for his actions, having taken on 'this Girl' as an 'incumbrance' to him 'at the useless and uncommon age of 12 years when she co'd be of no service to any one', and provided her with board and lodgings for five years ('such an expence for such a length of time, I trust you will conceive merited a Return'). Warming to his subject, Rogers began to rant in fragmented sentences ('it was at a time she wanted the care and Attention of a father, to Guide and protect her thru Life—and which called aloud for some severity'). The lawyer had been exposed as a cowardly sadist: he concluded by begging for the Governors' mercy, urging them to drop their prosecution of him:

> The Anxiety I have repeatedly felt on this Occasion is great...
> Under these Circumstances—Considering the great expences
> I have been at for 5 Years with so young a Girl—relieve me from
> the Prosecution without any expence and the same will impress
> a due sense of Acknowlegement [from] Your most Obedient
> Most humble Servant.[37]

In the long run, this episode did not hinder the man's legal career. His wife appeared before the General Committee on 4 April 1787 to plead (successfully) for the prosecution to be dropped, and Rogers succeeded in keeping the scandal away from the press. He practised as a solicitor until his death in 1836, having been a member of the Select Vestry of St Margaret's Westminster, a Churchwarden who succeeded in lowering the rates so that less money would be available to the 'undeserving', and solicitor to the 'Guardians of the Poor'.[38]

In extreme cases, foundling children lost their lives as a result not just of overwork, mistreatment, and poor living conditions, but because of the sadistic behaviour of their masters or mistresses. Foundling Mary Jones was sent to the parish of St Dunstan in the West to be engaged in household work aged eleven in May 1765.[39] Her master was James Brownrigg of Fetter Lane, and Mary narrowly escaped the clutches of his wife Elizabeth and son John, who displayed behaviour that might today be called psychopathic. She received a beating that nearly cost her an eye, and fled back to the Foundling Hospital for refuge, where the Governors, shocked at her injuries, obtained a discharge of her indentures. Two years later, the Brownrigg mother and son were indicted at the Old Bailey for 'wickedly, maliciously, and feloniously' beating another servant girl in their household, Mary Clifford, to death. For over a year, on 'divers other days and times', with 'divers large whips, canes, sticks, and staves', over her 'naked head, shoulders, back, and other parts of her naked body, in a cruel and in human manner, giving to her divers large wounds, swellings, and bruises; and with divers large hempen cords, and iron chains', Mary Clifford was beaten and imprisoned against her will in a cellar, before she eventually died of her injuries. The press gave a lurid report of Mrs Brownrigg's crimes and execution at Tyburn.[40]

Not all foundling apprentices escaped brutal and sadistic masters or mistresses; perhaps those sent to work in London found it easier to run back to the institution that had raised them than those who had been dispatched from a branch hospital to an area where there was less direct scrutiny by inspectors. Jemima Dixon was murdered by her master, William Butterworth, a Manchester weaver, whose brutality towards her was only revealed when there was an attempt to prosecute him for her death. He was found guilty but reprieved by a judge, a pardon that could not be overturned even by the intervention of the Hospital Governors.[41] In an age where networks of patronage and wealth were exercised to protect the interests of employers, where bribery and corruption were an accepted part of the political landscape, and where the legal system was unambiguously patriarchal in character, it was not uncommon for the death of a low-status woman like Jemima to go unpunished.[42]

Like other pauper apprentices, children who had been raised in the London Foundling Hospital and its branch institutions, once apprenticed, could use the bureaucratic mechanisms of inspections and local officials representing the Governors' interests to speak out about issues such as neglect, cruelty, and various forms of abuse which they suffered. Even by the standards of the late- eighteenth century, the details of such cases were considered harrowing, and in the extreme could result in the death of one or more children. There are numerous cases where the Foundling Hospital Governors were attentive to what children told them about abusive masters and mistresses, and could act swiftly to intervene, using powerful networks of patronage and social influence to advocate for the children deemed to be in their lifelong care. So when foundling apprentice Sarah Middlesex appeared at a committee to inform the Governors of her 'cruel treatment' at the hands of Mrs Coles, the wife of Sarah's second master who was a cabinet maker of Aldersgate Street, the committee, 'having reason to suppose her complaint to be well founded', placed her back with her original employer. Perhaps the most visible evidence to the Governors was that Sarah, no longer a girl but a sixteen-year-old young woman, was inadequately clothed when she appeared before them. This was to a degree that they found shocking, since they threatened her master Coles with 'a prosecution' which 'will be commenc'd against him by this Corporation', adding that 'this Committee expect[s] Mr Coles [sic] answer on or before Wednesday next'.[43]

Where magistrates failed to intervene or no satisfactory out-come resulted from statutory intervention to help a distressed apprentice, former children from the Foundling Hospital could find it to their advantage to have powerful Governors on their side who could threaten errant employers with prosecution, or be a source of appeal if they found themselves on the wrong side of the law, allegedly through no fault of their own. Foundling George Smith wrote a lengthy and impassioned letter, apparently in his own hand, from prison, where he had been thrown for absconding from his apprenticeship to George Bernfleet, an engraver of St Martins. George's letter was unusually fluent and well written, signed 'with the greatest respect, your grateful Obedient and Humble Servant'). His boldness was in complaining to his patrons that the magistrate who had committed him to prison 'has greatly prejudiced my Character', considering his treatment had been so abysmal. Bernfleet had not clothed the young man properly, which as George cannily expressed it 'were a disgrace to my master and myself'. His bedding had been inadequate, so he had arranged to share a bed in another lodging 'with a friend who was a foundling', and hid from view in his master's shop for the shame of wearing ragged clothes. As George phrased it eloquently in his own words:

> [Had] I been negligent of my masters business or had his circumstance rendered him Incapable of providing in a better manner I should have patiently submitted to all those Inconveniences but as I was convinced of the contrary, I humbly Conceive Gentleman I was not blameable in quitting his service.

Though the general correspondence and memoranda make no further reference to this case, the apprenticeship register indicates that George succeeded in securing his release from prison and was reapprenticed (suggesting the Governors 'repaired' the damage to his character, a vital matter for tradesmen if they wanted to secure good credit) to John Lockington, a copperplate engraver of St James, in November 1791. It is tempting to think that George's expression of sensibility and fluently respectful deference towards the Governors were instrumental in securing not only his release, but also his reapprenticeship to the 'liberal master' he had hoped for, in a much more affluent parish.[44]

There were different dimensions to the treatment of foundlings who found themselves the victims of injustice. How they were treated could be influenced by the disparity between the lower social status of farmers, manufacturers, or tradesmen who typically employed foundlings, and the high social rank of the Foundling Hospital Governors, on whose behalf the Hospital's officers acted. The Governors could issue thinly veiled threats to their social inferiors, or even legal action, and such displays of authority were not lightly bestowed or received. Foundlings in difficulty sometimes had access to powerful patronage through the institution that had raised them. However, the Governors were only too aware of the reputational damage that could potentially be done by foundlings exposed in notorious court cases reported in the press. For some, foundlings would always be 'bastards' who were simply acting out the low morals and criminal behaviour that many commentators believed would be the inevitable outcome of this expensive and grandiose experiment in social engineering.

The treasurer of the Foundling Hospital, George Whatley, showed that he was prepared to intercede on behalf of one vulnerable young woman, a foundling named Mabel Roper. Mabel had been apprenticed to a farmer from Skipton in Yorkshire named John Simpson, whose household she had left having served out her full seven years' apprenticeship, thereby demonstrating she was hardworking and of good character. She went on to work for another year after her apprenticeship was ended and was therefore entitled to wages. But by that time she had moved to London, and her former employer was still in possession of her clothing and a box containing all her possessions. The steward, who drafted the letter on behalf of the treasurer (with many crossings-out, hinting at the sensitive wording that was needed in this case), instructed Mabel's former master 'be pleased at the same time to enclose (in her Box)...5 guineas due to her at Michaelmas last for One Year's wages and a Receipt signed by herself shall be sent to you'. With the paternalistic force of the Foundling Hospital behind her, Mabel's employer was also issued with instructions about providing her with a reference:

> [The Treasurer hopes] you will not hesitate to give her a proper recommendation to help her to another Service in London wherefore he [the Treasurer] desires that you will transmit him in writing such a Character as you think she deserves, specifiying her qualifications, the length of time she was with you, signed with your name and be pleased to enclose it in the Box with her other Things.

Another remarkable feature of Mabel's story is that further inquiry was made into the circumstances of her leaving her clothing, belongings, and wages behind, and that the Foundling Hospital officers continued to be her advocate even when the full story was known. Her good conduct in fulfilling her apprenticeship had been established, but it transpired that she had left her employer's house after having been lured away to Doncaster by a young man who had seduced her. She walked all the way there via Leeds, which took her three days, and she waited in vain for a further week for the young man to appear. In a desperate state, Mabel sold what remaining clothes she had in order to pay her way to London, where she found shelter in a workhouse and contacted the Foundling Hospital steward. In a final twist to Mabel's tale, the steward, John Merryweather,

was presented with a moral dilemma about what to tell the treasurer to say to Mabel's former employer about why she had
absconded. This part of her story casts an intriguing light upon
what former foundlings chose to say about their origins and their
upbringing:

> Unless the Treasurer deems it necessary they may be left to their
> own conjectures [about the reason for Mabel's disappearance]
> nor does it appear requisite they should be acquainted this is a
> Foundling, she never having told them she was so, her Master
> and Mistress hav[in]g always looked upon her as being appren-
> ticed by the Parish to the Man she served her time with, not that
> she concealed that circumstance from shame or any other motive
> but as they imagined it to be so, it was of no consequence to
> undeceive them.[45]

At first this case is mystifying, since it is difficult to imagine how
Mabel's master and mistress could not have known that she was a
foundling. The apprenticeship register provides a plausible answer:
her first master was not John Simpson, but a man named John
Young, a farmer from Ripon in north Yorkshire, to whom she was
sent to work in November 1769. Reapprenticeship was an opportunity
for Mabel to reinvent her past as a parish apprentice, poor but not
stigmatized as presumed to be a bastard child. We should perhaps
be less surprised at the degree of initiative shown by young Mabel
in pretending she was a parish apprentice, than by the Foundling
Hospital's willingness to collude with her story. Ultimately, it was
in the interests of the Governors and of Mabel herself to secure her
belongings, wages, and the possibility of an honest living so that
she could be self-sufficient. Pragmatism ruled over prudery at the

Foundling Hospital in dealing with the consequences of seduction and failed elopement, although as time passed and attitudes hardened, their tolerance increasingly became a source of criticism in the Victorian world of evangelical social and sexual mores.

The Governors of the Foundling Hospital often provided lifelines to their former charges and a valuable safety net that was not available to poor people who had no connection with the charity. Though their efforts were directed towards making the children self-sufficient, and shifting the balance of responsibility for their welfare onto the parish system by securing settlements via employment, they continued to take an interest and provide practical help if they fell upon hard times in adulthood. Sometimes this took the form of small doles of money to help petitioners later in life if tragedy befell them. Stephen Grateful, to the best knowledge of the Governors, had been apprenticed to an apothecary at Holmfirth in Yorkshire in October 1767. Stephen turned up later in London, however, 'in great distress' having left his employment to go to sea and 'suffered Shipwreck'. His ambition was to get help so that he could get employment 'at Haymaking'.

The Governors sometimes resorted to public fundraising if the case was particularly poignant, and beyond their means to provide lifelong support. In a pamphlet entitled *The Case of Mercy Draper*, the Governors publicized the fate of a blind girl who had, unusually, been allowed to pursue a musical career, with solo parts at the Hospital Chapel; 'the Number of Persons who resorted to the Chapel of the Hospital to hear her sing' raised a 'considerable Benefit to the Charity', since her voice was 'uncommonly harmonious'.

In 1775, aged nineteen, Mercy was engaged to sing oratorios at Drury Lane under the patronage of Mr Stanley, a respectable citizen whose repertoire of sacred music made Mercy's career acceptable to the Governors. In 1777, she was taken into Mr Stanley's household 'where she was treated with great Tenderness and Affection', meeting 'universal applause' for her performances until 1782. It was hoped that her talent would bring her 'Competency for Life' and the means to earn her own living; however, the unfortunate young woman was struck down with 'a Disorder of the Brain, which has terminated in INCURABLE INSANITY'. Whereas individuals of means could be confined to a private madhouse and treated to the expensive tyranny of doctors (not least George III, the king himself), there was no public hospital for the likes of Mercy Draper ('open for the Reception of Patients afflicted with this most dreadful of all human Evils'). For a time she was confined to Bedlam, and then to a private facility, 'William Perfect's mad house' in Kent, but her benefactors died and an appeal was made to the public to raise money for her treatment. What made this 'poor forlorn young Woman' a member of the 'deserving poor' was that she had earned her keep for the Hospital that had raised her by singing ('being in her Turn a Benefactress to that Institution, which had extended its Bounty towards her'). The rhetoric of sentiment that accompanied this appeal emphasized that, having been saved from a young age 'from all the Horrors of want, Misery and Vice', and making a promising career for herself, her fortunes had now changed. Owing to her illness, Mercy was now 'more helpless than an Infant, more destitute than a forsaken Orphan' and played upon the public air of uncertainty about the tragic consequences of insanity for individuals, and the nation, at a time when George III's mental and physical health were uncertain ('Madness! Incurable Madness! Whither can it fly for Refuge?'). The Foundling Hospital recognized that some children with mental disabilities were vulnerable to abuse and could be exploited in the world outside the Hospital walls. Ann Twigg, a girl said to be 'deficient in understanding' and 'defective in capacity', was returned before her apprenticeship ended on the grounds 'that it may be hurtful to the Girl to be from under the immediate protection of this Charity'. Bartholomew Walbroke was said to be so unruly ('an idiot, mischievous and ungovernable') that he was sent directly to Bedlam rather than being returned to the Hospital.[46]

The Governors continued to exert clemency towards foundling girls in adulthood if they became pregnant out of wedlock, showing compassion at a time when attitudes were hardening towards illegitimacy. In 1788, former foundling Sarah Saunders, apprenticed to a hosier by the name of William Surgery in Leicester Fields, 'returned Thanks to the Committee for their kindness' in having admitted her child to the Hospital, 'upon the representation of her Master'. Assuming that there was nothing unduly sinister behind William's actions—that he was not the father of her child (which was often the case in households where one of the men had consensual sex or raped a young female servant), eighteen-year-old Sarah had few options. She was grateful that the Hospital provided for her illegitimate baby, and no doubt that her master showed compassion in liaising with the Governors on her behalf, bypassing the normal admission procedure. It was noted 'the Girl called in and admonish'd to be careful of her Character'. This was the most that someone in her situation could hope for.[47]

In adulthood, former foundlings made their own networks of allegiance, finding surrogate brothers and sisters, mentors, and parental figures. The process of finding an alternative family for themselves started while they were still at the Foundling Hospital, and continued when they went out into the world. The ties of mutual help and affection that they made could help them to get by and even prosper, though for many the limits of their expectations were very narrow. Many foundlings married and had families of their own, while others kept in touch with their 'schoolfriends' (as George King liked to refer to the boys he had known while he was growing up, fellow foundlings like himself). Small acts of friendship, kindness, and neighbourliness could be crucial to a poor person's survival and were documented in the incidental comments made in the Foundling Hospital correspondence. When Hannah Draper's master, an ironmonger of Holborn, went bankrupt, she moved from place to place until finally she fell ill and was confined to St Thomas's Hospital for a year. When she was discharged, she was no longer fit to work in domestic service, but avoided the workhouse because of her skill at needlework and 'the benevolence of her Friend at the House where she lodg'd'.[48] Another foundling, Charlotte Downing, the well-behaved servant whose 'excellent Character' earned her a gratuity for good behaviour throughout her apprenticeship, was taken ill shortly after going to work in a household in Fish Hill Street near the Monument (on the same street, coincidentally, as George King lived while an apprentice). She ended up in St Bartholomew's Hospital for a time. Charlotte was helped to find a place once she was well again by kindly Mrs Lyney, her former master's sister, 'in consideration of her good Conduct'. The same woman petitioned the Hospital Governors on Mary's behalf so that she could receive her rightful gratuity. Mrs Lyney described herself in another letter as Charlotte's 'Friend', a term that had considerable significance and a specific meaning at this time, as someone who could be an advocate for another person as though they were a blood relative.[49] Calling in her network of favours from respectable women known to the Hospital, Mrs Lyney also dropped in the letter that Charlotte was known to Mrs Coleman, 'a School Mistress at the Foundling [Hospital]'.

For some, but by no means all, foundlings, the haven of their early childhood was with their wet nurses and families. A few children managed to maintain contact with these motherly figures throughout their lives. The Foundling Hospital inspector in Chertsey reported that Adam Bell had turned up in Surrey having escaped from his master, a pocket book maker in London. He had 'come down to his Nurse to inform her that his Master has used him exceedingly ill & that he could not stay any longer with him'. The youth, who was fourteen years old at the time, was returned to London for examination by the Governors, bearing the inspector's letter.[50] When Honor Barnes's master, described as a 'Gentleman' of Southwark, died suddenly, she had the good fortune to be looked after by Ann Waterman, described as a woman who 'goes out ironing' for a living 'and has taken care of Honor Barnes'. The girl had been turned over by her master's widow, who soon remarried, to an 'undertaker and appraiser' and his wife. This unscrupulous woman, a seller of 'Oysters, Milk and Fruit', pawned Honor's things and kept the proceeds for herself. Ann was instrumental in helping Honor recover a petticoat and cloth apron, a far from trivial matter to the girl, since with these humble items of clothing she could earn a living and keep herself decently.[51]

The few mothers who sought to reclaim their infants from the Hospital were often unsuccessful because so many babies and young children died before they could be reclaimed. There is some evidence in the archive of the other side of the story, however: some foundlings who *did* survive wanted to know about their identity later in life. One such foundling was Rebecca Potter, received into the Hospital on 16 March 1760, and apprenticed on 14 June 1769 to William Hayes of Moor's Yard, Old Fish Street in the Parish of St Nichols, a tailor. She was employed in Hayes's household as a servant, and attended the sub-committee of the Foundling Hospital in person many years later, on 16 December 1786, at the age of twenty-six. In front of the assembled dignitaries, she requested 'their indulgence to acquaint her what name she was received with'. A note written at the head of the slip of paper that documented this extraordinary evidence of a foundling wanting to know more about her birth identity was that the 'Billets [were] ex[amin]d', but they yielded little information, and no further clue was given as to whether Rebecca ever learned more about the name her mother had given her, nor anything further about her true identity.[52]

Another foundling who wanted to know more about his identity was Thomas Radford. Thomas was bound apprentice to John Glover, a cutler, by the Governors of Ackworth Hospital on 21 March 1771, 'with whome he served honestly and faithfully the term limited'. The local schoolmaster, John Richardson, commissioned by Thomas for his superior letter-writing ability, wrote on behalf of Thomas in fine copperplate hand from Sheffield in May 1791. Thomas wished to thank 'the Patrons of his Youth' and said 'that he would be exceeding glad of a line in return', adding he would like to be told 'should any thing concerning his Relations or Parents ever have transpired or came [to] light, or may hereafter be known'.[53] Likewise, Elizabeth Larker, received 29 April 1769 at the age of two, was apprenticed in July 1777 to Ann Chambers of Poplar, a widow, as a household servant, and reassigned to Ann Hatley of Brook Street, Stepney. It was recorded at the Foundling Hospital that 'The above Eliz. Larker attends to request the Committee to Inform her of her parents if possible'.[54]

The Governors may have been surprised to find their former charges cared so deeply about the identity of their true parents. That the former foundlings had any opinions at all on the subject, and the gumption to ask them questions about how they had been treated as infants, was not always well received. Given the patrician attitudes of the times, the Governors would have been surprised if anyone of lowly rank had questioned them, or exhibited sentiments usually reserved for those of higher rank and finer feelings. In one small memorandum written for the General Committee, there is the trace of kindness on the part of a master towards his foundling apprentice that offsets the many cases of brutality that are also documented in the Foundling Hospital archives:

If the Committee should think proper to order Indentures for Apprenticing James Melling to Mr Newham whose Petition lies before them, He desired the Steward to inform the committee that he requests his own Name of Newham may be inserted in the Indentures instead of Melling if compatible with the rules of the House, as he intends to look upon him as a relation & call him so, and have him [left] something handsome when he dies if he finds he shall deserve it hav[in]g no Relations of his own to bequeath his Property to.[55]

It was not unusual for someone to take on the name of a benefactor, guardian, or godparent in the era before adoption became a legally recognized process, which did not happen in English law until 1926. Francis Newham, James's master, was a Whitechapel grocer, who had purchased a shop on Whitechapel Road in the 1750s and had taken ten-year-old James as his apprentice in September 1789. Newham was prosperous: he converted an alleyway into 'Newham Rents', four cottages to the rear of his shop. It may have been his intention to have secured an heir via the Foundling Hospital or this could have been a serendipitous plan that developed during James's apprenticeship. A footnote in a small, crabbed hand, records that the General Committee considered this unorthodox request, and noted dismissively that 'The Comm[itt]ee cannot change their Registers, Mr Newham may call the Boy by what Name he pleases'.

In the event, Francis Newham's plan to make a foundling his heir came to nothing, perhaps because the Governors' response was so dispiriting, or maybe the condition that the boy should behave well and merit his benevolence ('if he finds he shall deserve it') did not materialize. James was reapprenticed in 1794 to a woollen draper in St James, and again in 1796 to a warehouseman in St Mary Le Bow. His former master, Francis Newham, died in 1807 and divided the ownership of his business and property empire among relatives.[56]

Of the thousands of stories of foundling children who went out into the wider world beyond the Hospital walls, only a few have left traces in the archives, and those that have are often better documented because they were exceptional, whether because the children were the victims of cruelty and brutality, or had encounters with the law as the victims or perpetrators of crime. We have seen how some of them chose to reinvent their stories later in life so that the shame of being associated with bastardy was erased from their past, something which makes it harder still to trace them. For those who did not break the law, or girls whose names changed upon marriage, there are still fewer paper trails.

There were horrific examples of violence and abuse meted out to foundling children, who were among the most vulnerable members of Georgian society once they left the confines of the Hospital grounds. Their lives were often no more nor less impoverished and susceptible to illness and misfortune than others destined for the bottom of the social order. Yet in relation to their own quests for identity and resilience in the face of so many obstacles, the traces are there of resourcefulness, defiance, and gritted determination to survive. And, as we shall soon see, a small number of foundling children managed to escape the fate that had been planned for them by their social betters since before they were born.

·CHAPTER 8·

Outrageous Fortune

O NE OF THE most prominent figures to take an interest in the fortunes of children raised in the London Foundling Hospital was Charles Dickens. Born in 1812, his genteel upbringing in Chatham had ended with his family's move to London in the 1820s. Up until the age of twelve, the future novelist and tower of English literary culture had enjoyed every privilege, but, as his father's debts mounted, the family's future suddenly looked bleak. Charles's education was brought to an abrupt halt. His parents and younger siblings were thrown into the Marshalsea debtors' prison, and he was left to fend for himself in a lodging house, earning his keep in a blacking factory, pasting labels onto bottles.[1] Dickens looked back at his experience of being left without family as a child worker with horror, as he later told his biographer: 'No words can express the secret agony of my soul as I sunk into this companionship [of "common men and boys"]...The deep remembrance of the sense I had of being utterly neglected and hopeless; of the shame I felt in my position.'[2] It was during his early teenage years that Charles Dickens began his investigations into the darkest corners of London's poorest streets and the dire living conditions of the working classes. He built his literary career in the 1830s as a journalist, basing his fictional characters in the serialized *Pickwick Papers* on real-life scenarios and events that were familiar to his readers. He campaigned through his journalism and his novels to expose the harsh working lives of poor children. *Oliver Twist* (first published in serial form in 1837) was an attack upon the great expansion of workhouses that resulted from the reform of the Poor Law system in 1834. Dickens did more than any other author to provoke a public outcry that compelled successive government administrations to act to reform employment conditions in factories, and to improve children's education.

Interest in the Foundling Hospital was of a piece with Dickens's obsession with uncovering to public view the living conditions of poor children, and chimed with his own experiences of isolation, displacement, and loss. Interviews with real-life foundlings were part of his investigations into the charities upon whom so many indigent Londoners were dependent. In the widely read serial publication *Household Words* (1853), Dickens gave an account of the Hospital's origins and history, and evoked the bureaucratic processes of form filling by which a 'blank child' was admitted and given an identity and education. He was sympathetic to the cause ('This blank institution is by no means a blank place', he observed wryly). By the middle of the nineteenth century, the Hospital had acquired 'a warm, old fashioned, rich-relation kind of gravity, strongly indicative of Bank stock'.[3] He satirized the prurient critics who accused the institution of fostering sexual immorality, and sketched a picture of a lively and kindly place where the rigours of military drill were offset by raucous play with toys and a 'cheerful little uproar' among the children.

Whether by coincidence or journalistic conceit, he claimed to have witnessed on the very day of his visit a lad of fourteen being sent away to be apprenticed to a lithographic printer. The boy took with him a written reminder to go forth and live as a diligent and hardworking Christian. Dickens must have considered that the pathos of the wording would appeal to his readers, and the sober advice it contained, for he reprinted it in full:

> You were taken into it very young, quite helpless, forsaken, poor and deserted. Out of Charity, you have been fed, clothed and instructed, which many have wanted. You have been taught to fear God; to love him, to be honest, careful, laborious and dili-gent... [now go and] execute all lawful commands with Industry, Cheerfulness, and good Manners.

It was while on his visit to the Foundling Hospital that Dickens also claimed to have met 'a decently dressed woman', the wife of a former foundling, 'Joe', who had left the Hospital to become a cabin boy. Joe had experienced many ups and downs: 'in common with some other of his school-fellows, [he had] been assisted through life with temporary loans of money, the latest of which loans had enabled Joe to seek... [his] fortune in Australia'. He had risen in the world sufficiently to be able to pay for his wife and chil-dren to join him half-way around the world, and to send £10 to his former benefactors at the Foundling Hospital in gratitude for raising him.[4] Foundlings also appeared in Dickens's novels, most famously through the eponymous hero of *Oliver Twist*, an orphaned child who is reunited with his blood kin, his true identity confirmed by means of a token (a ring bearing his mother's name), left with him as an abandoned infant in a workhouse. The name of the maid 'Tattycoram' in *Little Dorrit* (1857) refers to the fact that she is a former foundling. Her character was the subject of sentimental reflection by her employer, Mrs Meagles, who visits the Foundling Hospital Chapel in the novel and wonders whether a 'poor child' there might ever know a mother's love, 'her kiss, her voice, even her name!'[5]

Dickens's real-life interview with the wife of former foundling 'Joe', unidentifiable from other sources of evidence as fact or fiction since he gave no surname, was a small glimpse of the varying fortunes of the foundling children who went out into the world. We may speculate that the vast majority did not deviate from the life courses that had been mapped out for them, constrained by poverty and limited opportunities for education. Many thousands left very few traces within the historical record, unless they repeatedly fell on hard times and returned to the Hospital's Governors for assistance, to parish authorities, or even ended up in the criminal courts, as the victims or perpetrators of crime. One such case came before the Old Bailey in December 1768. The accused, Bartholomew Fanton, was alleged to have made a criminal assault on Ann Roch, a former Foundling Hospital child. Though twelve years old, she was described as 'an infant', and had allegedly been assaulted on the king's highway by the prisoner, Fanton, who had used 'menaces, oaths, and imprecations' as well as violence to try and steal money that she was carrying in her hand. Roch gave her testimony in person at the Old Bailey against the man who had attacked her,

worth repeating in full as one of the very few first-hand accounts by
a young girl newly apprenticed from the Foundling Hospital about
her vulnerability on the streets of London:

> I was twelve years of age the 2 d. of June last, I came from the
> Foundling-hospital, to live with a gentlewoman on Clerkenwell-
> green. Last Tuesday night, about half an hour after six in the
> evening, my mistress sent me for two yards of three-penny ribbon;
> I had six pennyworth of halfpence in my hand; I was got but three
> doors from our house, the prisoner whom I had never seen before,
> to my knowledge, came and got hold of my hand; he tried to open
> it, and could not; he put a blue and white handkerchief to my
> mouth; and put his foot out and throwed me down upon the pave-
> ment; and tried to get my money out of my hand. I screamed out
> murder, for God's sake; he roiled me about, and made me very
> dirty. He run away at last, and a gentleman catched hold of him.

The Foundling Hospital records verify that Ann Roch was baptised
on 2 June 1756 and provide the additional information that she was
apprenticed in April 1766 to Mary Brown, a schoolmistress of
Clerkenwell Green in the parish of St James Clerkenwell, just as
Ann had testified.

When cross-examined and asked, 'Did the prisoner say nothing
to you?', Ann replied, 'He d[amn]d me, and said I was a b[itc]h,
and said he would tell my father, and that he knew him extremely
well; he had the blue and white handkerchief in his hand, when he
was brought to me again'. Perhaps emboldened since she knew
Fanton was lying—she had no father—Ann fought back. She produced her clothes in court to show they were 'all very dirty'. When
asked directly by the prisoner at the bar whether he had struck her,
Ann replied bravely, 'No, you throw'd me down though. There was

a halfpenny missing. I kept the rest in my hand.' A passer-by, Martha Wintles, reported that she had heard a child 'cry out bitterly', saying 'don't murder me for God's sake'. She ran and saw the prisoner make off: 'She had a lump on her head, by the fall, as big as an egg'. A male witness, Anthony Simpkin, verified that he saw the prisoner trip up the girl, and it was he who apprehended the accused ('I ran and catched him by the collar, before he got twenty yards from her'). In his defence, the prisoner claimed 'she ran against my head; I laid hold of one of her hands, and she fell down: she called out murder; I did not wilfully throw her down', adding, 'I am a paper-stainer, and work for Mr. Chitty'.

It was normal following 'hue and cry' (calling out to alert those nearby that a crime was taking place) for there to be a citizen's arrest, but it is intriguing to speculate whether Ann was emboldened to face her attacker in the dock by the support of the schoolmistress and gentlewoman, her employer Mary Brown, in the prosecution of this case. Ann had been trusted with 'ready money' to run an errand, and was confident in putting forward her version of events, an honest girl who was telling the truth. But the English legal system gave little credence to her testimony. 'Outed' as a foundling, her word as a female child did not count, nor did the corroborating testimonies, nor did the material evidence of her attack. Whether it was because of Ann's young age, her low social status as a former Foundling Hospital child, or the fact that her alleged attacker could claim to be a respectable tradesman's apprentice, her assailant was found not guilty.[6] It is hard to imagine how many of the former foundlings kept their spirits up in the face of such prejudice.

From its earliest days, the Foundling Hospital's harshest critics had claimed that the charity would undermine social morality and bring about chaos in the normal provisions made for the poor. There is very little evidence that any of these doom-laden predictions were realized. It might be expected that settlement disputes would follow in areas that received large numbers of foundling apprentices, but there is very little evidence of this in the Quarter Sessions records which dealt with such disputes in rural parishes. The East Riding of Yorkshire Quarter Sessions records yield no examples of local conflict over settlement of former foundlings. As we have seen, although many hundreds of children were sent to Yorkshire parishes, their distribution over a wide geographical area with only a small number per parish to a large number of masters who were in need of extra labour may be one explanation for this.

There are some traces of foundling children who stayed on in parishes where they were apprenticed. Ann Brent, apprenticed to a farmer in the parish of Wheldrake in 1768, was still a resident of that parish when she named the father of her illegitimate child before a Beverly magistrate in 1781. Some years later, in 1796, another former foundling, Edward Offley, apprenticed without fee as a farm labourer, was bound over to keep the peace with his wife in Great Driffield, the parish where he had been sent in December 1768, presumably (like Ann Brent) from the Ackworth branch of the Foundling Hospital.[7] It would be reckless to claim on the basis of these two cases that some foundlings turned out to be 'no better than they should be': the law-abiding, hardworking ones who never got in trouble with the law simply left no written record, or at least it may have been in their best interests to hide the fact of their unknown origins and upbringing at the Hospital's expense.

Thousands of children passed through the charity's care and many hundreds of these were known to the secretary of the Foundling

Hospital, Morris Lievesley. He remembered, perhaps because it was unusual, a case of disputed settlement involving a foundling who had been sent to work in York. It was not the foundling in this case, but his master, whose settlement was a matter of doubt. Morris Lievesley recalled that:

> Ezekiel Hulse No. 5852 was received into the Hospital on the day he was born viz 30th Sept 1757 and on the 10th Decr 1766 he was apprenticed to Joseph Jubb of Thurghland [Thurgoland] in the County of York Tailor whom he served faithfully at the expiration of his apprenticeship.

These details are extremely precise, and are corroborated by the apprenticeship register. Lievesley's recollection gives an insight into what could happen in later life to a former foundling. Once he had successfully completed his apprenticeship, Ezekiel 'removed into the neighbouring Parish of Hartley where he remained as a Master Tailor until 1843'. In this year, a dispute arose 'between the parishes of Wortley and Thurghland and Leeds as to the Settlement of the Children of Ezekiel it appeared in Sessions at Leeds'. In March 1843, it transpired that Ezekiel's former master, Joseph Jubb, had come to Thurgoland 'upon a Parish Certificate by which he gained no Settlement there nor at Wortley'. At the age of eighty-seven, Ezekiel had acquired a respectable reputation in his community (Lievesley calls him 'this deserving Man for industry—untainted and respected'), but found that 'his Children and grandchildren had no legal settlement or in the language of the overseers that they were *free people*'. Providence intervened for Ezekiel, however. Lord Wharncliffe of Wortley and his family had employed this honest tailor for upwards of sixty years and said to the old man, 'the decision of the Sessions shall not touch you—you shall remain at Wortley and I will assist you'. Lievesley added, 'Ezekiel at 87 can walk 30 miles within the day and is as upright as any man of 30'. The incidental detail of how a former foundling could earn a good living in a skilled trade, marry and have children and grandchildren, and gain the patronage and backing of a powerful 'leading citizen' in his community, provides a rare glimpse of a former foundling who lived a long life in good health and relative prosperity, able to marry and support a family of his own.[8]

Of the thousands of children to be raised by the Hospital up until the mid-Victorian period, a small number demonstrated that social mobility was possible, in spite of their humble origins.[9] For girls raised in the Foundling Hospital, whose trials of life were made harder by their limited education, and few opportunities for working women at this time, their small triumph lay in earning their own living and maintaining a good character in their neighbourhood. One such girl, Fanny Rose, was sent out into the world as a servant 'employed in household business' to Thomas Moor, a hatter. She served out her time as apprentice and stayed working for her master for over a year afterwards, which meant she was entitled to a parish settlement in St Botolph Without Aldgate. Since that time, it was reported 'she has got her livelihood by keeping a little school and working at her Needle at Camberwell', an appropriately modest, hardworking, and seemly life of which her former patrons would have approved. For Fanny, eking out a living was precarious, and she was admitted to the London Hospital in Whitechapel, after she had sold all her possessions so she could be cared for at home. The Hospital had discharged her 'better but not properly recovered' and the gentlemen of the committee raised £1 12s 6d for her relief. Fanny may have always had a delicate constitution (she was not apprenticed until she was nearly seventeen), but she seems always to have been able to make the best of her circumstances.[10]

Of course, it was boys, not girls, who were expected to make their way in the world and, though they started with very little, some male foundlings made remarkable careers for themselves. One such foundling was Paul Holton, received into the Hospital in 1760 wearing warm clothing (a blue and white checked gown) and a red and white ribbon as an identifying token. As an infant he was sent to nurse in Wokingham in Berkshire. The local Foundling Hospital inspector, John Bunce, reported back to the London Governors that a wine merchant in the neighbourhood, John Grassingham, had taken a liking to the boy. Paul spent much time at his house, and he had even been sent to school at Grassingham's expense. This was during the late 1760s and the Governors were stretched to their limits finding places for the bulk of children received during the General Reception. They therefore agreed for the normal procedures to be bypassed and for Paul to be sent directly to be Grassingham's apprentice at the unusually young age of six. In 1775, Paul assumed the sole management of the business following his master's death, working alongside his master's widow. In 1782, having prospered at his trade, he married Mary Feltham, a local girl. He was soon running his own business as a 'Wine and Brandy Merchant', and when his wife died in 1792 he inherited two properties from her. He afterwards married a wealthy widow, Ann Staverton, and became a 'leading citizen' in Wokingham, as a constable, freeman, burgess, and finally an alderman. As a magistrate and churchwarden, it was he who doled out justice and alms to the poorest in his local community, rather than being on the receiving end of charity himself. When he died in 1828, his household was considerable: at a time when many people struggled to furnish their home with 'necessaries', he bequeathed household goods, furniture, plate, linen and china, books, pictures, and prints, all of which he wanted to be sold to the benefit of his wife. He also left a generous legacy of £200 in investments to the Governors of the Foundling Hospital in his will, 'to be by them applied to the use of that Institution to which I bear most grateful remembrance'.[11]

John Brownlow is the most famous example of a former foundling whose life was one of extraordinary achievements. Admitted to the Foundling Hospital as an infant in August 1800, as a child Brownlow was bright and quick to learn. He caught the attention of the secretary of the Hospital, Morris Lievesley, who employed him as his clerk. The Hospital Governors were pleased with Brownlow's work, and promoted him to treasurer's clerk in 1828, giving him the means and security to marry and set up a household of his own. He lived with his wife, firstly at Heathcote Street, and then at no. 1 Handel Street, just opposite the front gates of the Foundling Hospital. John eventually succeeded in becoming the Hospital's secretary in 1849, a position that brought a salary of £460 a year, and which he held until 1872 when he entered a comfortable retirement. He and his wife Johanna had three daughters, one of whom, Emma, became an artist whose work is still exhibited today at the Foundling Museum. His many contributions to the Hospital included the foundation of a military band, which overturned the original ban on teaching the children to perform music, albeit within the suitably regimental regime of the Hospital's ethos. He also wrote a novel, *Hans Sloane: a tale illustrating the history of the*

Foundling Hospital (1831), in defence of the institution that had raised him. As Dickens had observed satirically, the Hospital's founding principles of compassion towards 'fallen' women and their illegitimate children were increasingly out of kilter with Victorian evangelical attitudes towards sexual morality. In Brownlow, the charity found a robust defender of its cause, and its first historian, the author of *Memoranda: or, Chronicles of the Foundling Hospital* (1847), which influenced Charles Dickens's account of the charity in *Household Words*. The continuing sensitivity of former foundlings' social status was no better illustrated than in Mrs Brownlow's objection to a public declaration on his proposed memorial in the Hospital Chapel of his sixty years of service. Anyone could do the maths and work out that he had lived there for a longer period of time than worked there. 'I think it unnecessary', she wrote to the secretary, 'to tell my grandchildren that their dear & honoured Grandfather was brought up at the Foundling Hospital'.[12]

But the most spectacular example of an unknown eighteenth-century foundling whose unpredictable life and fortunes intertwined with the nation's history, and whose travels took him across the globe, was that of George King. The Governors of the Foundling Hospital had sanctioned his apprenticeship to the honest trade of a confectioner, but George's decision to take his life into his own hands was a fateful one. He had fled from London, his master, and all that was familiar to him, on pain of trial and imprisonment. George's autobiography resumes the narrative of his life with an account of him as a young man on board the ship *Polyphemus*, an *Intrepid*-class ship of the line, bidding farewell to the white cliffs of Dover.[13]

He had in fact been caught up in the latest wave of impressment that was taking place to man the Royal Naval ships mustered in preparation to defend England's shores from French invasion. Here was a foundling caught at the front line of the struggle between Europe's great imperial nations. In 1803, Napoleon had once again turned his attentions to the invasion of Britain following a number of military campaigns to the south, in Egypt and Austria. The British declared war in May 1803, and Napoleon, bolstered by military victories on land, started to plan how to seize control of the Channel.[14] The main obstacle to his plans was the Royal Navy, under the command of a number of experienced tacticians in sea battles, including Vice Admiral Horatio Nelson and Admiral William Cornwallis, who had command of the English Channel fleet. As an army strategist, Napoleon had few rivals, but his knowledge of seafaring and naval logistics was limited. The English Channel and Mediterranean narrows, defended by British stations in Gibraltar and Malta, were the two greatest obstacles to Napoleon's expansionist ambitions. His troops assembled around Boulogne for the planned invasion of Britain. In July 1804, to the chagrin of the British public, the French dictator declared, 'Let us be masters of the Straits but for six hours and we shall be masters of the world'. Shortly afterwards, Napoleon ordered a trial run for the invasion, a disastrous foray in blustery weather that was contrary to his admirals' advice, wrecking thirty ships and losing several hundred men at sea.

Meanwhile, the French fleet was kept at bay, blockaded by the Royal Navy at Brest and Rochefort. Spain was neutral early on in this particular conflict, but the potential importance of Spanish ships to Napoleon's ambitions meant that the British had to keep a watchful eye on the Spanish ports of Ferrol and Cádiz.

In September 1804, the *Polyphemus* took part in the blockade of Cádiz, and diplomatic relations between the British and Spanish authorities deteriorated. Below decks, ordinary seaman George King witnessed action for the first time: the capture of two Spanish merchant vessels that had sailed from Buenos Aires 'laden with hides and tallow', and a third ship carrying gold doubloons. Every man on board the *Polyphemus* could look forward to the prospect of a share in the bounty once prizes were captured, but only after they were safely landed back in England and the Admiralty had placed a valuation upon confiscated enemy cargoes. George's first direct engagement in a sea battle came shortly afterwards, with the Spanish gunner, the *Santa Gertruda*, bearing chests of silver plate, spices, and pigs of silver metal from the New World.

George had played his part below decks in the decisive act of hostility that provoked the Spanish into a new alliance with Napoleon, doubling the French dictator's fleet to 102 ships of the line. Three Spanish ships had been seized and a fourth blown up, an act of aggression by the British that had killed among others the wife and daughters of a returning Spanish governor. George proudly recalled his part in this event in his autobiography. Once the Spanish prize had been captured, he was one of the crew members despatched to navigate on board while it was towed back to England. Their voyage back to safe English shores was a hard one: past Cape Finisterre the *Polyphemus* lost her rudder and mainmast in the high winds, and according to George 'the sea was mountains high' in the pitch black of night. The crippled vessels limped to safety past Land's End, rescued by Cornish pilot boats which steered them all the way back to Plymouth, still towing their Spanish prize. From his vantage point, still on board the Spanish vessel, the seventeen-year-old George watched agog as the cargo of silver was unloaded and fifty carpenters from Devonport dockyard boarded to make essential repairs.

Between the autumn of 1804 and spring of 1805, Napoleon developed no fewer than five new strategies for co-ordinating the combined naval forces at his disposal, a logistically complex problem since they were scattered across eight different ports and blockaded or under surveillance by the British Navy. Two French admirals were ordered to embark troops and take their ships to sea, where they would sail to the West Indies and attack British colonies there, forcing the Royal Navy to send ships to defend them, and leaving the Channel and English shores vulnerable to invasion. Nelson went in pursuit of Admiral Villeneuve, who had given his fleet the slip past the Straits of Gibraltar. Villeneuve and the allied fleet captured a British convoy in the West Indies, from whom he learned Nelson was in pursuit. He sailed at once for Europe, forgetting his orders from Napoleon to capture British colonies in the Caribbean. This escapade was evidently well known later among the able seamen on board Royal Naval ships: George King referred to it in his autobiography as Nelson's 'chase around the West Indies'.

During the summer of 1805, Napoleon's invasion force of 93,000 troops, held at Boulogne, was still waiting for transportation. The Russian and Austrian armies had begun manoeuvres to the south, which meant he would have to redirect them towards the Rhine and away from Britain's shores. The prospects of the Franco-Spanish fleet at Cádiz making a successful attempt against the British blockade were lessened still further by redirecting reinforcements in his combined fleet towards southern Italy to assist with troop movements against Austria. By September, the *Polyphemus* sailed to join Rear Admiral John Orde and his five ships of the line that were blockading six Spanish ships and one French vessel in port at Cádiz under the command of Admiral Collingwood. On Monday 14 September, George recalled, they were joined by Lord Nelson in his ship *H. M. S. Victory*, and on 28 September Nelson resumed command of the British fleet.

In the early days of October, the senior officers of the combined fleet were uncertain what to do. They had been hung out to dry by Napoleon, but wanted to avoid the appearance of cowardice. Collingwood, a supreme strategist, believed the enemy would come out of port on the attack, but it was Nelson's tactics that offered the bait. Six ships of the line, including the *Polyphemus*, departed and made as if to sail for Gibraltar to replenish with supplies, while in fact keeping over the horizon, with frigates stationed on the lookout. On 19 October, they saw the entire combined fleet setting sail and heading for the Straits of Gibraltar.

As part of Nelson's decoy squadron, George King and the rest of the crew of the *Polyphemus* set sail under the command of Captain Robert Redmill and proceeded to the Gut of Gibraltar. There they waited. During the night of 20/21 October, George recalled overhearing a conversation between Nelson himself and the ship's captain. At about

> ten minutes to twelve we drifted alongside the Commander in Chief when we were hailed by his Lordship who accosted us thus "what ship?" The Captain answered "Polyphemus", when his Lordship said "Redmill, I suppose we shall have a warm day tomorrow" [and] ... the Captain answered "I hope so my Lord".

George helped keep watch until 4am and barely had time to return to his hammock when the signal was made that the French fleet was in sight. 'We were then entirely fit for action', he recalled, and the British fleet was soon in a two-line formation, the first time such a manoeuvre had been tried. At eight o'clock, George recalled:

we piped the breakfast it being Monday Banyon Day. The most part eat [ate] their dinner for breakfast and each man was served with half a pint of wine. We had three butts of water on the lower deck and three on the main deck with the heds [*sic*] knocked in. Our bread bags with our other provisions were stowed in the launch on the boons.[15]

At half past nine in the morning on the day of the Battle of Trafalgar, former foundling George King wrote, 'Nelson made the signal that England expects every man will [do] his duty'. The officers were encouraged by their commander in chief to urge their men to behave gallantly, and three hurrahs were given by the ship's company. George had a moment to notice the mild wind, smooth sea, and the 'beautiful view of the combined fleets which had formed a crescent and the centre of the enemys [sic] line was the Spanish Admiral his flag flying on board the *Santissima Trinidada*'. The British fleet had twenty-seven ships against the combined fleet's thirty-three. Nelson issued a plan of attack to his officers in three parts, the last of which was to be used at the discretion of his trusted officers at decisive moments of battle: 'I think it will surprise and confuse the enemy. They won't know what I am about. It will bring forward at pell-mell battle, and that is what I want.'[16] While the French traditionally 'fired high', aiming for masts and rigging, the British Navy had established a convention of running swiftly into the single line of enemy ships before discharging fire fast, low, and at close quarters.[17] George witnessed this for himself: Collingwood's ship the *Royal Sovereign* commenced the battle at ten minutes to twelve, 'by running under the stern of a Spannish three-decker and a French Eighty' and 'pouring a few broadsides into the stern of one and the bow of the other'.[18] The English ships were nimble with superior gunnery tactics. The larboard 'bumpkinshead' of the *Polyphemus* was shot off, but this mishap did not prevent her from running under a French ship and a Spanish ship, pouring broadside ammunition into each. 'There not being sufficient wind to carry away the smoke, we could hardly see the ship we was engaging', recalled George, writing in a way that directly conjures his speaking voice as he told the story of the most heroic moment of his life. It was 'a very warm sultry day we stripped ourselves to trousers only and blazed away for three hours, I being quartered at the second gun on the Forecastle'. By 4pm, shrouded in a pall of smoke, the men could make out that the French ship *Achille* was on fire. Peering over the hammock netting that covered the larboard, George could see as the smoke cleared that a number of ships 'both of us and the enemy totally dismasted and all appeared to be in confusion'. Two more hours passed, and smaller vessels were sent to retrieve hundreds of drowning men from the waters, just as the *Achille* 'blew up with a tremendous explosion burying all the slain and wounded'. Some 200 French prisoners were brought on board the *Polyphemus* and placed below deck under guard. Then, George mentioned perfunctorily, 'The Commander in Chief being slain, Admiral Collingwood shifted his flag from the *Royal Sovereign* into the *Euryalus* frigate and at this time it commenced to blow a fresh breeze'. Four hundred and forty-nine British men lost their lives that day, including Admiral Lord Nelson, with the combined fleet suffering about ten times as many fatalities.[19]

The action was over, and all hands were put towards securing the vessel and repairing damage. At midnight, the men took their first refreshment since that morning's breakfast, and fell upon any bread, cheese, or meat they could find, and another half-pint of wine each. As a caution, each man retired to his hammock armed with a cutlass and a brace of pistols. But he was not yet out of danger. Having survived the perils of battle, George turned over in exhausted sleep and accidently flashed one of the brace of pistols 'with the muzzle direct in my left arm pit which...did not go off otherwise it might have cost my life'. The following day, Admiral Collingwood toured the fleet and according to George, 'the ships company manned the Rigging and saluted the Hero with three hearty cheers'. The privilege fell to the *Polyphemus* to tow *H. M. S. Victory*, bearing their slain commander, through to safe port in Gibraltar.

George's account of his seafaring adventures continued in great detail and portrayed his experiences of serving over a remarkably long career, from the time he had fought at the Battle of Trafalgar to his discharge from sea-service nearly three decades later, with a final few years as a merchant seaman. His autobiography paints a vivid picture of his daily life at sea. He noted how, each time he and the crew of the *Polyphemus* were given their wages, Jewish traders crowded on board via the 'Bum boats' carrying rum, grog, tobacco, and women. On such occasions he became, by his own admission, 'a little elevated', blowing all his money and receiving a lashing from time to time for being drunk on duty. The close camaraderie of the men, forged in fear of mortal danger, and the scrapes and tribulations of gaining money and losing it, meant George found a place in the strict hierarchies and routines of life on board ship. This was a 'wooden world' of its own in which his uncertain identity on land was left far behind. He recalled a feeling of belonging (his shipmates called him a 'damn good fellow' for pulling out a bottle of rum which according to them 'sav'ed our lives') and happy times 'singing some of Charly Dibdins songs and others dancing to the fife... [played by] a Dublin man of the name of McGee'. Among this company, he sailed as far as South America, reaching Santiago ('St. Iago') in January 1807. The British army had been engaged in Buenos Aires, receiving back-up in the form of troops and additional supplies from the Navy, including the *Polyphemus*, which reached the Pacific Ocean towards Montevideo, from where they rescued retreating troops and made a hasty retreat.

Throughout George's diary, he observed the misfortunes that brought home the fragility of men's lives, not just in the theatre of war but in everyday tragedies. In one 'unlucky accident' the mainmast topman fell off his post and landed dead on the brass stanchions below, not a foot away from the admiral and his secretary ('his body... bent the stanchions nearly double', noted George, for this particular sailor had been 'a strong bodied man'). A man who came on board in Cork to welcome the crew home, bringing wives and daughters to reunite with their menfolk, got drunk, fell overboard, and drowned, 'a sad sight for his wife and daughter'. George's keen eye for detail and unswerving account of the hardships he endured suggest he would have made a fine journalist, at least when sober. Even allowing for the exaggeration to which sailors were notoriously prone, he showed remarkable courage and resilience in facing the horrors of life at sea, witnessing post-battle surgeons 'using their tourniquets' on limbless men who begged to die, and standing next to a coxswain on one raid whose head was blown clean off, spattering him with gore.

In January 1808, having been given his share of bounty for capturing French frigates off the coast of Rochefort, ordinary sea- man George King landed at Portsmouth and recalled how good it felt to be alive:

> I jumped out of the boat for the first time on English ground since July 1804. I being so much overjoyed and four guineas in my pocket I took a run and did not feel the ground under me. I think a greyhound wou'd hardly head me for the first hundred yards.

Still only in his late teens and with money in his pocket, each time he was on shore George frittered it away on girls and grog, and he became wise to the low cunning of men who stole his small bounty by various tricks. He continued his service with the Royal Navy, joining the *Melpomene* in February 1808, which took him to Barbados, Jamaica, and Havana, and further standoff with the French fleet. On his intermittent returns to London, he took part in press gangs, more drinking, and borrowing money from 'Bum boat women' or 'Doxies', prostitutes who knew him well enough to know that they would be repaid when the Admiralty doled out the prize money from his most recent voyage.

This foundling saved for the nation did his patriotic duty, fighting for his country in one of the most iconic and decisive battles of British maritime history. He also helped to safeguard the precious cargoes of luxuries imported on the merchant ships belonging to the East India Company off the coast of Spain, adding to the *specie* seized from rival trading nations. At Westminster, the mercan- tilist foreign policy of successive British governments had directed resources into making the Royal Navy the finest in the world.

Under the ideology of British imperialist expansion, seizure by force of the property and territories of other sovereign powers, peoples, and nations was regarded as perfectly legitimate, and even ordinary soldiers and seamen such as George King could expect their share of the rewards. While cruising off the coast of Norway, the *Melpomene* seized a fine Danish vessel laden with cochineal and indigo, expensive cargoes bound from Batavia to Sweden. Brimstone, silver and gold, and even Arabian horses were among the exotic and expensive cargoes seized on his travels, and his trips to London were punctuated with visits to Somerset House to find out whether the Admiralty were willing to settle his share of prize money.

George must have kept a diary while he was on board ship, given the extraordinary level of incidental detail and accuracy of the dates he included in his autobiography. This was common practice for the officers on board who were schooled as gentlemen and who had better literacy, but unusual for a sailor of George's lowly rank. He found a way of earning himself a few extra 'Spanish dollars' once some 'young gentlemen, midshipmen' discovered he could write their reports—routine quarter watch and station logs—for them. George proudly recorded, 'The gentlemen's names were Lord Edward Russell, Honble Mr. Ryder, Honble Mr Anson and Honble Mr. Telbot who paid me well for my trouble'.[20] Even allowing for a little hyperbole on the part of this sea-dog and his tales, George had an inherent love of writing which gave him opportunities not afforded to others of his rank. This was made possible by the education imparted by his Foundling Hospital schoolmaster, Mr Atchison. Unlike the formal reports he composed for the naval officers, in his private autobiography his prose was full of salty language and sailor's slang ('dowesd the glim' was to 'put out the light', and in one entry he referred to his personal bearing as his 'gib').

Institutionalized as a boy at the Foundling Hospital, George King fully embraced a second institutionalization in the Navy. His sense of humour in the face of the trials he endured at sea is often endearing and reveals a fully rounded personality that seldom emerges from other kinds of evidence about the lives of foundling children. He recalled that he enjoyed fishing ('a sport I used to love'), and caught mackerel from casting a line out to sea whenever he had the chance. On a shore visit near the Gulf of Venice, he got into a scrape stealing honey with his friends while they were sent to draw water. Another sailor filled his hat with the sweet spoils, while George tried unsuccessfully to keep the bees at bay with a tree branch ('they pretty well punished us'). He wrote that the best time of his life was on board the new frigate *Orlando*, from 1811 to 1814, with a captain and officers who were well liked by their crew: 'I must certainly say that while I was on board of her, it was the happiest days of my life and were I fit to serve again I would with pleasure join the same officers again and that ships company'. Of his inner life, George occasionally gave insights into his feelings regarding his lost friends and lack of family. He never forgot his 'dear friend Rivington', his surrogate brother and fellow foundling, whom he tried to contact when his ship docked in Malta, where Henry's battalion, the 10th Regiment of Foot, was stationed.[21] He was 'overjoyed' at the prospect of seeing his friend again, but sadly their reunion was never to take place.

By 1815, though still a young man under thirty, the physical demands of being a sailor and recurrent bouts of dysentery began to take their toll on George. Repatriated to recover from his illness, he again walked all the way from London to Chatham, as he had done as a runaway apprentice over a decade earlier. He again tracked down Rivington's regiment, only to be told 'that Serjeant Rivington died on the Isle of Wight after coming from the Recruiting Service'. George noted sadly, 'I then lamented his death'. Perhaps he began to feel his sense of being lonely and adrift in the world, for after learning of Henry's demise he briefly visited his 'good old schoolmaster', Mr Atchison, at the Foundling Hospital, who had now retired. George soon realized he had little prospect of work in his former employment as a confectioner 'in consequence of being so many years from the business'. Since he had no family ties he resolved to leave London, and joined another frigate bound for the Cape of Good Hope. His memories of this period became more brief, and suggest that his seafaring was a trial for a number of years, dogged by ill health. He soon caught typhus fever and was again sent back to London to recover. He reported to the Board of Admiralty at Greenwich to inquire after being invalided, and was told that he was entitled to receive a pension of £10 4 shillings per year, the equivalent of a modest servant's wage at that time. He was also told that if he served a further seven years, he would be able to 'augment my pension' by putting in a full twenty-one years' service. That length of service, in the face of so many perils and diseases, was a feat that few rank-and-file seamen achieved, but it gave him a sense of purpose to aim for it.

During the summer of 1818, while still recuperating in London, George had more luck in finding old friends. He found James Gardner, who had been the original cause of his seafaring life, living in Bow Street; 'we had a glass or two together', he recalled. On the

Sunday following the pair 'visited our old school', as he still called the Foundling Hospital, but discovered that 'our old schoolmaster had gone to sleep'. The hardened sailor who had faced his own mortality so many times could not bring himself to write of Mr Atchinson's death without recourse to metaphor. His old friend James Gardner had married and successfully set up his own household, which served as a haven in which George could recover his health ('I remained with Gardner and his wife three weeks').

Once he was back on his feet, George returned briefly to sea again, determined to serve out his twenty-one years of service. He was in Barbados when news of Queen Charlotte's death in November 1818 reached his crew (although he did not give a date for when they learned of the event), noting that it was marked by a seventy-gun salute. It was not long before he was invalided again from service, and this time his loneliness and rootlessness were more explicit: 'myself having no home to go to, no relative living, I was like a lost sheep and obliged to live as I could'. He was taken in again by Gardner, his old friend, with whom he stayed until his money ran out and he once again returned to sea, this time on 'light duties' as a ship's painter.

The next few years of George's life were spent alternating between brief voyages abroad and recurrent bouts of illness, including 'nodes on the shin bones' which were cured eventually by a Plymouth doctor. He lived off his erratic wages and occasional prize money payments. Then, without warning (perhaps fed up with feeling like a 'lost sheep'), he recorded that on 4 March 1825, 'I got married'. He did not name his wife, nor would he perhaps have expressed his sentiments about this rite of passage in his ship's diary. Matrimony did not seem to alter his habit of life, however, which was unsettled, and his fortunes unpredictable. By 1828, he had notched up enough time in the Navy so that he was just three months short of his twenty-one years' service, his best hope of gaining a decent pension. He did not stop once he passed this landmark, however, but spent the next three years plying the route from Malta to the Greek Islands and Dardanelles. His ship, the *Windsor Castle*, was despatched to ensure British interests were secured against the encroachment of Russian trading vessels.[22] In Gibraltar on the return journey to England the ship took in an entire army regiment, together with their wives and 152 children. It was, he recalled, a 'tedious' voyage home. While he was away at sea, his wife must have died, since George recorded that he visited his 'late' wife's father and mother in Cork, though he gave no further details. He went to the Admiralty in London shortly afterwards to confirm his entitlement to a navy pension following twenty-four years' service, and the prospect of £16 a year.

Perhaps because his prospect of having a domestic life had ended, George decided to join the merchant navy and made his way to Liverpool, where wealth from the African slave trade continued to bring lucrative rewards for merchant sailors. And so, at the ripe old age of forty-four, he became steward on board the merchant vessel *Celia*. In January 1832, following several months at sea, George found himself in Charlestown, despatching paying passengers who rewarded him for taking care of them on their arduous voyage. He had nothing more onerous to do than buy meat for the crew, despatch the captain's linen to be cleaned, and resupply the ship with quantities of grog. The temptations of life in the newly independent American town were immediately apparent and unsurprisingly his captain urged him not to 'disappear', as doubtless many had done before him. George slept in a boarding house on shore, breakfasted on beefsteak, coffee, and 'New York whisky', and proceeded to a shoemaker's shop, 'where I purchased a new pair of shoes for one dollar and a quarter'.

Evidently a great walker, George started out on the road to Augusta, some 90 miles south, with no particular plan. He hitched a wagon ride with an Irishman, Richard O'Brien, and they stopped for the night to camp by the road, gathering wood that they found and lighting a bonfire (having 'got some firing from some of the Negroes from a rice plantation'). George was impressed that his companion gave him a half-pint of New York whiskey from 'his thirty-eight gallon cask...besides five demijohns, each holding three gallons'. When it was time to sleep, the men lay down with their soles towards the fire; 'in a little while we were burning at the feet and nearly freezing at the head'. George was obviously contemplating settling in America for good, since he discussed with O'Brien whether work was available as a painter on the railroad construction business, 'to which he said there was no chance'. Instead, the honest Irishman offered him a teaching post in Walterborough, the small town where he lived, and promised 'that he would ensure me the Committee would give me two hundred dollars yearly', a prospect that made George's heart leap. Sure enough, his 'true friend' the Irishman ensured that he received a warm welcome when they arrived in town.

In 'Walterborough' (or Walterboro, a small town in South Carolina), George was treated with great hospitality and immediately welcomed as their new schoolmaster-in-waiting while the schoolhouse was being built. In describing the months he spent there, George's prose again becomes fulsome, recalling a bucolic life in a small town in the Deep

South that was entirely unfamiliar to him, but where he found a temporary home and family of sorts. He fished in the rivers with O'Brien's sons and accompanied the men on deer hunts. He found local people were willing to put him up for no charge, and he feasted aplenty at the regular gatherings for communal celebrations.

One day, he was invited to a wedding, where the ceremony was conducted simply and without church formality, and he was included in the party afterwards, one of the best nights of his life: 'We all sat down to an excellent supper, a profusion of every description and the room beautifully arranged with lights. I then instantly thought of the different [life] I was placed in that [to] . . . what I was for twenty four [years] previous.' Looking around at the happy townsfolk among whom he had been welcomed, George reflected on how he had risen in the world, from a penniless London foundling and runaway apprentice, through his ups and downs over more than two decades at sea. He had progressed from being one of the 'scum of the earth', a press-ganged sailor, and now had acquired respectability as an accepted member of a community half-way round the world. He discharged his duties as a schoolmaster to the satisfaction of all, serving out a quarter-year term teaching the local children, and even becoming a teetotaller for a short time out of respect for the Puritan sensibilities of the house in which he lodged. At the end of this time, he received his due payment of 50 dollars, for which he had to make a journey to Charleston to draw upon a bank order.

By the time he boarded a wagon for Charleston, a bottle of New York whiskey under his arm, the barometer had risen to 84 degrees. Whether it was his 'falling off the wagon', the unrelenting heat, or the torrential rain that followed that changed his mind, George did not say, but when he reached Charleston he wrote a letter saying farewell to his true friend Richard O'Brien and took working passage on the first English vessel to leave port. It was a merchant ship registered in New York, the *Thule*, sailing on 10 June 1832 for Liverpool, laden with 680 bales of slave-grown cotton that were destined for the textile mills of northern England. Just one year before the abolition of slavery in the British Empire in August 1833, George King completed the 'return passage', the final leg of the notorious triangular trade that had passed between the British Isles, the West Coast of Africa, and the New World for over 200 years, claiming in that time the lives of between 1 and 2 million African slaves.

He had just one final voyage to make. George King docked at Liverpool in April 1833, following his ultimate 'tedious and wet passage' of fifty-three days as a merchant sailor. He said goodbye to his life at sea by heaving his sodden bedding overboard and announcing to his shipmates in a nearby inn (where they had all gone, inevitably 'to take a parting glass') that he would 'not go to sea any more having been twenty-seven years'.

He was soon back in London, where he went immediately to Somerset House to check if any prize money was payable to him for any of the ships he had served in wartime, dating back to his time on the *Melpomene*. This yielded slim pickings. He hoped he might secure a position in the newly formed police service, and secured a reference from a former captain. When he turned up at Scotland Yard, he failed to tip half a crown so that his failure to meet the regulation height for admission could be overlooked. Though he tried to call in favours, George was 'completely lost for the want of a friend', a foundling once again. Like many demobbed servicemen, he tried but failed to secure work in labouring jobs, walking through the London docks in search of work, and even as far as Maidstone in Kent to see if he could scrape a living as a hop picker. He eked out a meagre subsistence between pension days, when he went to Tower Hill to receive his quarterly naval pension. In desperation, his thoughts turned to 'making an application to the Lord Commissioners of the Admiralty'. And so, George King joined the mass of old sailors who assembled on the day that the admiralty board met to see whether they could gain admission to Greenwich Hospital.

Greenwich Hospital was one of the great charitable institutions of England's capital city, built to provide refuge and a dignified retirement for sailors fallen upon hard times. The idea of a sea-man's hospital had been conceived during the reign of James II, but was taken up and developed during the time of William and Mary at the end of the seventeenth century, in response to the Queen's compassion for disabled, sick, and impoverished sailors.[23] Like the Foundling Hospital, its foundation had relied upon the patronage of royalty and wealthy donors. The services of the architect of St Paul's Cathedral, Sir Christopher Wren, had been commissioned to produce a grandiose design for the building in English Baroque style. Costs were a recurring problem for parlia-ment, and it remained unfinished until 1751. Eventually, however, its four great courts were completed, divided into wards that were named after warships and admirals. The living conditions and regulations of the hospital for its 1,700 pensioners were suited to ex-Naval servicemen, who lived 'decently' in private 'cabin' quar-ters or communal dormitories. Foreign visitors noted that these were often decorated with maps and sea and land charts, marking out the memories of their voyages and battles.[24] The fame and model of benevolence of Greenwich Hospital was such that its grand buildings, close by the Thames on the south side of the river, had been immortalized in one of the council room paintings on display at the London Foundling Hospital (Figure 8.1).

And so, for the second time in his life, George's fate would be determined by lottery. On the first occasion, some forty-seven years earlier, his destiny had been sealed when his birth mother, Mary Miller, drew a white ball from a bag, by which she gained admittance for her baby son to the Foundling Hospital. On the second occasion,

FIGURE 8.1 George King's refuge in old age: Greenwich Hospital for old sailors. Samuel Ware (1721–86), *Greenwich Hospital.*

in middle age, and facing destitution, George entered the number of his seaman's pension ticket at the Admiralty Office. The odds were not good. The first time he tried, in December 1834, there were 300 men applying for thirteen places. The second time, in January 1835, he arrived at the Admiralty Office and 100 men were waiting, of whom only fifty were admitted for consideration by the board. There were only nine vacancies. George recalled, 'I did not expect to be admitted, but one of the Lords asked me my service and also my Pension to which I answered him twenty-four years and sixteen pounds Pension'. He was ushered into the inner hall and awaited the sea lords' decision.

George was one of the lucky ones that day. He received a note immediately to 'repair down to Greenwich Hospital'. By 4pm, he and another old sailor had made their way as fast as they could south across London to the main entrance. George offered up the precious note of admission to the Regulating Boatswain, yet one more gatekeeping, charitable official he had encountered who had the power to save his life. He ended his autobiography with the post script that he was 'placed on the books upwards of seven years since, and thus ends the sequel of my story'.

George's own account of his life ends there, but it is not quite the end of his story. The records of Greenwich Hospital indicate that George King, born in Hertfordshire (he was evidently still claiming to have come from Hemel Hempstead), was admitted to the Hospital as a pensioner on 2 January 1835, aged forty-nine. The age is correct, as is the record of the ship in which he last served, the *Windsor Castle*.[25] He was five foot seven inches tall. His pensioner's ticket number (1,352) was recorded, just as he had been given a number at five months old when he was 'processed' through the Foundling Hospital. George received an in-kind dole of money and lived as an out-pensioner to begin with, but the records show that he applied to transfer from being an out-pensioner to an in-pensioner in December 1834 and again in January 1835 (which tallies with the two attempts documented in his diary, the second time successfully).[26] He was provided with the standard-issue blue jacket with gold buttons and breeches on the day of his admission. This pensioners' uniform signified his membership of an institution, but this one certainly worn with pride, as the old soldiers in Chelsea Pensioners' uniform continue to do today.

George King was not the only foundling to go to sea, nor the only one to end up a Greenwich pensioner, but his first-hand account of his life is uniquely recorded in his own words. According to the Hospital secretary, Morris Lievesley, another foundling, John Hunt, was 'Apprenticed to a Mariner' who took him 'from the Hospital to his House gave him refreshments and immediately proceeded with him to his Ship in the River Thames'. After several voyages, John was '[im]pressed on board a Man of War and his Apprenticeship expired whilst serving his Country'. He received an injury in his fingers, 'for which he got a Ticket of Pension from Greenwich Hospital'. The precarious livelihoods of foundlings who went to sea were remarked upon by the secretary of the Foundling Hospital: in John's case, 'having not slept on shore during the term of his Apprenticeship, he attained no settlement'.[27] Like George King, whose indentures ended up being thrown by a press gang into the sea, sailors could not fall back upon parish relief once they were no longer able to earn their living. The American novelist Nathaniel Hawthorne's most famous work *The Scarlet Letter* (1850) dealt with questions of Puritan sexual morality, adultery, and illegitimate birth. He observed Greenwich Hospital and its pensioners first hand while he lived on Blackheath during his stay as an American consul between 1853 and 1857, noting, 'It seemed to me that the Greenwich pensioners are the petted children of the nation, and that the government is their dry-nurse, and the old men themselves have a childlike consciousness of their position'.[28] Hawthorne could not have known how near the mark his comment came in relation to George King, wet nursed at charitable expense in infancy, and 'dry nursed' by the state in old age. The novelist concluded with his commentary upon the old sailors of Greenwich Hospital with the verdict that 'Their chief discomfort is probably for lack of something to do or think about'.[29]

In one final twist, rather than living in the childlike dependency of Hawthorne's imagination, we find George King of Hemel Hempstead, the place where he had been raised as an infant out of the Foundling Hospital, was discharged from the Greenwich Hospital and paid off in January 1848. By 1851, the time of the national census, he was living at no. 2 Thames Street, Greenwich, with his second wife, Caroline. She was forty-five, he sixty-three. Considering his institutionalized life, it is plausible that she had been George's nurse, or employed in another capacity at the Hospital. At the time of the census, George's occupation was given as 'Clerk of Greenwich Hospital and Chapel'.[30] His small amount of extra schooling all those years earlier in the Foundling Hospital by his old mentor, the schoolmaster Mr Atchison, enabled him to live independently and with dignity to the end, a married man with a responsible administrative role at Greenwich Hospital. But George was never fully free of institutional life: the records indicate he was 'DD'—discharged dead—as was the customary term for old sailors, and was buried on 31 July 1857, in the Royal Hospital cemetery in East Greenwich, at the venerable age of seventy.[31]

CHAPTER 9

Epilogue

WELFARE, PHILANTHROPY,
AND THE FUTURE

T HE NUMBERS OF children apprenticed out of the
Foundling Hospital dwindled after 1771, and by the time
the British Government began the slow process of reforming
children's employment, many of the more egregious cases of child
cruelty through batch employment to industry had ceased. The
1802 Health and Morals of Apprentices Act provided systematic
regulation of the employment of children in textile mills, although
by this stage this was a fairly small proportion of the number of
children working in England at the time.[1] Overseers and guardians
were appointed to keep a register of children apprenticed, and the
Elizabethan Statute of Artificers was finally repealed in 1814. This
meant that it was no longer necessary for a person to have completed an apprenticeship to set themselves up in a trade, although
the mechanism of pauper apprenticeship continued well beyond
the Poor Law reforms of 1834, into the 1870s and beyond.[2]

Thomas Coram revealed in a letter that his original design, one which was to be put into effect on an unprecedented scale, had been 'Rescuing poor Miserable Exposed Newborn Infants or Foundlings from the Cruelties of their own Parents or Barberous Nurses'.[3] His view, and that of the benefactors of the Foundling Hospital, and eventually the British government, was that removing infants from their families was preferable to the risk of having them starved, neglected, and 'exposed'. Coram's charity, it was thought, would provide a better alternative to being raised in poor families with desperate parents. This germ of an idea translated into institutional care, of which the Foundling Hospital was the earliest and most ambitious example in Britain. It was to have enormous consequences for the care of children born into poverty in Britain over the next 250 years. This particular experiment in social welfare was carried out originally in the name of Christian charity and humanity, but also in the service of an empire in whose mission the ready supply of innumerable labourers was an essential ingredient. The example of the Foundling Hospital project is another dimension to the discovery that imperial ambitions shaped society within the British Isles (the 'inner empire') as much as in the 'outer empire' of overseas colonies. Since the days of the Elizabethan Poor Laws, the state had intervened in the business of raising pauper children. Though the full terms of the Foundling Hospital Charter referred to the institution providing for children who were 'expos'd' and 'deserted', as it turned out many of the infants given over to the Hospital's care had at least one parent surviving. Controversially, Coram's legacy was not only to save orphans, but effectively to create them.

In subsequent decades after the Hospital's foundation, the imperialist attitudes of Thomas Coram and the Hospital's patrons and

Governors were to become a cornerstone of the Foundling Hospital's mission. The institution's ethos was to end the 'wasteful' loss of human life at the metropolitan core of the British Empire, and to produce productive, self-sufficient citizens who would go on to win gainful employment and lead upright lives, albeit within the narrow orbit of the labouring poor. For a time, the running of the Foundling Hospital became a truly national concern, through the system known as the General Admission funded by the Westminster parliament, with babies being trafficked from the farthest corners of the country so that parishioners would not have to pay for unwanted children from the local Poor Law rates. Having experimented with the creation of a proto-welfare system, politicians quickly realized the escalating costs and unintended social consequences, and stopped direct funding within the decade. Post-General Admission, during the French Revolutionary Wars of the 1790s, subsidies were given to the Hospital to take in the orphans of servicemen killed in action. The idea of the sacrificial father was propagated and continued to have currency as the British Empire expanded, right through to the end of the Victorian era and the early years of the twentieth century.[4]

During the nineteenth century, industrial-scale approaches to solving the problem of urban poverty were introduced through a more extensive system of parish workhouses instituted by the Poor Law Reform Act of 1834. This strengthened the distinction between 'deserving' and 'undeserving' poor. The Foundling Hospital's clemency towards 'fallen' women and their illegitimate offspring was increasingly regarded as of a piece with Georgian mores and the Old Poor Laws, and out of step with new Victorian attitudes to social and moral reform. A new rhetoric about the Hospital, reinforced through regular sermons in the chapel, stressed the importance of redemption and the fatal consequences of sin for unmarried mothers and their offspring. Discipline and order were emphasized by those who, like former foundling John Brownlow, sought to defend the charity from its severest critics. The military character of the Hospital was strengthened through regular drilling of the children and the introduction of a marching band at Brownlow's instigation. Right through to the early twentieth century, the children were dressed in the regimented uniforms that would have been familiar in Hogarth's day.[5]

After the First World War, rising costs and changing attitudes towards institutional care and children's education forced change. In 1926, the charity abandoned its London premises to move, first to Redhill in Surrey, and then in 1935 to purpose-built accommodation in Berkhamsted. This had smaller dormitories than in the London Foundling Hospital premises, and better sports and school accommodation. The site of the Hospital in Bloomsbury was sold in 1925 to a property developer, with some land bought back (including the children's play area known today as Coram's Fields) with the help of Lord Rothermere. In 1936, by Act of Parliament, the remit of a charity known today as Coram Family was set out in relation to the welfare and education of children in need, including a welfare centre, nursery and school, and a hostel for expectant mothers and babies. The emergence after 1945 of new fields of inquiry into child psychology and development led to a watershed in the understanding of the detrimental effects of institutional care upon children, and orphanages began to close. In 1954 the name of the Foundling Hospital was changed to the Thomas Coram Foundation for Children, by which time the Berkhamsted school had scaled back its activities, with boarders sent to foster families and day pupils mixed into a single secondary modern school. The Coram campus in London became the home of Coram Family, the leading children's charity in the UK. In 1971, Coram became a registered adoption agency, and remains active in its support to children's welfare to the present day. The historic art collections and some of the interiors of the original building opened in 2004 as the Foundling Museum at 40 Brunswick Square.[6]

The figure of the foundling continues to exert a powerful influence on cultural imagination in our own time. The character of Hetty Feather, as imagined by children's author Jacqueline Wilson, has moved thousands of young readers to contemplate the fate of Victorian children raised in the Foundling Hospital. She has succeeded in imagining the emotional lives of foundling children, their wet nurses and foster families, where the archives are silent.[7] Jamila Gavin's book *Coram Boy*, published in 2000, was dramatized at the National Theatre in 2005. The poet Lemn Sissay experienced being raised by adoptive parents who put him back into care when he became a teenager, and gives a powerful voice to the feelings of isolation and search for identity that many 'looked-after' children experience. The Foundling Museum continues under the direction of Caro Howell to act as a hub for the arts, commissioning and exhibiting works by leading contemporary artists such as Tracey Emin, Paula Rego, and Cornelia Parker, stimulating debate about child poverty and social exclusion today in a powerful way, attracting national and international interest. Poetry, literature, art, and music continue to call attention to the plight of orphaned and abandoned children, even though the term 'foundling' has fallen from our vocabulary. Themes of isolation, dislocation, and a search for identity still cluster powerfully around the idea of the child who does not know where they are from and who has no family or 'friends' in the world.

History has its part to play in this attempt to empathize with the foundling, with what is, ultimately, an extreme distillation of the *anomie* of the human condition. Attempting to make lugubrious claims about how we can learn directly from the 'lessons of history' is usually a doomed enterprise. The contexts are so different, the worlds and mentalities of our ancestors so remote. But my main conclusion from reading the heart-rending and voluminous documents in the Foundling Hospital archive over many years is that the state has never been, is not, and cannot be a good parent. The foundling children at the heart of this book knew as much, but it seems we have learned little since the eighteenth century. At least children raised within the care of the Foundling Hospital, for all its institutional lovelessness, knew they had a place to return to if they were in trouble or faced abusive masters or mistresses. The archives suggest that many did indeed use the protection of the Foundling Hospital Governors as a safety net. As late as the 1960s, the Thomas Coram Foundation maintained accommodation in London which could be used as a place of safety by adults who had been brought up in the Foundling Hospital and its associated institutions. The original eighteenth-century Governors of the Foundling Hospital, though distastefully paternalistic to modern eyes, were powerful lobbyists whom few dared to take on in the face of children's complaints in cases of abuse and neglect. Moreover, when children spoke out about their abuse, there is evidence that they were often believed, something which we have dismally failed to do in more recent times. Former foundlings knew they had the Governors to look after their interests: but few children in care today receive such lifelong back-up, in spite of the statutory obligation for local councils to safeguard their interests until the age of twenty-one. I am not suggesting that we should return to the standards of the eighteenth century, but that now, as then, there are large numbers of children for whom the state cannot and ought not to provide care, as the disaster of the General Reception proved over two and a half centuries ago. Children's services seem to have better outcomes when delivered at a local scale, keeping it small and personal (a model favoured by the modern hospice movement). Like the Foundling Hospital, the modern-day charity Kids Company was built on the charismatic leadership of its founder, but quickly scaled up too fast, with catastrophic consequences. History suggests that sustainability and careful scaling according to local needs, free from a centralized, state-driven, 'one-size-and-solution-fits-all' approach, may be the key.

We live now in a time when 'blended' families are becoming the norm—when the majority of children in the UK are now born to unmarried parents, and the high rate of divorce means that it is common for children to be raised alongside others who are half-siblings or not blood relations at all. This ought to mean that there is greater understanding shown towards those in care, or 'looked-after' children (as they are called today, with no trace of irony), who are not part of conventional mother-father-two-children families, since what constitutes a 'normal' family is by no means certain any more. But, sadly, we still have a long way to go. Institutions like the Foundling Hospital were closed after World War II in England, following the widespread recognition by government, local authorities, and voluntary organizations that fostering and adoption into loving families offered the best hope for children whose parents or family could not raise them. But it is still the case that many children raised in care face significant social stigma and diminished life chances. A disproportionately high percentage end up in prison and have complex issues with mental health problems, addictions, and poor prospects. And this is just the UK: if we widen the discussion to think about the prospects of children, whether in the affluent Global North war-torn Middle East, or across the Global South the scale of the problem is truly overwhelming, and there are no easy solutions.

Among its many achievements, the modern-day charity Coram brokers 10 per cent of all adoptions in England, just one legacy of the philanthropic efforts of the original Foundling Hospital and its many benefactors through history. One of Coram's recently commissioned studies highlighted the thousands of migrant children in the UK who have no access to a British passport, and who find themselves in limbo as a result, without eligibility for education, health care, or work.[8] Thomas Coram, whose name the charity bears, would surely have been astonished that the ends of his philanthropy are still being achieved, if not by the means of which he could ever have dreamed.

ACKNOWLEDGEMENTS

Historians are trained to be scientific and rigorous in their work, and are supposed to maintain a forensic and clinical objectivity at all times. This is a very important corrective to the enterprise of generating 'fake news', but it would make pretty dull reading to be so disengaged from archival research that all empathy is lost with the suffering of people who died many centuries ago. It requires more of an imaginative leap the further back in time you go, perhaps, than when studying the lives of people in the more recent past who left immediately accessible traces, such as films, photographs, and sound recordings.

When I started my research on the London Foundling Hospital archive I had no idea that it would affect me so personally or engage my emotions so directly, and frankly I didn't like it. Historians often have a deep-seated reason for engaging with their chosen research topic, revealed in a strong affinity for an individual, a cause, a political venture, or a social justice campaign. Like the proverbial elephant in the corner of the room, the historian's subjectivity is never supposed to be mentioned, although it's always there, staring back at us with an unblinking, reproachful look.

I didn't anticipate that I would find myself caring so passionately about the foundlings whose traces I found in the voluminous bundles of documents at the London Metropolitan Archive, and I was afraid that I wouldn't be able to complete the project. Every bundle of curl-edged parchments retrieved from the store contained so much emotion—in years of working with archives, I hadn't encountered anything like it. Even bureaucratic-sounding records, like apprenticeship indentures, could be interleaved with surprises— tiny slips of paper written in an eighteenth-century hand, with the barest of details, like Lady Elizabeth Marchmont, the Foundling Hospital's inspector in Hemel Hempstead who gave George King his name, who mentioned in one of her letters: 'very sorry to send an account of the death of another foundling. There is a disorder among the Children about us, that has carried off several young Infants.' I worked under time pressure on research visits to London, thumbing through each distracting scrap, aware as I did so that at every turn another scant trace of a human life was being skimmed over. I tried to proceed carefully and respectfully, treading lightly upon these fragile traces.

No matter how hard I tried to disengage emotionally, their voices kept crowding in, countless stories demanding to be told. I was on the serious quest for occupational data, but out fell a letter from a nurse, her milk ready for a newborn, requesting she be sent an infant to suckle, her good character attested with the initials at the foot of a page of a respectable citizen of her parish. Another time while I was combing for evidence of the procedure of Foundling Hospital management, a young servant girl appeared, trembling before the aristocratic might of the General Committee to plead to know the name she had been given upon admission to the Hospital. Then there were the accounts of foundlings who were returned to the Hospital by force, having run away to their country nurses in spite of the best efforts to raise them institutionally. The bonds of family affection gripped these children at a young age and compelled them to try and return to the only place they had known as home and experienced human love. The rational, critical historian's voice in my head kept drawing me back from subjects that were too difficult for me to address personally. Where can we go, beyond sentimentality, if we want truly to understand more about what this all means? What about the fact that the wet nurse of good character was being paid a premium to keep infants in her care alive for a year, since so many of them usually died? Or that the vast majority of foundlings never knew the identity of their parents, let alone were reunited with them? Beyond empathizing with their plight, what can we *do* with the story of Foundling Hospital children, to make sense of what happened to them and to think about the lasting issues that their experiences still address today? I made an early decision not to repeat the serial number given to each child upon admission in the main text (with a few exceptions), although these are added to the footnotes, in the hope that this will be useful should anyone be engaged in tracing particular children in the future. The Foundling Hospital archive, which today is still owned by the children's charity Coram that bears Thomas Coram's name, can only be served with the level of careful research it deserves once it is fully digitized, which would allow cross-referencing between the many different kinds of evidence contained in this Kafka-esque repository. Until then, anyone who wants to discover a foundling ancestor will find they have a very difficult task indeed beyond a preliminary name search in the billet (admission) books. I am hoping Lemn Sissay, a powerful advocate for 'looked-after' children like himself in our own time, might take up this cause.

For deciding who and who isn't 'legitimate', who gets to know their parents and who doesn't, is or rather ought to be part of our collective consciousness, as a society and a nation. I gradually became aware that the story of orphaned, abandoned, and illegitimate children was part of my family history, as for so many others. In October 2014, while I was researching this book, my Nan, Ida Mary Bamsey, known as Mary (my Mum's mother), died at the age of 100. Born in the year that saw the outbreak of World War I, she lived all her life with the stigma of illegitimacy. The daughter of an unmarried teenage mother, she was fostered by a Salvation Army family. She grew up to have a huge personality, and in spite of her modest circumstances and limited educational opportunities, had an indomitable spirit and charisma. She married and had three children of her own, Iraeila, Hilary, and Julia (my mother), the eldest of whom, Iraeila, died at a young age following birth complications. Mary lived through the Great Depression, having to decide whether to buy medicine for her sick baby, or food. During the Blitz in Plymouth she did a 'man's job' selling insurance and went on to become a successful businesswoman in her own right after the war, the matriarch of a family that she lived to see extend into its fourth generation.

Not so much a foundling as a fostered child, who knew the identity of her birth mother but was raised in a family of foster-siblings, my Nan's life story seemed to echo with so many of those I was researching in the archives. Alas, there was no female equivalent of George King in the eighteenth century whom I could find. So few working-class girls in that period could write, and if they did they tended to confine their written words to practical matters. Anecdotes about my Nan's life brought home the fact that it was not so very long ago that unmarried mothers faced terrible stigma, and that children raised knowing they were illegitimate had to find somehow a strength of character, and make their own way in a 'friendless' world. Her story shows that triumph over adversity was and is possible. This book is dedicated to her memory.

I'm indebted to a large number of people without whom this book would never have been written. The original idea for working on Thomas Coram came from a lunchtime discussion with my wonderful editor at Oxford University Press, Luciana O'Flaherty. I discovered that there is already a comprehensive biography on Coram by Gillian Wagner (much cited in this book), but was drawn into the astonishing richness of the Foundling Hospital archive, housed today at the London Metropolitan Archives in Farringdon. I calculated that the shelf length which the archive occupies is the equivalent of seventeen double-decker buses. As research became more convoluted, it became clear why more isn't written on the contents—it is truly overwhelming, minutely recording the daily operation over many decades of what was in effect a prototype department of the welfare state. I'm extremely grateful to Philippa Smith and staff at the London Metropolitan Archives for early meetings about this project and help on numerous trips there, and to David (D. S.) Allin, Yvonne Tomlinson, and the Friends of the Foundling Museum for their generosity in sharing so much of the research that they have conducted over many years. Janette Bright, whose own contribution to research on the Foundling Hospital archive is breaking new ground, was extremely generous with her time in helping me find key documents and understand their significance. I owe a huge debt to Stephanie Chapman and Alison Duke of the Foundling Museum, who put me onto the extraordinary diary of George King. As every reader of this book will appreciate, George's diary was crucial to introducing a human dimension to this story from the perspective of an eighteenth-century foundling. I do not share the transcriber's verdict that his diary is of limited value, owing to his being 'mostly drunk'. The director of the Foundling Museum, Caro Howell, is doing a fine job of keeping the Museum engaged with contemporary issues relating to children's welfare, and its long association with the arts. Her personal tour of the Museum, and her insights into the portraits of its Governors, were a particular inspiration, and helped shape Chapter 3. The former archivist at Coram, Melanie Peart, was also a kind and encouraging supporter during an early phase of this project, and Margaret McCollum, the treasurer at Coram, generously gave of her time in touring the premises and providing a personal account of the incredible work done by the present-day children's charity. I have benefitted as well from the scholarly friendship and intellectual generosity of John Styles, whose pioneering work on the textile collection contained in the billet books has revolutionized our knowledge of 'tokens' left with foundling infants, and so much more about the texture and colour of the lives of ordinary people in the eighteenth century.

I am indebted to the help of a community of researchers whose skills and expertise went into gathering and analysing the data that went into this book. Tim Wales has a truly remarkable knowledge of, and love for, historical archives, and gathered much of the material used in these pages. He is a remarkable scholar, and his insights into youth and pauper apprenticeship were particularly helpful. Ria Snowdon is a very able historian and researcher who completed the database that helped me cope with the sheer volume of archival evidence, and provided excellent assistance with illustrations. My colleague in archaeology from the McCord Centre for Landscape Studies at Newcastle University, Caron Newman, did a fantastic job of mapping the destination and occupational profile of the children who survived being raised in the Foundling Hospital. Any errors in my attempts to interpret this and other historical evidence are of course my own. I'm very appreciative to the following for generous invitations to share work in progress: Leigh Shaw-Taylor, Amy Erickson, and the Cambridge Group for the History of Population and Social Structure (April 2016); Perry Gauci, Joanna Innes, and the Oxford Long Eighteenth-Century History Seminar at Lincoln College, Oxford (May 2016); and the organizers of the 'Affective Families' conference at the University of Sheffield (March 2017). I acknowledge with thanks the financial help of a British Academy Small Grant (SG122254) which enabled the research that went into this book to be completed, and research support from the School of History, Classics, and Archaeology, and Faculty of Humanities and Social Sciences at Newcastle University.

My agent Jonathan Conway has been a brilliant source of critical friendship over a number of years, and I'm very lucky that he was as insightful as he is patient in waiting for the final typescript to be delivered. Anthony Fletcher and Elizabeth Foyster have, as ever, been stalwart friends and critics of early drafts, for which I am deeply grateful. Elizabeth Eger, Karen Harvey, and Amanda Vickery were wonderful co-conspirators and took a lively interest in counting foundlings in Yorkshire on a mischief-filled historians' retreat in the south of France in 2015, and again on a similar adventure to the equally glamorous shores of Filey in 2016. My friend Ali Azfar generously provided a sanctuary and some lively discussions during that time. Nigel Thornton, Catherine Cameron, and Bessie and

Acknowledgements

James Thornton gamely took on spotting anything to do with foundlings, not least *Hetty Feather*. Their hospitality and enthusiasm for this project have been truly marvellous. Among many friends and colleagues, Beattie, Freddie, and Theo Azfar, the late Graham Butler, David Creese, Pauline Dixon, Liam Donaldson, Quinn Fidler, Victoria Gardner, Christopher Hartley, Kathryn Hollingsworth, Alysa Levene, Gill McRae, Caroline Neilsen, April Pudsey, Annie Tindley, and David Saunders provided insightful comments and practical support. I'm also extremely fortunate to be working with Jeremy Boulton, even if expertise on the Bills of Mortality and the lives of London's poor has a predictably dampening effect on the spirits at times. His steadying influence in the face of my wilder flights of fancy about historical evidence, and intellectual generosity, are very much appreciated. It was attending the launch event for a *festschrift* in honour of Keith Wrightson at the Newcastle Mining Institute in 2014 that brought the idea for me to work on something more *serious* into focus. My best hope is that I might also continue to inspire my PhD students to do better well into their middle age.

Julia Berry, who is not by nature serious, has made me remember recently that nothing is so bad in life that it can't be cured by having a laugh over a coffee with your Mum. I realize how lucky I am to have known my own mother, and to have had the good fortune to be parented by someone who is not only resilient, but an optimist, and great fun. My final and greatest debt is to Fiona Hartley, who has had to live with my daily attempt at seriousness for a number of years. Beware promising to listen to someone's stories as a wedding vow—they may well take you up on it.

Morpeth
June 2018

NOTES

1. Empire

1. *The Times* (22 May 1844; 2 August 1844).
2. *The Times* (3 April 1845); the medal was reproduced in the *Illustrated London News* (5 April 1845).
3. *Illustrated London News* (12 April 1845).
4. According to the Foundling Hospital secretary, Morris Lievesley, King was certainly invited, and since he was employed at Greenwich it is reasonable to assume he was in attendance, although there was no roll call on the day. His Naval service is verifiable in several Admiralty records, including TNA, microfilm ADM 171, *Admiralty and Ministry of Defence, Navy Department: medal rolls, 1793–1827*, which records the award of the Naval General Service Medal to George King of the *Polyphemus* under the Trafalgar list, f. 266. See also LMA/A/FH/F/12/001/001, Morris Lievesley, 'A book of reminiscences of behaviour of Governors, staff and pupils of the Foundling Hospital', f. 34.
5. The original autobiography of George King has been on loan to the Foundling Hospital Museum from the National Maritime Museum, Greenwich, since 1973. I am very grateful to staff for a copy of the transcript, from which the account of George King is quoted throughout.
6. Julian Hoppit questions some of the received wisdom about the South Sea Bubble, including whether it can be properly labelled the

first example of a 'stock market crash', although this is how it is most commonly known: see 'The myths of the South Sea Bubble', *Transactions of the Royal Historical Society*, 6: 12 (2002), 141–65.

7. See Jeremy Black, *Britain in the Age of Walpole* (London, 1984).

8. John Brewer, *The Sinews of Power: War, Money, and the English State, 1688–1783* (Boston, MA, 1990), xiii–xiv and *passim*.

9. Julian Hoppit, *A Land of Liberty? England, 1689–1727* (Oxford, 2000), 124–9.

10. N. A. M. Rodger, *The Command of the Ocean: a naval history of Britain, 1649–1815* (London, 2004), 442.

11. T. H. Breen, *The Marketplace of Revolution: how consumer politics shaped American independence* (New York and Oxford, 2004).

12. Linda Colley, *Britons: Forging the Nation, 1707–1837* (New Haven, CT and London, 1992), 101.

13. Hoppit, *Land of Liberty?*, 427.

14. Joyce Ellis, 'The "Black Indies": economic development of Newcastle, c.1700–1840', in R. Colls and B. Lancaster (eds), *Newcastle upon Tyne: a modern history* (Chichester, 2001), 1–26.

15. John Gay, *Trivia, or the Art of Walking the Streets of London* (1716), Book II.

16. Paul Griffiths and Mark S. R. Jenner (eds), 'Introduction', in *ibid.* (eds), *Londinopolis: Essays in the cultural and social history of early modern London* (Manchester, 2000).

17. Lievesley, 'Book of reminiscences', f. 6.

18. See Robert Shoemaker, *Prosecution and Punishment: petty crime and the law in London and rural Middlesex, c.1660–1725* (Cambridge, 1991).

19. On the moral dimensions of luxury and its putative 'feminizing' effects upon men see most recently Peter McNeil and Giorgio Riello, *Luxury: a rich history* (Oxford, 2016), 15–25, 40–5.

20. Romola Davenport, Leonard Schwarz, and Jeremy Boulton, 'The decline of adult smallpox in eighteenth-century London', *Economic History Review* 64: 4 (2011), 1289–314.

21. Alysa Levene, *Childcare, Health and Mortality at the London Foundling Hospital, 1741–1800: 'Left to the mercy of the world'* (Manchester, 2007), 48.

22. Angus McLaren, *Reproductive Rituals: the perception of fertility in England from the sixteenth century to the nineteenth century* (York, 1984).

23. See especially Levene, *Childcare, Health and Mortality*, ch. 7.

24. David R. Weir, 'Rather never than late: celibacy and age at marriage in English cohort fertility, 1541–1871', *Journal of Family History*, 9: 4 (1984), 340–54.

25. E. A. Wrigley, *Energy and the English Industrial Revolution* (Cambridge, 2010), table 5.3, 'Estimated county net migration totals, 1600–1851', 124; Wrigley, 'Men on the land and men in the countryside: employment in agriculture in early nineteenth-century England', in L. Bonfield, R. M. Smith, and K. Wrightson (eds), *The World We Have Gained: histories of population and social structure* (Oxford, 1986), 295–336; Wrigley, 'English county populations in the later eighteenth century', *Economic History Review*, 60 (2007), 35–69.

26. Robert Shoemaker, *The London Mob: violence and disorder in eighteenth-century England* (London, 2007), 12–14.

27. E. A. Wrigley and R. Schofield, *The Population History of England* (Cambridge, 1981), 231.

28. T. Hitchcock, P. King, and P. Sharpe, 'Introduction', in *Chronicling Poverty* (London, 1997), 9–10. In acknowledgement of this term 'making shift', see also Paul Slack, *Poverty and Policy in Tudor and Stuart England* (Oxford, 1988).

29. See Joanna Innes, ' "The mixed economy of welfare" in early modern England: assessments of the options from Hale to Malthus (c. 1683–1803)', in M. Daunton (ed.), *Charity, Self-Interest and Welfare in the English Past* (London, 1996), 139–80.

30. Roy Porter, *London: a social history* (Cambridge, MA, 1994), 52–4.

31. M. Dorothy George, *London Life in the Eighteenth Century* (London, 1925, reprinted Harmondsworth, 1992), 45–8.

32. The contrast between attitudes to sexual activity among the general population compared to those in positions of authority is explored further in Faramerz Dabhoiwala, *The Origins of Sex: a history of the first sexual revolution* (Harmondsworth, 2012).

33. George, *London Life*, 51.

34. Erica Charters, 'The caring fiscal-military state during the Seven Years War, 1756–63', *Historical Journal*, 52: 4 (2009), 921–41.

35. Brewer, *Sinews of Power*, 183.

36. Jeremy Boulton, 'Indoors or outdoors? Welfare priorities and pauper choices in the metropolis under the Old Poor Law, 1718–1824', in C. Briggs, P. M. Kitson, and S. J. Thomson (eds), *Population, Welfare and Economic Change in Britain, 1290–1834* (Woodbridge, 2014), 175; Tim Hitchcock, 'Unlawfully begotten on her body': illegitimacy and the parish poor in St Luke's Chelsea', in Hitchcock et al., *Chronicling Poverty*, 75.

37. Caroline Withall, 'Shipped out? Pauper apprentices of port towns during the Industrial Revolution, 1750–1870', unpublished DPhil thesis, University of Oxford (2014).

38. Gillian Wagner, *Thomas Coram, Gent. (1668–1751)* (Woodbridge, 2004), 77–8.

39. Donna Andrew, *Philanthropy and Police: London charity in the eighteenth century* (Princeton, NJ, 1989); Hugh Cunningham and Joanna Innes (eds), *Charity, Philanthropy and Reform from the 1690s to 1850* (Basingstoke, 1998).

40. Charters, 'Caring fiscal-military state', 921–41.

2. 'My Darling Project'

1. Thomas Coram to Benjamin Colman, 30 April 1734, in 'Letters of Thomas Coram', *Proceedings of the Massachusetts Historical Society*, 3rd ser., 56 (1922–3), 20.

2. Ibid., 55.

3. John Brownlow, *The History and Objects of the Foundling Hospital with a Memoir of the Founder* (3rd edn, London, 1865), 1.

4. For studies of other foundling hospitals on the continent, see Alysa Levene, 'Health and survival chances at the London Foundling Hospital and the *Spedale Degli Innocenti* of Florence, 1741–99', unpublished PhD thesis (University of Cambridge, 2002); Rachel Fuchs, *Abandoned Children, Foundlings and Child Welfare in Nineteenth-Century France* (Albany, NY, 1984).

5. Richard Steele, *Guardian* (11 July 1713).

6. Keith Wrightson, 'Infanticide in earlier seventeenth-century England', *Local Population Studies*, 15 (1975), 10–22; see also Laura Gowing, 'Secret births and infanticide in seventeenth-century England', *Past and Present*, 156 (1997), 87–115.

7. Alysa Levene, *Childcare, Health and Mortality at the London Foundling Hospital: 'left to the mercy of the world'* (Manchester, 2007), 3.

8. Brownlow, *History and Objects*, 100.

9. Ruth McClure, *Coram's Children: the London Foundling Hospital in the eighteenth century* (New Haven, CT and London, 1981), 18.

10. John Brewer, *The Sinews of Power: war, money, and the English state, 1688–1783* (Boston, MA, 1990).

11. Gillian Wagner, *Thomas Coram, Gent.* (Woodbridge, 2004), 187–8.

12. Brownlow, *History and Objects*, 101.

13. Anon., *Essay on the Character of Capt. Thomas Coram* (London, 1751), 6 (my emphasis).

14. BL Add MS 32692, f. 536, Thomas Coram to the Duke of Newcastle (n.d.).

15. Anon., *The Rise and Progress of the Foundling Hospital Considered* (London, 1761), 41–3.

16. 'Letters of Thomas Coram', 55.

17. Wagner, *Thomas Coram*, 79–80; Alessandra Maggi, *The Renaissance of Children: the hospital of the innocents and the taking in of children in the 1400s and 1500s* (Florence, 2007), 12–13. I am very grateful to Liam Donaldson for this last reference.

18. Jenny Uglow, *Hogarth: a life and a world* (London, 1997), 329.

19. Wagner, *Thomas Coram*, 81–2.

20. Ibid., 82–3.

21. McClure, *Coram's Children*, 23 and appendix 1, 256–7.

22. For an overview, see Ingrid Tague, 'Aristocratic women and the ideas of family in the early eighteenth century', in H. Berry and E. Foyster (eds), *The Family in Early Modern England* (Cambridge, 2007), 184–208. An important new study of the experience of eighteenth-century illegitimacy, including among royalty and the aristocracy, is Kate Gibson, 'The experience of illegitimacy in England, 1660–1834', unpublished PhD thesis, University of Sheffield (2018).

23. McClure, *Coram's Children*, 44.

24. Brownlow, *History and Objects*, 4.

25. McClure, *Coram's Children*, 34.

26. Ibid., 28.

27. Quoted from Wagner, *Thomas Coram*, 145.

28. Tanya Evans, '"Unfortunate objects": London's unmarried mothers in the eighteenth century', *Gender and History*, 17: 1 (2005), 127–53.

29. McClure, *Coram's Children*, 140.

30. Quoted in Ibid., 51.

31. Ibid.

32. Wagner, *Thomas Coram*, 145.

33. A classic collection of essays comparing family size and structure in colonial North America with Europe and Japan from early modern to modern times is Peter Laslett and Richard Wall (eds), *Household and Family in Past Time* (Cambridge, 1972).

34. Heliodorus, *Ethiopian Story*, transl. Sir William Lamb (London, 1997), Book IV, 88–90. The reason for the baby's fair skin was owing to the idea of 'maternal imagination'—the mother was thinking of the goddess Andromeda at the moment of the baby's conception. I am indebted to Dr David Creese for this reference.

35. Laurence Simon-Donnadieu, '*L'assistance aux enfants abandonnés à Montpellier au 18e siècle*', *Mémoire de Maîtrise d'Histoire Moderne de l'Université Montpellier*, III (Montpellier, 1994).

36. McClure, *Coram's Children*, 48.
37. The collection of textiles is beautifully documented in John Styles, *Threads of Feeling: the London Foundling Hospital's textile tokens* (London, 2010), 19 and throughout. Also by the same author, *The Dress of the People: everyday fashion in eighteenth-century England* (New Haven, CT and London, 2007), 114–22 and *passim*.
38. The tokens still provoke a strong emotional reaction today among visitors who view them on display at the Foundling Hospital Museum in London.
39. This may have been done at the time, or later when the archive was put in order in the nineteenth century.
40. Originally sealed inside the folded 'billets' containing the details about each infant upon admission, some were first opened and exhibited as early as 1858, by which time they had ceased being used as identifiers of reclaimed children. Earlier generations were also touched by the sentiments aroused by the tokens: they were first displayed to the public at the South Kensington Museum, now the Victoria and Albert Museum, with the aim of raising public sympathy and donations to the charity. See Janette Bright and Gillian Clark, *An Introduction to the Tokens at the Foundling Hospital Museum* (London, 2014), 6.
41. A deep-time and cross-cultural comparison of the evolution of systematic recording of people's lives is Keith Breckenridge and Simon Szreter, *Registration and Recognition: documenting the person in world history* (Oxford, 2012), including a chapter by one of the editors on the registration of identities in early modern English parishes. Though not the first recording system, the Foundling Hospital kept unusually extensive, systematic, and accurate records from its inception.
42. Wagner, *Thomas Coram*, 148.
43. Dido was the subject of the film *Belle* (2013, dir. Amma Asante); see also Sarah Minney, 'The search for Dido', *History Today*, 55: 10 (2005), 2–3.

44. East Riding Record Office [ERRO]/DDGR/42/21/f. 68, Thomas Collingwood (secretary to the London Foundling Hospital), letter to Mr Hargreaves, Ackworth Hospital (11 July 1771).
45. Caro Howell, *The Foundling Museum: an introduction* (London, 2014), 23.
46. Foundling no. 10,125. Apprenticeship register, LMA/A/FH/A12/003/[n.f.]; see also Howell, *Foundling Museum*, 76.
47. Morris Lievesley, 'A book of reminiscences of behaviour of Governors, staff and pupils of the Foundling Hospital', LMA/A/FH/F/12/001/001, f. 10. Lievesley was secretary to the hospital from 1799 to 1849.
48. For an introduction to the idea of race in Enlightenment thought see Nicholas Hudson, 'From "nation" to "race": the origin of racial classification in eighteenth-century thought', *Eighteenth-Century Studies*, 29: 3 (1996), 247–64.
49. Styles, *Threads of Feeling*, 17.
50. Alysa Levene, *Childcare, Health and Mortality at the London Foundling Hospital: left to the mercy of the world* (Manchester, 2007), 18, 33–5.
51. McClure, *Coram's Children*, 50.
52. Levene, *Childcare, Health and Mortality*, 31.
53. Levene estimates that 30–34 per cent of foundlings were born to married parents, based upon samples of sources such as admission billets and petitions to reclaim children where the marital status of the parents is given. This is inherently difficult to verify, however, and may present a skewed picture of the overall percentage, since couples may have only claimed children if they were subsequently able to marry and set up a household (they had to demonstrate to the Governors that they could support their child). They may also have been lying about their marital status. Ibid., 31–5.
54. This principle was changed after 1770, when a written explanation was required to be submitted to the Governors with the infant.
55. McClure, *Coram's Children*, 138–9.
56. Ibid., 139.

57. Evans, ' "Unfortunate objects" ', 129.
58. Anon., *The Curiosities of London and Westminster*, II (1783), 90.
59. Levene, *Childcare, Health and Mortality*, 94–6.
60. Ibid., 92.
61. LMA/A/FH/A6/9/5/1- [n.f.], letter of recommendation for Anne Green from H. Conyers, 17 August 1767; LMA/A/FH/A6/9/12/1- [n.f.], printed form recommending Elizabeth Wylkerson of Farnham aged about thirty years 'as a fit Person to be a wet Nurse', signed William Burgess, undated [1770].
62. Levene, *Childcare, Health and Mortality*, 94.
63. Ibid., 94, 127–8.
64. Ibid., 12.
65. Lievesley, 'A book of reminiscences', f. 1.
66. Anon., *Essay on the Character of Thomas Coram* (1751), 12.
67. Wagner, *Thomas Coram*, 100–6.
68. T. Bernard, *An Account of the Foundling Hospital, in London, for the Maintenance and Education of Exposed and Deserted Young Children* (2nd edn, London, 1799), 24.

3. A Fashionable Cause

1. See Jenny Uglow, *The Lunar Men: the friends who made the future* (London, 2002); Roy Porter, *Enlightenment: Britain and the creation of the modern world* (London, 2001).
2. John Brown, *An Estimate of the Manners and Principles of the Times* (1758), 19; N. A. M. Rodger, *The Wooden World: an anatomy of the Georgian Navy* (London, 1986), 265–6.
3. This anonymously authored work claimed to be based upon the life of an anonymous Frenchwoman. All of the most *outré* novels were translated from the French, or purported to be.
4. Anon, *The Perjured Lover* (London, 1790).
5. Sigmund Freud, 'The family romance of the neurotic' (1909), in *Family Romances: the standard edition of the complete psychological works of*

Sigmund Freud, volume IX (1906–1908), ed. James Strachey (London, 1955), 235–42. See also Kate Gibson, 'The experience of illegitimacy in England, 1660–1834', unpublished PhD thesis, University of Sheffield (2018), p. 66.

6. Seth Denbo, 'Speaking relatively: a history of incest and the family in eighteenth-century England', unpublished PhD thesis, University of Warwick (2001).

7. Henry Fielding, *The History of Tom Jones: a Foundling* (London, 1749), Wordsworth Classics edition (Ware, 1992), 3–6, 7, 10–11, 33, 70, 79.

8. Ibid., 39.

9. Helen Berry and Elizabeth Foyster, 'Childless men' in *The Family in Early Modern England* (Cambridge, 2007).

10. Martin C. Battestin, 'Fielding, Henry (1707–1754)', *Oxford Dictionary of National Biography*, Oxford University Press, 2004, www.oxforddnb. com/view/article/9400, accessed 18 Aug 2016; see also Gillian Wagner, *Thomas Coram, Gent.* (Woodbridge, 2004), 168.

11. Stefano Filipponi, Eleonora Mazzocchi, and Ludovica Sebregondi (eds), *The Museo degli Innocenti* (Florence, 2016).

12. Jenny Uglow, *Hogarth: a life and world* (London, 1996), 429–30.

13. Ibid., 430.

14. Ibid., 332–4, 436.

15. Ibid., 431–2.

16. Ibid., 434.

17. Caro Howell, *The Foundling Museum: an introduction* (London, 2014), 71–5.

18. Lawrence Klein, 'Politeness and the interpretation of the British eighteenth century', *Historical Journal* 45: 4 (2002), 869–98.

19. John Cannon's calculations, cited here, excluded aristocratic women as being of little political significance, a view that has since been revised: *Aristocratic Century: the peerage of eighteenth-century England* (Cambridge, 1984), table 3, 32 and *passim*; for a revised interpretation, see Elaine Chalus, 'Elite women, social politics, and the

political world of late eighteenth-century England', *Historical Journal*, 43: 3 (2000), 669–97.

20. The modern analogy would be access to an expensive and exclusive club (maybe under the aegis of a leisure activity, such as playing golf) that brings members into a common network of sociability, leisure, and benevolence (such as charitable galas and fundraising) and spin-off benefits such as business deals sealed over drinks in the bar. This fluidity between different kinds of capital was well understood by nineteenth-century American philanthropist Andrew Carnegie, much criticized for his love of golf and 'leisure', who had a canny understanding of the importance of networking. Such behaviour was already well embedded in eighteenth-century patrician social circles. See Charles Harvey, Mairi Maclean, Jillian Gordon, and Eleanor Shaw, 'Andrew Carnegie and the foundations of contemporary entrepreneurial philanthropy', *Business History*, 53: 3 (2011), 425–50.

21. Peter Marshall, 'Legge, William, second earl of Dartmouth (1731–1801)', *Oxford Dictionary of National Biography*, Oxford University Press, 2004; online edn, September 2013, www.oxforddnb.com/view/article/16360, accessed 17 Aug 2016.

22. G. E. Cokayne, *The Complete Peerage of England, Scotland, Ireland, Great Britain and the United Kingdom*, vol. II (London, 1912), 82–3.

23. Howell, *Foundling Museum*, 53.

24. Olaudah Equiano, *The Interesting Narrative of the Life of Olaudah Equiano* (1789).

25. Howell, *Foundling Museum*, 52–3. Emerson's non-conformity, and consequent debarring from public office, may be one reason for his omission from the *Oxford Dictionary of National Biography*.

26. BL Mss EurG37/57/1, ff. 87–8, Thomas Collingwood to Robert Clive (24 April 1769).

27. Somendra C. Nandy, 'Amir Chand (d. 1758)', *Oxford Dictionary of National Biography*, Oxford University Press, 2004, www.oxforddnb.com/view/article/63551, accessed 17 August 2016.

28. Ian Christie, *Stress and Stability in Late Eighteenth-Century Britain: reflections on the British avoidance of revolution* (Ford Lectures, Oxford, 1984), particularly lectures III 'Factors of Social Cohesion', 54–93 and IV 'Social Support: the Poor Law', 94–123.

29. Simon Szreter and Armine Ishkanian (eds), *The Big Society Debate: a new agenda for social welfare?* (London, 2012); see also Szreter's summary of key debates at www.historyandpolicy.org/news/article/the-old-poor-law-and-the-economic-rise-of-england.

30. Christie, *Stress and Stability*, 43.

31. James Stephen Taylor, *Jonas Hanway, Founder of the Marine Society: charity and policy in eighteenth-century Britain* (London and Berkeley, CA, 1985), 15–16.

32. Ibid., 48.

33. Ibid., 59.

34. For a fascinating recent study of the 'decoding' of visual and textual cues under conditions of censorship in late-seventeenth-century print culture, see Adam Morton, 'Intensive ephemera: the Catholick gamesters and the visual culture of news in Restoration London', in Simon F. Davies and Puck Fletcher (eds), *News in Early Modern Europe* (Leiden and Boston, MA, 2016).

35. Jonas Hanway, *A Candid Historical Account of the Hospital for the Reception of Exposed and Deserted Young Children* (2nd edn, London, 1760), 10–11.

36. Rodger, *Wooden World*, 284–6.

37. Ibid., 278–82.

38. Donna T. Andrew, *Philanthropy and Police: London charity in the eighteenth century* (Princeton, NJ, 1989), 57–64.

39. Beatrice Scott, 'Ackworth Hospital, 1757–1773', *Yorkshire Archaeological Journal*, 61 (1989), 157–8.

40. Howell, *Foundling Museum*, 53.

41. D. S. Allin, 'The early years of the Foundling Hospital, 1739/41–1773', unpublished thesis, London Metropolitan Archives deposit (2010), 63.

42. Jane Humphries, 'English apprenticeship: a neglected factor in the first industrial revolution', in Paul A. David and Mark Thomas (eds), *The Economic Future in Historical Perspective*, vol. 13 (Oxford, 2006), 74–8.

43. K. D. M. Snell, *Parish and Belonging: community, identity and welfare in England and Wales, 1700–1950* (Cambridge, 2006), 86–7.

44. Steve Hindle, *On the Parish? The micro-politics of poor relief in rural England c.1550–1750* (Cambridge, 2004), 6–7 and *passim*.

45. Ibid., 7; see also Tim Hitchcock, Peter King, and Pamela Sharpe (eds), *Chronicling Poverty: the voices and strategies of the English Poor, 1660–1840* (Basingstoke, 1997).

46. Jeremy Boulton, 'The poor among the rich: paupers and the parish in the West End, 1600–1724', in Paul Griffiths and Mark Jenner (eds), *Londinopolis: essays in the cultural and social history of early modern London* (Manchester, 2000), 201.

47. M. B. Rose, 'Social policy and business: parish apprentices and the early factory system, 1750–1834', *Business History*, 31: 4 (1989), 7.

48. Joanna Innes, *Inferior Politics: social problems and social policies in eighteenth-century Britain* (Oxford, 2009), 59–61.

49. Ibid.

50. Anon., *The Tendencies of the Foundling Hospital in Its Present Extent Considered* II (London, 1760), 13.

51. Anon., *The Rise and Progress of the Foundling Hospital Considered: and the reasons for putting a stop to the general reception of all children* (London, 1761), 22–3, 28, 30, 33 and *passim*.

52. For the best authoritative account of childrearing practices at the Foundling Hospital, see A. Levene, *Childcare, Health and Mortality at the London Foundling Hospital, 1741–1800: 'Left to the mercy of the world'* (Manchester, 2007).

53. Foundling no. 16,208: Gillian Clark (ed.), *Correspondence of the Foundling Hospital Inspectors in Berkshire, 1757–68*, Berkshire Record Society, I (1994), 82–3.

54. Levene, *Childcare, Health and Mortality*, 12.
55. Ibid., 103–6.
56. Ibid., 36–7.
57. Rodger, *Wooden World*, 108, 162.
58. Ibid., 286.
59. Allin, 'Early years', 63.
60. Ibid., 57.
61. Selections by Hanway from the Register of the Parish Infant Poor (1766), quoted in M. Dorothy George, *London Life in the Eighteenth Century* (1925, reprinted Harmondsworth, 1922), appendix IIC, 403.
62. Taylor, *Jonas Hanway*, 110–15.
63. Hanway was also a victualling commissioner for the Royal Navy; see Jonas Hanway, *Reasons for Augmentation of at Least 12,000 Mariners to Be Employed in the Merchants-Service and Coasting Trade* (London, 1759), 13; Taylor, *Jonas Hanway*, xi–xii.

4. Foundling Education

1. Admission records LMA/FH/A8/1/1/17; George King's admission details are the same as in the Apprenticeship Register, LMA/A/FH/A12/003/[n.f.].
2. Some former foundlings in adulthood did request to know more details about their birth mothers but no evidence was found that George was one such petitioner. See Chapter 7 for further examples.
3. Mary Miller to the Foundling Hospital Governors, Petitions for Admission, LMA/A/FH/A8/1/1/17.
4. Billet LMA/A/FH/A/09/001/192; Nursery book—LMA/A/FH/A/10/003/007; date of admission LMA/A/FH/A/08/001/001/017. I am very grateful indeed to Janette Bright for locating these records.
5. Hume, Ian Maitland, 'Campbell, Hugh Hume, third earl of Marchmont (1708–1794)', in *Oxford Dictionary of National Biography*, online edn, ed. David Cannadine (Oxford, 2004), www.oxforddnb.com/view/article/14143 (accessed 26 July 2017).

6. Quoted in Katie Barclay, *Love, Intimacy and Power: marriage and patriarchy in Scotland, 1650–1850* (Oxford, 2013), 89 (my italics).

7. Lady Marchmont to Mr Merryweather, Secretary, LMA/A/FH/A/006/001/044/012/5 (28 August 1791).

8. Lady Marchmont to Mr Merryweather, Secretary, LMA/A/FH/A/006/001/044/012/3 (23 January 1791).

9. Lady Marchmont to Mr Merryweather, Secretary, LMA/A/FH/A/006/001/040/012/8 (9 November 1787).

10. General Correspondence, LMA/A/FH/A/06/001/045/012/10 (28 October 1792).

11. Quoted in Wendy Moore, *How to Create the Perfect Wife* (London, 2013), 64–4.

12. Sub-Committee Minutes, LMA/A/FH/A/03/005/005 (January 1762).

13. General Correspondence, LMA/A/FH/A12/23 (16 January 1791), n.f.

14. Foundling no. 13,718, General Correspondence, LMA/A/FH/A6/9/12/[1769], n.f.

15. Some moving twentieth-century memoirs include Tom H. Mackenzie, *The Last Foundling: the memoir of an underdog* (London, 2012). Part of the last class to be admitted to the Hospital in 1939, the author recalled his fear of being in dormitories, and bullying. Gordon Aspey, *All at Sea: memories of a Coram Boy* (Emsworth, 2010).

16. Gillian Pugh, *London's Forgotten Children: Thomas Coram and the Foundling Hospital* (Stroud, 2007), ch. VII.

17. John Styles, *The Dress of the People: everyday fashion in eighteenth-century England* (New Haven, CT and London, 2007), especially ch. 18.

18. Ruth McClure, *Coram's Children: the London Foundling Hospital in the eighteenth century* (New Haven, CT, 1981), 193.

19. Anthony Fletcher, *Gender, Sex and Subordination in England, 1500–1800* (New Haven, CT and London, 1995), 208–9.

20. Anthony Fletcher, *Growing Up in England: the experience of childhood, 1600–1914* (New Haven, CT and London, 2008), 3–4.

21. One particularly lengthy rant is Anon., *The Tendencies of the Foundling Hospital in Its Present Extent* (London, 1760). See also Lisa Cody, *Birthing the Nation: sex, science and the conception of eighteenth-century Britons* (Oxford, 2005).

22. John Locke, *Some Thoughts Concerning Education* (London, 1693), section VII, 'I will also advise his *feet to be wash'd* every day in cold water, and have his *shoes* so thin, that they might leak and *let in* water'.

23. Sir Thomas Bernard, Foundling Hospital treasurer (1799) quoted in Pugh, *London's Forgotten Children*, 69.

24. Moore, *Perfect Wife*, 45–6, 142–4 and *passim*. Ann Kingston, found-ling no. 4,579, and Dorcas Car, no. 10,413, appear in the Foundling Hospital register confirming the details of their apprenticeship: see Apprenticeship Register, LMA/A/FH/A12/003/001 [n.f.].

25. See Jonathan Israel, *Democratic Enlightenment: philosophy, revolution, and human rights 1750–1790* (Oxford, 2013).

26. The controversy over this issue was started many years ago by Lawrence Stone in *The Family, Sex and Marriage in England, 1500–1800* (London, 1977); less controversially, see Linda A. Pollock, *Forgotten Children: parent-child relations from 1500 to 1900* (Cambridge, 1983).

27. Pugh, *London's Forgotten Children*, 67–70. This account of the Foundling Hospital's regime was recorded by the Hospital's treasurer, Sir Thomas Bernard, in 1799.

28. Anon., *An Account of the Hospital for the Maintenance and Education of Exposed and Deserted Young Children* (1759), 69.

29. Jonas Hanway, *Christian Knowledge Made Easy: with a Plain Account of the Sacrament of the Lord's Supper. To which are added, The Seaman's faithful companion, with an Historical Account of the Late war. The whole calculated for the use of young Persons* (1763), xxviii.

30. Quoted in Levene, *Narratives of the Poor*, 29.

31. John Brownlow, *Memoranda: or, Chronicles of the Foundling Hospital* (1847), 95–7.

32. Jonas Hanway, *A Proposal for Saving From 70,000L to 150,000L to the Public; at the same time rendering 5000 young persons of both sexes more*

happy in themselves and more useful to their country, than if so much money were expended on their account (1764), *passim*.

33. McClure, *Coram's Children*, 221–4. This compared to just 60 per cent of semi-skilled tradesmen and 35–40 per cent of labourers and servants at the time, although these figures varied between London and provincial England and were not necessarily a gauge of literacy since someone could sign their name and write nothing else.

34. Pugh, *London's Forgotten Children*, 65.

35. 'Autobiography of George King, Seaman and Greenwich Hospital Pensioner', 19th century, f. 1.

36. Thomas Bernard, *Account of the Foundling Hospital* (2nd edn, 1799), 72–3 confirms the accommodation of two military corps within the Hospital grounds at this time: the Light Horse volunteers and Bloomsbury and Inns of Court Association.

37. 'Autobiography of George King', f. 1.

38. Ibid.

39. Pugh, *London's Forgotten Children*, ch. VII.

40. Alysa Levene, *Narratives of the Poor in Eighteenth-Century Britain*, vol. 3 (London, 2006), 20–5.

41. Anon., *Regulations for Managing the Foundling Hospital* (1796), 50.

42. Pugh, *London's Forgotten Children*, 68–9.

43. Alice Dolan, 'The fabric of life: linen and life cycle in England, 1678–1810', unpublished PhD thesis, University of Hertfordshire (2015), 99–100. Dolan's calculation of the volume of garments produced (and worn) by foundling children at this time is a remarkable scholarly achievement.

44. Alysa Levene, *Childcare, Health, and Mortality at the London Foundling Hospital, 1741–1800: 'Left to the mercy of the world'* (Manchester and New York, 2007), 162–4.

45. Pugh, *London's Forgotten Children*, 69.

46. Dolan, 'Fabric of life', particularly ch. 2.

47. Ibid., 108.

48. Beatrice Scott, 'Ackworth Hospital, 1757–1773', *Yorkshire Archaeological Journal*, 61 (1989), 163.

49. Pugh, *London's Forgotten Children*, 53, records that £200 was raised per annum by the sale of children's handicrafts in the aftermath of the General Reception.

50. McClure, *Coram's Children*, 226–7.

51. Ibid., 230–1.

52. Anon., *Regulations for Managing*, 86.

53. McClure, *Coram's Children*, 229.

54. Jonas Hanway, *Reasons for Augmentation of at Least 12,000 Mariners to Be Employed in the Merchants-Service and Coasting Trade* (London, 1759), 111.

55. LMA/A/FH/Q/74, *Psalms, Hymns and Anthems for the Use of the Children of the Hospital for the Maintenance and Education of Exposed and Deserted Young Children* (York, 1767), 16.

56. 'Autobiography of George King', f. 4.

57. K. D. M. Snell, *Annals of the Labouring Poor: Social Change and Agrarian England, 1660–1900* (Cambridge, 1987), 232–6; Ilana K. Ben Amos, *Adolescence and Youth in Early Modern England* (New Haven, CT, 1994), 81.

58. Jane Humphries, 'English apprenticeship: A neglected factor in the first industrial revolution', in P. A. David and M. Thomas (eds), *The Economic Future in Historical Perspective* (Oxford and New York, 2003), 74.

59. Levene, 'Parish apprenticeship', table 2, 925; mean age calculated from the Apprenticeship Register, LMA/A/FH/A12/003/001.

60. S. Horrell and J. Humphries, 'Child labour and British industrialization', in M. Lavalette (ed.), *A Thing of the Past? Child labour in Britain in the nineteenth and twentieth centuries* (Liverpool, 1999), table 3.4, 88, 97.

61. See for example Abraham Western (no. 5035) apprenticed at the age of five on 27 January 1762 to John Richardson, an Essex farmer, whose wife had wet nursed the boy. Circumstantial details emerge from comparing the Apprenticeship Register entry

with the Sub-Committee Minutes Sub-Committee Minutes of the General Committee of the Foundling Hospital LMA/A/FH/A/03/005/005, January 1762.

62. General Committee minutes, LMA/A/FH/K02/05–06 (1755–7), 14 January 1756, ff. 19–20.

63. General correspondence, LMA/A/FH/A6/9/5/1 [n.f.] undated [1767].

64. General correspondence, LMA/A/FH/A12/23/1 [n.f.]; Apprenticeship register LMA/A/FH/A12/003/001, apprenticeship of George Grafton, foundling no. 16,644.

65. LMA/A/FH/A6/9/5/1 [n.f.] undated [1767].

66. Campbell, *London Tradesman* (1747), 331–40. See also Patrick Wallis, 'Apprenticeship and training in premodern England', *Journal of Economic History*, 68: 3 (2008).

67. General correspondence, LMA/A/FH/A12/23/1 [n.f.].

68. General correspondence, LMA/A/FH/A12/003/327, child no. 16,327.

69. Copy of Apprenticeships noted in General Committee Minutes made by Thomas Collingwood, Secretary to the Hospital: LMA/A/FH/A/06/007/016/011a [f. 2], [21 March 1764], list of items 'Given with each Child Apprentice'.

70. *Account of the Hospital* (1749), 46.

71. Foundling no. 832, LMA/A/FH/A/06/007/016/011a [f. 2].

72. Foundling no. 5,035, Apprenticeship Register, LMA/A/FH/A12/003/001 [n.f.].

73. Foundling no. 677, Apprenticeship Register, LMA/A/FH/A12/003/001 [n.f.]; LMA/A/FH/A/06/007/016/011a [f. 2].

5. Finding Work

1. 'Autobiography of George King, Seaman and Greenwich Hospital Pensioner', 19th century, f. 1. 'Fish Street Hill' is mistranscribed in the Foundling Museum's copy as Fleet Street Hill—the former is correct given the reference to the Monument.

2. Apprenticeship Register, LMA/A/FH/A12/003/[n.f.].
3. The classic article on this subject is E. A. Wrigley, 'A simple model of London's importance in changing English society and economy 1650–1750', *Past and Present*, 37 (1967): 44–70; more recently by the same leading historian, *Energy and the English Industrial Revolution* (Cambridge, 2010), particularly ch. 3.
4. John Styles, *The Dress of the People: everyday fashion in eighteenth-century England* (New Haven, CT and London, 2010), especially ch. 10.
5. An excellent introduction to this subject which has generated an extensive bibliography in recent years is Maxine Berg and Elizabeth Eger (eds), *Luxury in the Eighteenth Century: debates, desires and delectable goods* (London, 2003).
6. Christopher Brooks, 'Apprenticeship, social mobility and the middling sort, 1550–1800', in Jonathan Barry and Christopher Brooks (eds), *The Middling Sort of People: Culture, society and politics in England, 1550–1800* (Basingstoke, 1994).
7. The phenomenon of a young apprentice marrying his former master's widow provided rich grounds for satire, but there were strong economic reasons on both sides for wanting to enter such marriages. See Peter Earle, 'The middling sort in London', in Barry and Brooks, *Middling Sort of People*, 154–5.
8. Caroline Withall, 'Shipped out? Pauper apprentices of port towns during the Industrial Revolution, 1750–1870', unpublished DPhil thesis, University of Oxford (2014).
9. Memorandums of Complaints between Masters and Apprentices, LMA/A/FH/A12/23/[11 August 1791], n.f.
10. LMA/A/FH/D4/6/2, 'A list of the Orphan Children Apprenticed in the Year 1767 belonging to the Hospital for the maintenance and Education of Exposed and Deserted young Children'. The register is approximately twenty pages in length with ten apprentice names per page.
11. Foundling no. 93, LMA/A/FH/A12/003/[n.f.].

12. A sample of eleven apprentice names recorded on p. 1 of the Chester register (LMA/A/FH/D4/6/2) indicated a 100 per cent correlation with information recorded about the child's name, number, master/mistress details, and location in the London register (LMA/A/FH/A12/003/001-411), suggesting a remarkably high level of accuracy in record keeping on the part of Foundling Hospital administrators.

13. Ruth McClure, *Coram's Children: the London Foundling Hospital in the eighteenth century* (New Haven, CT, 1981), 132.

14. Sara Horrell and Jane Humphries, 'Child labour and British industrialization', in M. Lavalette (ed.), *A Thing of the Past? Child labour in Britain in the nineteenth and twentieth centuries* (Liverpool, 1999), 76.

15. For a comprehensive overview in a comparative European perspective, see R. Floud, J. Humphries, and P. Johnson (eds), *The Cambridge Economic History of Modern Britain, Vol. I: 1700–1870* (2nd edn, Cambridge, 2014).

16. Leigh Shaw-Taylor and E. A. Wrigley, 'Occupational structure and population change', in Floud et al., *Cambridge Economic History*, table 2.2, 59.

17. Ibid., 72.

18. The term is most usually associated with Jan de Vries, *The Industrious Revolution: consumer behaviour and the household economy, 1650 to the present* (Cambridge, 2008).

19. Charles H. Feinstein, 'Pessimism perpetuated: real wages and the standard of living in Britain during and after the Industrial Revolution', *Journal of Economic History* 58: 3 (1998): 625–58.

20. Shaw-Taylor and Wrigley, 'Occupational structure', 66–70.

21. A useful overview is Duncan Bythell, 'Cottage industry and the factory system', *History Today*, 33: 4 (1983), 17–23; also by the same author, *The Sweated Trades* (Batsford, 1978).

22. Adam Smith, *Wealth of Nations* (1776) Book I, ch. 1, 'On the division of labour'.

23. Memorandums of complaint, LMA/A/FH/A12/23 [n.d.], n.f., Account of 'Mrs Smith's business' making components for the 'Master Pin Makers'.

24. Jane Humphries, *Childhood and Child Labour in the British Industrial Revolution* (Cambridge, 2010), 39.

25. Ibid.

26. Other conditions for gaining a settlement, such as having a father with a settlement claim, office holding, or tenure of property, were largely inapplicable to the socio-economic conditions of foundlings. See K. D. M. Snell, *Parish and Belonging: Community, identity and welfare in England and Wales, 1700–1950* (Cambridge, 2006), 86–7.

27. Patrick Wallis, 'Apprenticeship and training in premodern England', *Journal of Economic History*, 68: 3 (2008), 855.

28. McClure, *Coram's Children*, 221–4.

29. B. Scott, 'Ackworth Hospital, 1757–1773', *Yorkshire Archaeological Journal*, 61 (1989), 162, 166.

30. Apprenticeship Register, LMA/A/FH/A12/003/[n.f.].

31. Peter Kirby, 'A brief statistical sketch of the child labour market in mid-nineteenth century London', *Continuity and Change*, 20 (2005), table 2, 234.

32. E. A. Wrigley, 'English county populations in the later eighteenth century', *Economic History Review*, 60: 1 (2007), 39–40.

33. McClure, *Coram's Children*, 128. The Apprenticeship Register contains two additional girls apprenticed to Arbuthnot.

34. There is a discrepancy here between the numbers of actual indentures issued according to the register, and the resolution of the General Committee, who could sanction a course of action that was not necessarily enacted in full. McClure relies upon the latter evidence, *Coram's Children*, 128, n. 15, which is repeated by Katrina Honeyman, *Child Workers in England, 1780–1820: parish workers and the making of the early industrial labour force*, (Aldershot, 2007), 219, n. 10.

35. Peter Kirby, *Child Labour in Britain, 1750–1870* (Basingstoke and New York, 2003), 52.

36. The designation of John Bowles' (foundling no. 5's) employer as 'Esq.' in the Apprenticeship Register suggests he was not the baronet Sir Stephen Beckingham (a London lawyer), whose wedding was painted by Hogarth, but the Stephen Beckingham Esq. who married heiress Catherine Corbett, inheritor of Bourne Place, and died in 1756. A slight modification may be needed to the account in Caro Howell, *The Foundling Museum: an Introduction* (London, 2014), 34. Details are verified in the Apprenticeship register, LMA/A/FH/A12/003/n.f.; see also W. H. Ireland, *England's Topographer: or, A New and Complete History of the County of Kent* (London, 1829), 458–9.

37. Scott, 'Ackworth Hospital', 157–8.

38. Ibid., 158–9; E. A. Wrigley, 'Rickman revisited: the population growth rates of English counties in the early modern period', *Economic History Review*, 62: 3 (2009), table 4, 723.

39. Kirby, *Child Labour in Britain*, 52.

40. Wrigley, *Energy and the English Industrial Revolution* (Cambridge, 2010), table 5.3, 256–7.

41. B. Bailyn, with the assistance of B. DeWolfe, *Voyagers to the West: a passage in the peopling of America on the eve of the revolution* (New York, 1986), especially 374–429.

42. Scott, 'Ackworth Hospital', 166.

43. Humphries, *Childhood and Child Labour*, 211–13.

44. Foundling no. 8874, LMA/A/FH/A12/003/n.f.

45. William Gifford, *Memoir of William Gifford/Written by Himself* (London, 1827), 1–12.

46. George Nugent Banks (ed.), *Autobiography of Sgt. William Lawrence* (London, 1886), 1–6.

47. D. S. Allin, 'The early years of the Foundling Hospital, 1739/41–1773', unpublished thesis (2010), 340.

48. Gillian Pugh, *London's Forgotten Children: Thomas Coram and the Foundling Hospital* (Stroud, 2007), 46.

49. Mary B. Rose, 'Social policy and business: parish apprentices and the early factory system, 1750–1834', *Business History*, 31: 4 (1989), 7–11; Honeyman, *Child Workers*, 99, 103.

50. The exact figure is 35 per cent. See H. Berry, 'Occupational destinations of Foundling Hospital children, c.1741–1851' (forthcoming).

51. N. Terpstra, 'Working the cocoon: gendered charitable enclosures and the silk industry in early modern Europe', in K. Kippen and L. Woods (eds), *Worth and Repute: valuing gender in late medieval and early modern Europe: essays in honour of Barbara Todd* (Toronto, 2011), 39–72. See also Sandra Cavallo, *Charity and Power in Early Modern Italy* (Cambridge, 1995), *passim*.

52. Horrell and Humphries, 'Child labour', 97.

53. General Receipts, LMA/A/FH/A12/19/[23 September 1768], n.f.

54. Humphries, *Childhood and Child Labour*, see particularly table 7.2; Katrina Honeyman, 'Compulsion, compassion and consent: parish apprenticeship in early-nineteenth century England', in N. Goose and K. Honeyman (eds), *Childhood and Child Labour in Industrial England: diversity and agency, 1750–1914* (Basingstoke, 2013), 73.

55. *Leeds Intelligencer* (24 July 1770).

56. See for example General Committee minutes, LMA/A/FH/K02/05-06 (1755–7), 14 January 1756, ff. 19–20.

57. *Account of the Hospital* (1749), 46.

58. Scott, 'Ackworth Hospital', 166; on the fluctuating population of Westmoreland (in decline between the 1760s and 1780s), see Wrigley, 'English county populations', table 5, 55.

59. *Derby Mercury* (6 June 1760).

60. See also William Pitt, *A Topographical History of Staffordshire* (London, 1817), 486.

61. Alysa Levene, 'Honesty, sobriety and diligence: master-apprentice relations in eighteenth- and nineteenth-century England, *Social History*, 33: 2 (2008), 195–6.

62. Foundling no. 214. LMA/A/FH/A12/003/005/[n.f.].
63. Apprenticeship details confirmed in LMA/A/FH/A12/003/[n.f.], letter quoted in Allin, 'Early years of the Foundling Hospital', 335.
64. See works by Levene, Honeyman, Horrell, and Humphries cited in this chapter.
65. 'Autobiography of George King', f. 3.

6. Industry and Idleness

1. Jenny Uglow, *Hogarth: a life and a world* (London, 1997), 438–52.
2. An accessible overview of this subject is Duncan Bythell, 'Cottage industry and the factory system', *History Today*, 33: 4 (1983), 17–23; also by the same author, *The Sweated Trades* (Batsford, 1978).
3. On the new vogue for domestic furnishing and comfortable interior design in the eighteenth century, see Amanda Vickery, *Behind Closed Doors: at home in Georgian England* (New Haven, CT, 2009).
4. John Richard Burton, *A History of Kidderminster* (London, 1890), 180, 183.
5. Their world is vividly reconstructed in Zara Anishanslin, *Portrait of a Woman in Silk: hidden histories of the British Atlantic world* (New Haven, CT and London, 2016).
6. Foundling no. 1,704. Testimonies of the character of masters, &c., LMA/A/FH/A6/9/12/[1770], n.f.; entered in the apprenticeship register as 'transfer' apprenticeship to Hewitt on 1 August 1770.
7. Foundling no. 16,891. Memorandums of Complaints between Masters and Apprentices, LMA/A/FH/A12/23/n.d., n.f.
8. Foundling no. 16,794. Memorandums of Complaints between Masters and Apprentices, LMA/A/FH/A12/23/n.d., n.f.
9. Foundling no. 17,293. Memorandums of Complaints between Masters and Apprentices, LMA/A/FH/A12/23/[23 May 1792], n.f.
10. Foundling no. 15,893, Correspondence, LMA/A/FH/A6/9/12/ [1770], n.f.; Memorandums of Complaints between Masters and Apprentices, LMA/A/FH/A12/23/[1772], n.f.

11. Memorandums of Complaints between Masters and Apprentices, LMA/A/FH/A12/23/20 [November 1784], n.f.

12. Foundling no. 16,945. General Correspondence, LMA/A/FH/A12/23/1 (20 November 1784), n.f. and (3 August 1774).

13. 'Black Book', LMA/A/FH/A9/16/1.

14. Foundling no. 11,536. Memorandums of Complaints between Masters and Apprentices, LMA/A/FH/A12/23/ (10 February 1759), n.f.

15. Foundling no. 16,804, Memorandums of Complaints between Masters and Apprentices, LMA/A/FH/A12/23/n.d., n.f.

16. Foundling no. 16,000. Memorandums of Complaints between Masters and Apprentices, LMA/A/FH/A12/23/(8 January 1785), n.f.

17. Foundlings no. 16,967 and foundling no. 16,952. Memorandums of Complaints between Masters and Apprentices, LMA/A/FH/A12/23/n.d., n.f.

18. Memorandums of Complaints between Masters and Apprentices, LMA/A/FH/A12/23/(23 April 1785), n.f.

19. See a recent overview in Peter Kirby, *Child Workers and Industrial Health in Britain, 1780–1850* (Woodbridge, 2013), 1–35.

20. See for example S. L. Newman and R. L. Gowland, 'Dedicated followers of fashion? Bioarchaeological perspectives on socio-economic status, inequality, and health in urban children from the Industrial Revolution (18th–19thC), England', *International Journal of Osteoarchaeology*, 27: 2 (2017), 217–29, which traces the health inequalities of four London parishes from the skeletal evidence of 403 children (0–17 years) between 1712 and 1854.

21. 'Black Book', LMA/A/FH/A9/16/[11 April 1818].

22. Foundling no. 16,869. Memorandums of Complaints between Masters and Apprentices, LMA/A/FH/A12/23/n.d., n.f.

23. Tim Wales, ' "Living at their own hands": policing poor households and the young in early modern rural England', *Agricultural History Review*, 61: 1 (2013), 19–39.

24. Register entry for Matilda Bell (no. 12,373), LMA/A/FH/
    A12/003/[n.d.], n.f.; correspondence in LMA/A/FH/A12/23/1
    (2 April 1775).

25. Paul Griffiths, *Youth and Authority: formative experiences in England,
    1560–1640* (Oxford, 1996), and 'Masterless young people in
    Norwich, 1560–1645', in S. Hindle, A. Fox, and P. Griffiths (eds),
    The Experience of Authority in Early Modern England (London, 1996);
    I. K. Ben-Amos, *Adolescence and Youth in Early Modern England*
    (New Haven, CT, 1994).

26. Foundling no. 16,858, Memorandums of Complaints between
    Masters and Apprentices, LMA/A/FH/A12/23/n.d., n.f.

27. Foundling no. 16,556, Memorandums of Complaints between
    Masters and Apprentices, LMA/A/FH/A12/23/[4 October,
    1787] n.f.

28. Foundling no. 13,718, Correspondence, LMA/A/FH/A6/9/12/
    [1770], n.f.

29. Foundling no. 16,893. Memorandums of Complaints between
    Masters and Apprentices, LMA/A/FH/A12/23/[15 January
    1791], n.f.

30. Memorandums of Complaints between Masters and Apprentices,
    LMA/A/FH/A12/23/[21 July 1790], n.f.

31. Petitions for Gratuities, LMA/A/FH/A12/7/[2 October
    1800], n.f.

32. Foundling no. 17,465. Petitions for Gratuities, LMA/A/FH/
    A12/7/[22 August and 20 October 1800], n.f.

33. Petitions for Gratuities, LMA/A/FH/A12/7/[3 December
    1800], n.f.

34. Foundling no. 17,554. Petitions for Gratuities, LMA/A/FH/
    A12/7/[15 May 1801], n.f.

35. Foundling no. 17,441, Apprenticeship register, admitted 5 May
    1779, apprenticed 30 October 1793 to William Sibley, a baker of
    Old Change; see also Petitions for Gratuities, LMA/A/FH/
    A12/7/[n.d.], n.f.

36. Foundling no. 17,479, Petitions for Gratuities, LMA/A/FH/A12/7/[24 September 1800], n.f.

37. Foundling nos 17,063 and 16,855. Petitions for Gratuities, LMA/A/FH/A12/7/[2 October 1800], n.f. It was not possible to locate marriage registers for Hussey and John.

38. Married women could not take on apprentices in their own right, nor could they own property, although in practice there were loopholes which some women in trade were able to exploit. See Alexandra Shepard, 'Minding their own business: married women and credit in early-eighteenth-century London', *Transactions of the Royal Historical Society*, 25 (2015), 53–74.

39. Foundling no. 17,149. Memorandums of Complaints between Masters and Apprentices, LMA/A/FH/A12/23/[5 January 1788], n.f.

40. This and subsequent references in this chapter are from 'Autobiography of George King', ff. 3–9.

41. Alysa Levene, 'Parish apprenticeship and the Old Poor Law in London', *Economic History Review*, 63, 4 (2010), 924 and *passim*.

42. Two years older than George, James Garden, foundling 17,990, was apprenticed to Samual Davis of Poppins Court, Fleet Street, a leather case maker, on 20 February 1799, and later reassigned to Capt. Johnson Walmsley. No further details are contained in the apprenticeship register.

7. Cruelty and Kindness

1. Elizabeth Foyster, *Marital Violence: an English family history, 1660–1857* (Cambridge, 2005).

2. Foundling no. 8,702, General Correspondence, LMA/A/FH/A6/9/12/[1770], n.f.

3. Foundling no. 15,666, General Correspondence, LMA/A/FH/A6/9/12/[1770], n.f.

4. Memorandums of Complaints between Masters and Apprentices, LMA/A/FH/A12/23/[22 July 1775], n.f.

5. Foundling no. 16,734, General Correspondence, LMA/A/FH/A6/9/12/[1770], n.f.

6. Foundling no. 16,569, General Correspondence, LMA/A/FH/A12/23/[1787?], n.f.

7. See Jeremy Boulton, 'Indoors or outdoors? Welfare priorities and pauper choices in the metropolis under the Old Poor Law, 1718–1824', in Chris Briggs, P. M. Kitson, and S. J. Thomson (eds), *Population, Welfare and Economic Change in Britain, 1290–1834* (Woodbridge, 2014).

8. Removal order, St Giles Cripplegate, Catherine Horton aged twenty-one, City of London Poor Law Records, Vol. 4, 1581–1899, GL Ms8912, Box 2.

9. Foundling no. 5,043, Memorandums of Complaints between Masters and Apprentices, LMA/A/FH/A12/23/[n.d.] n.f.; General Committee Minutes (21 May 1788).

10. Memorandums of Complaints between Masters and Apprentices, LMA/A/FH/A12/23/n.d., n.f.

11. Memorandums of Complaints between Masters and Apprentices, LMA/A/FH/A12/23/n.d., n.f.

12. Memorandums of Complaints between Masters and Apprentices, LMA/A/FH/A12/23/[13 April 1793], n.f.

13. Foundling no. 7,623, Memorandums of Complaints between Masters and Apprentices, LMA/A/FH/A12/23/n.d., n.f.

14. Memorandums of Complaints between Masters and Apprentices LMA/A/FH/A12/23, n.d., n.f.

15. Foundling no. 16,917, Memorandums of Complaints between Masters and Apprentices LMA/A/FH/A12/23 [16 August 1786]. The boy had been apprenticed on 19 October 1785.

16. LMA/A/FH/A12/003/001-; for example, William Spadewell (no. 626) died on the coast of Guinea (December 1770); Charles

Bristed (no. 18,940) drowned [no date]; William Pen (no. 533), admitted to the Hospital, 1 September 1749, apprenticed 2 April 1760, 'killed on the spot' July 1767.

17. Jane Humphries, 'English apprenticeship: A neglected factor in the first industrial revolution', in Paul A. David and Mark Thomas (eds), *The Economic Future in Historical Perspective* (Oxford and New York, 2003), 77–8.

18. Foundling no. 5,938, Memorandums of Complaints between Masters and Apprentices LMA/A/FH/A12/23, n.d., n.f.

19. *The World* (5 September 1791).

20. *The World* (12 September 1791).

21. Apprenticeship Register, LMA/A/FH/A12/003/[n.f.]. These were: Maud Archer, Frances Bonner, Elizabeth Brooks, Susan Bridgeman, Matilda Burr, Letitia Bury, Tabitha Carter, Sarah Hawson, Sarah Langford, Mary Pigot, and Jane Thwaites.

22. Memorandums of Complaints between Masters and Apprentices, LMA/A/FH/A12/23/[13 July 1780], n.f.

23. Beatrice Scott, 'Ackworth Hospital, 1757–1773', *Yorkshire Archaeological Journal*, 61 (1989), 163–4.

24. Ibid., 166.

25. Ibid., 164.

26. Ibid., 165.

27. Foundling no. 19, 712, Lievesley, 'Account', LMA/A/FH/F/12/001/ff. 18–19 (19 September 1846).

28. Lievesley, 'Account', LMA/A/FH/F/12/001/f. 10.

29. Ibid., f. 31.

30. Ibid.

31. Summarized in McClure, *Coram's Children*, 134–5.

32. As evidenced in the work of the worldwide anti-slavery campaigning organizations such as www.antislavery.org and www.unseenuk.org.

33. Foyster, *Marital Violence*.

34. The reference here may have resonated in relation to Blackstone's infamous 'rule of thumb' by which a man might beat his wife or servants with a stick no bigger than a man's thumb in circumference. See Ibid.

35. Memorandums of Complaints between Masters and Apprentices, LMA/A/FH/A12/003/[23 November 1786], n.f.

36. Anthony Fletcher, *Gender, Sex and Subordination in England, 1500–1800* (New Haven, CT and London, 1995), 302–3 and plates 35–7.

37. Memorandums of Complaints between Masters and Apprentices, LMA/A/FH/A12/003/[28 March 1787], n.f.

38. *Gentleman's Magazine*, 160 (July 1836), 440; Will of John Warrington Rogers, Manchester Buildings, Westminster, TNA/PROB11/1867/178.

39. Foundling no. 735. Apprenticeship register LMA/A/FH/A12/003/[n.f.].

40. *Old Bailey Proceedings Online* (www.oldbaileyonline.org, version 7.2, 26 August 2017), September 1767, trial of James Brownrigg, Elizabeth his wife, James Brownrigg, John their son (t17670909-1).

41. McClure, *Coram's Children*, 134–5.

42. Garthine Walker, *Crime, Gender and Social Order in Early Modern England* (Cambridge, 2003).

43. Memorandums of Complaints between Masters and Apprentices, LMA/A/FH/A12/23/[5 December 1787], n.f.

44. Foundling no. 16,791. Memorandums of Complaints between Masters and Apprentices, LMA/A/FH/A12/23/[n.d.], n.f.

45. Foundling no. 13,724 in the Apprenticeship Register, LMA/A/FH/A12/003/[n.f.]: see also Memorandums of Complaints between Masters and Apprentices, LMA/A/FH/A12/23/[n.d.], n.f.

46. These cases are explored in Ashley Mathisen, 'Treating the children of the poor: institutions and the construction of medical authority in eighteenth-century London', unpublished DPhil thesis (University of Oxford, 2011), 209–10.

47. Memorandums of Complaints between Masters and Apprentices, LMA/A/FH/A12/23/[n.d.], n.f.; General Committee Minutes, 2 July 1788; details of Sarah Saunders's apprenticeship, foundling no. 16,650 verified in the Apprenticeship Register, LMA/A/FH/A12/003/[n.f.].

48. Foundling no. 11,536, Memorandums of Complaints between Masters and Apprentices, LMA/A/FH/A12/23/n.d., n.f.

49. Petitions for Gratuities, LMA/A/FH/A12/7/[21 October 1800], n.f.; see also Naomi Tadmor, *Family and Friends in Eighteenth-Century England* (Cambridge, 2001).

50. Foundling no. 17,116. Memorandums of Complaints between Masters and Apprentices, LMA/A/FH/A12/23/[16 February 1791], n.f.; the Apprenticeship Register gives Adam Bell's admission date as 5 June 1776.

51. Foundling no. Memorandums of Complaints between Masters and Apprentices, LMA/A/FH/A12/23/[inventory taken 18 September 1776] n.f.; Sub-Committee Minutes (28 September 1776) refer to this case.

52. Foundling no. 16,078; Memorandums of Complaints between Masters and Apprentices, LMA/A/FH/A12/23/n.d., n.f.

53. Foundling no. 16,185, Memorandums of Complaints between Masters and Apprentices A/FH/A12/23/[8 May 1791], n.f.

54. Foundling no. 16, 608, Memorandums of Complaints between Masters and Apprentices LMA/A/FH/A12/23, n.d., n.f.

55. Foundling no. 17,391, Memorandums of Complaints between Masters and Apprentices LMA/A/FH/A12/23, n.d., n.f.

56. Will of Francis Newman, gentleman, of Mile End, Middlesex, TNA/PROB11/1459/77.

8. Outrageous Fortune

1. Michael Slater, 'Dickens, Charles John Huffam (1812–1870)', in H. C. G. Matthew and Brian Harrison (eds), *Oxford Dictionary of National Biography* (Oxford, 2004); online edn, ed. David Cannadine,

September 2014, www.oxforddnb.com/view/article/7599 (accessed 29 July 2017).

2. Ibid.

3. Charles Dickens, *Household Words*, no. 156 (19 March 1853).

4. Ibid.

5. Jenny Bourne Taylor, 'Received, a blank child: John Brownlow, Charles Dickens and the London Foundling Hospital—archives and fictions', *Nineteenth-Century Literature*, 56: 3 (2001), 330–1, 346.

6. *Old Bailey Proceedings Online* (www.oldbaileyonline.org, version 7.2) (11 August 2017), December 1768, trial of Bartholomew Fanton (t17681207-57). The Foundling Hospital apprenticeship register gives Ann Roch or Rock as foundling no. 3,920.

7. Recognizance of William Clough of Wheldrake, servantman, and Ann Brent of Wheldrake, singlewoman, East Riding Records Office [ERRO]/QSF/294/C/11 (19 September 1780); Recognizance of Edward Offley of Great Driffield, ERRO/QSF/251/C/8 (11 February 1796). The Foundling Hospital register records Ann Brent's apprenticeship as foundling no. 6,356, and Edward Offley as foundling no. 1,185.

8. LMA/A/FH/A/F12/001/001; Morris Lievesley, 'A book of reminiscences of behaviour of Governors, staff and pupils of the Foundling Hospital by Secretary to the Hospital', f. 18.

9. It would take many years of research in local archives and record offices to piece together the stories of each surviving foundling, work that has only just begun.

10. Memoranda of Complaints, LMA/A/FH/A12/23/n.d., n.f.

11. Will of Paul Holton, Wine and Brandy Merchant of Workingham, TNA/PROB11/1758/197, proved 2 July 1829. The majority of research for Paul Holton's story (foundling no. 15,297) was conducted by Janette Bright, as acknowledged by Caro Howell, *The Foundling Museum* (London, 2014), 90–1. Her research illustrates the potential for further foundling histories in future, although her remarkable talent for locating records and unlocking the intricacies

of the Foundling Hospital archive which is presently not digitized must be noted.

12. Howell, *Foundling Museum*, 94–5.
13. 'Autobiography of George King, Seaman and Greenwich Hospital Pensioner', 19th century. The following narrative of George's life and career is drawn from the pages of his transcribed diary, ff. 9–64.
14. The account of Franco-British military and naval strategies 1803–5 in this chapter is taken from the authoritative account of leading naval historian N. A. M. Rodger in *The Command of the Ocean: a naval history of Britain, 1649–1815* (London, 2004), 528–44.
15. 'Banyan Day, A sea term for those days on which no meat is allowed to the sailors: the term is borrowed from the Banyans in the East Indies, a cast[e] that eat nothing that had life'. Francis Grose, *Dictionary of the Vulgar Tongue* (London, 1811).
16. Rodger, *Command of the Ocean*, 538.
17. Ibid., 541.
18. Ibid., 542. The Spanish three-decker *Santa Ana* suffered double the losses of Collingwood's *Royal Sovereign*.
19. Ibid.
20. Lord (later Vice Admiral) Edward Russell, Honble Mr Ryder (later Sir Alfred Phillips Ryder, Admiral of the Fleet), Honble Mr Anson (possibly Hon. George Anson, a Major General in the British Army), and Honble Mr Talbot (possibly Admiral the Honourable Sir John Talbot).
21. Henry's regiment, the 10th (later North Lincolnshire) Regiment of Foot, took part in the Peninsular Wars and was frequently stationed in Malta from 1812 to 1814, as confirmed in Richard Cannon, *Historical Record of the 10th, or the North Lincolnshire Regiment* (London, 1847), 56–62. Unfortunately, beyond the records of the Foundling Hospital, it has proven impossible conclusively to locate Henry's service records or other documentation relating to his life or death.

22. Admiralty records confirm that Able Seaman George King entered service with the *Windsor Castle* on 4 June 1828 and was discharged on 20 June 1831 at Plymouth. British Royal Navy Personnel (1831), TNA/ADM/35/4523 and 37/7828.

23. Clive Aslet, *The Story of Greenwich* (London, 1999) , 141–2.

24. Ibid., 164.

25. Entry Book of Pensioners, Greenwich Hospital, 1833–40, TNA/ADM/73/68.

26. Applications for admission into Greenwich Hospital as in-pensioners (after service in the Royal Navy, Royal Marines, or the Naval Dockyards), December 1834–January 1835, TNA/ADM/6/241/45.

27. Lievesley, 'A book of reminiscences', ff. 30–1.

28. Nathaniel Hawthorne, *Our Old Home* (1863, revised edn, Boston, MA, 1883).

29. Aslet, *Story of Greenwich*, 166–7.

30. National census, England, Wales, and Scotland (1851), TNA/HO.107/1586.

31. Greenwich Hospital and Schools: Baptisms and Burials, TNA/ADM/73/40; TNA/RG/8/17 (31 July 1857).

9. Epilogue: Welfare, Philanthropy, and the Future

1. Peter Kirby, *Child Workers and Industrial Health in Britain, 1780–1850* (Woodbridge, 2013), 25–7.

2. Jane Humphries, 'English apprenticeship: A neglected factor in the first industrial revolution', in Paul A. David and Mark Thomas (eds), *The Economic Future in Historical Perspective* (Oxford and New York, 2003), 78; on the enduring use of apprenticeships, see Caroline Withall, 'Shipped out? Pauper apprentices of port towns during the Industrial Revolution, 1750–1870', unpublished DPhil thesis, University of Oxford (2014).

3. 'Letters of Thomas Coram', *Proceedings of the Massachusetts Historical Society*, 3rd ser., 56 (1922–3), 20 (22 September 1738), 43.

4. Erica Charters, 'The caring fiscal-military state during the Seven Years War, 1756–63', *Historical Journal*, 52: 4 (2009), 921–41.

5. Gillian Pugh, *London's Forgotten Children: Thomas Coram and the Foundling Hospital* (Stroud, 2007), 94–6.

6. Ibid., 107–16, 154–63.

7. Jacqueline Wilson, *Hetty Feather* (London, 2009).

8. See Coram: Digest of Achievements 2016–17, www.coram.org.uk/news-events/press-office.

SELECT BIBLIOGRAPHY

Manuscript Sources

British Library

Add MS 32692 Correspondence of the Duke of Newcastle, 1739
Mss Eur G37 Papers of Robert Clive, 1728–1832

East Riding Record Office

DDGR Correspondence of John Grimston
QSF East Riding Quarter Sessions Records

Foundling Museum, London

Autobiography of George King, Seaman and Greenwich Hospital Pensioner, 19th century MRF/85 [Catalogue reference, National Maritime Museum, Greenwich]

London Metropolitan Archive

A/FH/A London Foundling Hospital archive
  General Committee Minutes
  General Correspondence
  General Court Minutes
  Sub-Committee Minutes

A/FH/A/09/001/192 Billet books

A/FH/A/10/003/007 Nursery books

A/FH/A/12/001/001-104 Petitions to take apprentices

A/FH/A/12/002/002 Certificates of good character and settlement of masters, 1769

A/FH/A/12/003/001-411 Apprenticeship register

A/FH/A/12/004/001-158 Apprenticeship indentures, 1751–1834

A/FH/A/12/006/001-013 Apprenticeship transfers 1763–78

A/FH/A/12/007/001-043 Petitions of apprentices for gratuities

A/FH/A/12/010/001 and A/FH/A/12/010/088 Testimonials of characters of apprentices from their masters for gratuities—girls and boys

A/FH/A/12/011/002 Bond testimonials from Foundling Hospital governors to apprentices with address to foundlings on leaving at end of apprenticeship up to 1832

A/FH/A/12/015/001 Rough notes on apprentices punished, 1769–72

A/FH/A/12/023/001 Letters and memoranda concerning apprentices including complaints from masters, 1775–91

A/FH/A/F12/001/001 Lievesley, Morris, 'A book of reminiscences of behaviour of governors, staff and pupils of the Foundling Hospital by Secretary to the Hospital'

A/FH/A8/1/1/17 Admission records

A/FH/A12/1/001 Petitions to the General Committee

A/FH/A12/23 Memorandums of complaints between masters and apprentices

A/FH/D01/006/001-15 Application by masters to take apprentices

National Archives, Kew

ADM/6/241 Applications for admission into Greenwich Hospital as in-pensioners, 1834–5

ADM/73/40; RG/8/17 Greenwich Hospital and Schools: Baptisms and Burials, 1857

ADM/73/68 Entry Book of Pensioners, Greenwich Hospital, 1833–40

ADM/171 Admiralty and Ministry of Defence, Navy Department: Medal Rolls, 1793–1827

HO.107/1586 National census, England, Wales, and Scotland, 1851

PROB11/1459/77 Will of Francis Newman, gentleman, of Mile End, Middlesex

PROB11/1758/197 Will of Paul Holton, Wine and Brandy Merchant of Workingham

Primary Printed Sources

Books / Pamphlets

Anon., *Essay on the Character of Thomas Coram* (London, 1751).

Anon., *The Tendencies of the Foundling Hospital in Its Present Extent Considered* II (London, 1760).

Anon., *The Rise and Progress of the Foundling Hospital Considered: and the Reasons for Putting a Stop to the General Reception of All Children* (London, 1761).

Anon., *The History of Maria Farrell: or, the Beautiful Foundling. Containing a Variety of Strange Accidents and Wonderful Love Adventures Scarcely Equall'd in History* (1790?).

Brownlow, *History and Objects of the Foundling Hospital with a Memoir of the Founder* (3rd edn, London, 1865).

Bernard, Thomas, *An Account of the Foundling Hospital, in London, for the Maintenance and Education of Exposed and Deserted Young Children* (2nd edn, London, 1799).

Brownlow, John, *Memoranda, or, Chronicles of the Foundling Hospital: Including Memoirs of Captain Coram* (London, 1847).

Clark, Gillian, ed., *Correspondence of the Foundling Hospital Inspectors in Berkshire 1757–68* (Berkshire Record Society, 1994).

Fielding, Henry, *The History of Tom Jones, a Foundling*, 3 vols (London, 1749).

Ford, W. C., ed., 'Letters of Thomas Coram', *Proceedings of the Massachusetts Historical Society*, 3rd ser., 56 (1922–3), 15–68.

Grose, Francis, *Dictionary of the Vulgar Tongue* (London, 1811).

Hanway, Jonas, *Reasons for Augmentation of at Least 12,000 Mariners to Be Employed in the Merchants-Service and Coasting Trade* (London, 1759).

Hanway, Jonas, *A Candid Historical Account of the Hospital for the Reception of Exposed and Deserted Young Children* (2nd edn, London, 1760).

Hanway, Jonas, *Christian Knowledge Made Easy* (London, 1763).

Hanway, Jonas, *A Proposal for Saving From 70,000L to 150,000L to the Public; at the same time rendering 5000 young persons of both sexes more happy in themselves and more useful to their country, than if so much money were expended on their account* (London, 1764).

Newspapers and Periodicals

Derby Mercury
Guardian
Household Words
Illustrated London News
Leeds Intelligencer
The Times
The World

Secondary Sources

Britain and Empire

Aslet, Clive, *The Story of Greenwich* (London, 1999).

Bailyn, Bernard, with the assistance of DeWolfe, Barbara, *Voyagers to the West: a passage in the peopling of America on the eve of the revolution* (New York, 1986).

Brewer, John, *The Sinews of Power: war, money and the English state, 1688–1783* (London, 1994).

Charters, Erica, 'The caring fiscal-military state during the Seven Years' War, 1756–1763', *Historical Journal* 52: 4 (2009), 921–41.

Cody, Lisa, *Birthing the Nation: sex, science and the conception of eighteenth-century Britons* (Oxford, 2005).

Coffey, John, ' "Tremble, Britannia!": fear, providence and the abolition of the Slave Trade, 1758–1807', *English Historical Review* 127: 527 (2012), 844–81.

Colley, Linda, *Britons: forging the nation, 1707–1837* (New Haven, CT and London, 1992).

Colley, Linda, *Captives: Britain, empire and the world, 1600–1850* (London, 2002).

Conway, S., *War, State and Society in Mid-Eighteenth-Century Britain and Ireland* (Oxford, 2006).

Gradish, S. *The Manning of the British Navy during the Seven Years' War* (London, 1980).

Hoppit, J., 'Political arithmetic in eighteenth-century England', *Economic History Review*, 49 (1996), 516–40.

Innes, Joanna, 'The domestic face of the fiscal-military state: government and society in eighteenth-century Britain', in Stone, Lawrence (ed.), *An Imperial State at War: Britain from 1688 to 1815* (London, 1994).

Innes, Joanna, *Inferior politics: social problems and social policies in eighteenth-century Britain* (Oxford, 2009).

Land, Isaac, 'Bread and arsenic: citizenship from the bottom up in Georgian London', *Journal of Social History* 39: 1 (2005), 89–110.

Pietsch, Roland, *The Real Jim Hawkins: ships' boys in the Georgian Navy* (Barnsley, 2000).

Rodger, N. A. M., *The Wooden World: an anatomy of the Georgian Navy* (London, 1986).

Rodger, N. A. M., *The Command of the Ocean: a naval history of Britain, 1649–1815* (London, 2004).

Childhood, Youth, and Apprenticeship

Ben Amos, I. K., 'Failure to become freemen: urban apprentices in early modern England', *Social History*, 16: 2 (1991), 155–72.

Ben Amos, I. K., *Adolescence and Youth in Early Modern England* (New Haven, CT, 1994).

Brooks, Christopher, 'Apprenticeship, social mobility and the middling sort, 1550–1800', in Barry, J. and Brooks, C. (eds), *The Middling Sort of People: culture, society and politics in England, 1550–1800* (Basingstoke, 1994).

Cunningham, H., 'The employment and unemployment of children in England, c.1680–1851', *Past and Present*, 126 (1990), 115–50.

Fletcher, Anthony, *Growing Up in England: the experience of childhood, 1600–1914* (New Haven, CT and London, 2008).

Hanawalt, Barbara, 'Medievalists and the study of childhood', *Speculum*, 77 (2002), 440–60.

Honeyman, Katrina, 'Compulsion, compassion and consent: parish apprenticeship in early-nineteenth century England', in Goose, Nigel and Honeyman, Katrina (eds), *Childhood and Child Labour in Industrial England: diversity and agency, 1750–1914* (Basingstoke, 2013).

Horrell, Sara and Humphries, Jane, 'Child labour and British industrialization', in Lavalette, Michael (ed.), *A Thing of the Past? Child labour in Britain in the nineteenth and twentieth centuries* (Liverpool, 1999).

Humphries, Jane, 'English apprenticeship: a neglected factor in the first industrial revolution', in David, Paul A. and Thomas, Mark (eds), *The Economic Future in Historical Perspective* (Oxford and New York, 2003).

Humphries, Jane, *Childhood and Child Labour in the British Industrial Revolution* (Cambridge, 2010).

Humphries, Jane, 'Childhood and child labour in the British industrial revolution', *Economic History Review*, 66: 2 (2013), 395–418.

Kirby, Peter, *Child Labour in Britain, 1750–1870* (Basingstoke and New York, 2003).

Kirby, Peter, 'A brief statistical sketch of the child labour market in mid-nineteenth century London', *Continuity and Change*, 20 (2005), 229–45.

Lane, J., 'Apprenticeship in Warwickshire cotton mills, 1790–1830', *Textile History*, 10 (1979), 161–74.

Lane, J., *Apprenticeship in England, 1600–1918* (London, 1996).

Levene, Alysa, 'Honesty, sobriety and diligence: master-apprentice relations in eighteenth- and nineteenth-century England', *Social History*, 33: 2 (2008), 183–200.

Levene, Alysa, 'Parish apprenticeship and the Old Poor Law in London', *Economic History Review*, 63: 4 (2010), 915–41.

Rose, Mary B., 'Social policy and business: parish apprentices and the early factory system, 1750–1834', *Business History*, 31: 4 (1989), 5–32.

Taylor, James Stephen, 'Philanthropy and empire: Jonas Hanway and the infant poor of London', *Eighteenth-Century Studies*, 12: 3 (1979), 285–305.

Wales, Tim, ' "Living at their own hands": policing poor households and the young in early modern rural England', *Agricultural History Review*, 61: 1 (2013): 19–39.

Wallis, Patrick, 'Labor, law and training in early modern London: apprenticeship and the city's institutions', *Journal of British Studies* 51: 4 (2012), 791–819.

Wallis, Patrick, 'Rules and reality: quantifying the practice of apprenticeship in premodern England', *Economic History Review*, 65: 2 (2012), 556–79.

Wallis, Patrick and Minns, Chris, 'The price of human capital in a preindustrial economy: premiums and apprenticeship contracts in eighteenth-century England', *Explorations in Economic History*, 50: 3 (2013), 335–50.

Wallis, Patrick, Webb, Cliff, and Minns, Chris, 'Leaving home and entering service: the age of apprenticeship in early modern London', *Continuity and Change*, 25: 3 (2010), 377–404.

Wrightson, Keith, 'Infanticide in European history', *Criminal Justice History*, 3 (1982), 1–20.

Foundling Hospitals: General History

Aspey, Gordon, *All at Sea: Memories of a Coram Boy* (Emsworth, 2010).

Bright, Janette and Clark, Gillian, *An Introduction to the Tokens at the Foundling Hospital Museum* (London, 2014).

Compston, Herbert Fuller Bright, *Thomas Coram, Churchman, Empire Builder and Philanthropist* (London, 1918).

Howell, Caro, *The Foundling Museum: an introduction* (London, 2014).

Levene, Alysa, 'The origins of the children of the London Foundling Hospital: a reconsideration', *Continuity and Change* 18: 2 (2003), 201–36.

Levene, Alysa (ed.), *Narratives of the Poor in Eighteenth-Century Britain*, vol. 3 (London, 2006).

Levene, Alysa, *Childcare, Health, and Mortality at the London Foundling Hospital, 1741–1800: 'left to the mercy of the world'* (Manchester and New York, 2007).

Mackenzie, Tom H., *The Last Foundling: the memoir of an underdog* (London, 2012).

McClure, Ruth, *Coram's Children: the London Foundling Hospital in the eighteenth century* (New Haven, CT, 1981).

Nichols, R. H. and Wray, F. A., *The History of the Foundling Hospital* (Oxford, 1935).

Pugh, Gillian, *London's Forgotten Children: Thomas Coram and the Foundling Hospital* (Stroud, 2007).

Scott, Beatrice, 'Ackworth Hospital, 1757–1773', *Yorkshire Archaeological Journal*, 61 (1989), 155–71.

Styles, John, *Threads of Feeling: the London Foundling Hospital's textile tokens, 1740–1770* (London, 2010).

Taylor, James Stephen, *Jonas Hanway, Founder of the Marine Society: charity and policy in eighteenth-century Britain* (London and Berkeley, CA, 1985).

Ulbricht, Otto, 'The debate about foundling hospitals in Enlightenment Germany: infanticide, illegitimacy and infant mortality rates', *Central European History*, 18 (1985), 211–56.

Wagner, Gillian, *Thomas Coram, Gent. (1668–1751)* (Woodbridge, 2004).

Poverty and the Poor Laws

Boulton, Jeremy, 'Indoors or outdoors? Welfare priorities and pauper choices in the metropolis under the Old Poor Law, 1718–1824', in

Briggs, Chris, Kitson, P. M., and Thomson, S. J. (eds), *Population, Welfare and Economic Change in Britain, 1290–1834* (Woodbridge, 2014).

Ely, James W., 'The eighteenth-century Poor Laws in the West Riding of Yorkshire', *American Journal of Legal History*, 30: 1 (1986), 1–24.

Evans, Tanya, *Unfortunate Objects: lone mothers in eighteenth-century London* (Basingstoke, 2005).

Fideler, Paul A., *Social Welfare in Pre-Industrial England* (London, 2006).

Hitchcock, Tim, *Down and Out in Eighteenth-Century London* (London, 2004).

Hitchcock, Tim, King, Peter, and Sharpe, Pamela, *Chronicling Poverty: the Voices and Strategies of the English Poor, 1640–1840* (Basingstoke, 1997).

Hitchcock, Tim, Shore, Heather, and Porter, Roy, *The Streets of London: From the Great Fire to the Great Stink* (London, 2003).

Humphries, Jane, 'Care and cruelty in the workhouse: children's experiences of residential poor relief in eighteenth- and nineteenth-century England', in Goose, Nigel and Honeyman, Katrina (eds), *Childhood and Child Labour in Industrial England: diversity and agency, 1750–1914* (Basingstoke, 2013).

Innes, Joanna, 'Parliament and the shaping of eighteenth-century English social policy', *Transactions of the Royal Historical Society*, 5th ser., 40 (1990), 63–92.

Innes, Joanna, 'The mixed economy of welfare in early modern England: assessments of the options from Hale to Malthus (1683–1803)', in M. Daunton (ed.), *Charity, Self-Interest and Welfare in the English Past* (London, 1996).

Innes, Joanna, 'Power and happiness: empirical social inquiry in Britain, from "political arithmetic" to "moral statistics"', in *Inferior Politics: social problems and social policies in eighteenth-century Britain* (Oxford, 2009).

Kirby, Peter, *Child Labour in Britain, 1750–1870* (Basingstoke and New York, 2003).

Kirby, Peter, 'A brief statistical sketch of the child labour market in mid-nineteenth century London', *Continuity and Change*, 20 (2005), 229–45.

Levene, Alysa, 'Parish apprenticeship and the Old Poor Law in London', *Economic History Review*, 63: 4 (2010), 915–41.

Levene, Alysa, 'Charity apprenticeships and social capital in eighteenth-century England', in Goose, Nigel and Honeyman, Katrina (eds), *Childhood and Child Labour in Industrial England: diversity and agency, 1750–1914* (Basingstoke, 2013).

Snell, K. D. M., *Annals of the Labouring Poor: social change and agrarian England, 1660–1900* (Cambridge, 1987).

Snell, K. D. M., *Parish and Belonging: community, identity and welfare in England and Wales, 1700–1950* (Cambridge, 2006).

Wallis, Patrick, 'Apprenticeship and training in premodern England', *Journal of Economic History*, 68: 3 (2008), 832–61.

Social and Economic History

Andrew, Donna, *Philanthropy and Police: London charity in the eighteenth century* (Princeton, NJ, 1989).

Berry, Helen and Foyster, Elizabeth (eds), *The Family in Early Modern England* (Cambridge, 2007).

Cavallo, Sandra, *Charity and Power in Early Modern Italy* (Cambridge, 1995).

Erickson, Amy Louise, 'Eleanor Mosley and other milliners in the City of London companies, 1700–1750', *History Workshop Journal*, 71: 1 (2011), 147–72.

Foyster, Elizabeth, *Marital Violence: an English family history, 1660–1857* (Cambridge, 2005).

George, M. Dorothy, *London Life in the Eighteenth Century* (London, 1925, reprinted Harmondsworth, 1992).

Goose, Nigel and Honeyman, Katrina (eds), *Childhood and Child Labour in Industrial England: diversity and agency, 1750–1914* (Basingstoke, 2013).

Honeyman, Katrina, *Child Workers in England, 1780–1820* (Aldershot, 2007).

Kirby, Peter, *Child Workers and Industrial Health in Britain, 1780–1850* (Woodbridge, 2013).

Muldrew, Craig, ' "Th'ancient distaff"and "whirling spindle": measuring the contribution of spinning to household earnings and the national economy in England, 1550–1771', *Economic History Review*, 65: 2 (2012): 498–526.

Porter, Roy, *London: a social history* (Cambridge, MA, 1994).

Schwarz, Leonard, *London in the Age of Industrialization: entrepreneurs, labour force and living conditions, 1700–1850* (Cambridge, 1992).

Sharpe, Pamela, *Adapting to Capitalism: working women in the English economy, 1700–1850* (Basingstoke and New York, 1996).

Sharpe, Pamela, *Women, Gender, and Labour Migration: historical and global perspectives* (New York: Routledge, 2001).

Shaw-Taylor, Leigh and Wrigley, E. A., 'Occupational structure and population change', in Floud, R., Humphries, J., and Johnson, P. (eds), *The Cambridge Economic History of Modern Britain, Vol. I: 1700–1870* (2nd edn, Cambridge, 2014).

Shepard, Alexandra, 'Poverty, labour and the language of social description in early modern England', *Past and Present*, 201 (2008), 51–95.

Shoemaker, Robert, *Prosecution and Punishment: petty crime and the law in London and rural Middlesex, c.1660–1725* (Cambridge and New York, 1991).

Shoemaker, Robert, *London Mob Violence and Disorder in Eighteenth-Century England* (London, 2007).

Styles, John, *The Dress of the People: everyday fashion in eighteenth-century England* (New Haven, CT and London, 2007).

Tadmor, Naomi, *Family and Friends in Eighteenth-Century England* (Cambridge, 2001).

Terpstra, Nicholas, 'Working the cocoon: gendered charitable enclosures and the silk industry in early modern Europe', in Kippen, K. and Woods, L. (eds), *Worth and Repute: valuing gender in late medieval and early modern Europe: essays in honour of Barbara Todd* (Toronto, 2011).

Tuttle, C., *Hard at Work in Factories and Mines: the economics of child labor during the British Industrial Revolution* (Boulder, CO, 1999).

Uglow, Jenny, *Hogarth: a life and a world* (London, 1997).

Wrigley, E. A., 'English county populations in the later eighteenth century', *Economic History Review*, 60: 1 (2007), 35–69.

Wrigley, E. A., 'Rickman revisited: the population growth rates of English counties in the early modern period', *Economic History Review*, 62: 3 (2009), 711–35.

Wrigley, E. A., *Energy and the English Industrial Revolution* (Cambridge, 2010).

Wrigley, E. A. and Schofield, R. S., *The population history of England, 1541–1871: a reconstruction* (Cambridge, 1981).

Unpublished Theses

Allin, D. S., 'The early years of the Foundling Hospital, 1739/41–1773', unpublished thesis, London Metropolitan Archives deposit (2010).

Dolan, Alice, 'The fabric of life: linen and life cycle in England, 1678–1810', unpublished PhD thesis, University of Hertfordshire (2015).

Gibson, Kate, 'The experience of illegitimacy in England, 1660–1834', unpublished PhD thesis, University of Sheffield (2018).

Mathisen, Ashley, 'Treating the children of the poor: institutions and the construction of medical authority in eighteenth-century London', unpublished DPhil thesis, University of Oxford (2011).

Neilsen, Caroline, 'The Chelsea out-pensioners: image and reality in eighteenth-century and early nineteenth-century social care', unpublished PhD thesis, Newcastle University (2014).

Withall, Caroline, 'Shipped out? Pauper apprentices of port towns during the Industrial Revolution, 1750–1870', unpublished DPhil thesis, University of Oxford (2014).

PICTURE
ACKNOWLEDGEMENTS

Figure 1.1 Heritage Image Partnership Ltd/Alamy Stock Photo.

Figure 1.2 Artokoloro Quint Lox Limited/Alamy Stock Photo.

Figure 1.3 Wellcome Library, London.

Figure 1.4 Wellcome Library, London.

Figure 2.1 William Hogarth, *Portrait of Thomas Coram*, 1740; © Coram in the care of the Foundling Museum, London.

Figure 2.2 Nathaniel Parr, *An Exact Representation of the Form and Manner in Which Exposed and Deserted Young Children Are Admitted into the Foundling Hospital*, 1747; © Coram in the care of the Foundling Museum, London.

Figure 2.3 © Coram in the care of the Foundling Museum, London.

Figure 2.4 London Metropolitan Archives, City of London, A/FH/A/009/001/192. © Coram.

Figure 2.5 Chronicle/Alamy Stock Photo.

Figure 3.1 Wellcome Library, London.

Figure 3.2 William Hogarth, *Moses Brought Before Pharaoh's Daughter*, 1746; © Coram in the care of the Foundling Museum, London.

Figure 3.3 William Hogarth, original sketch for Arms for the Foundling Hospital, 1747; © Coram in the care of the Foundling Museum, London.

Figure 3.4 Wellcome Library, London.

Figure 3.5 Joseph Highmore, *Portrait of Thomas Emerson*, 1731 © Coram in the care of the Foundling Museum, London.

Figure 3.6 © Trustees of the British Museum.

Figure 4.1 © Coram in the care of the Foundling Museum, London.

Figure 4.2 London Metropolitan Archives, City of London, A/FH/A/008/001/001/017. © Coram.

Figure 4.3 Wellcome Library, London.

Figure 6.1 agefotostock Art Collection/age fotostock.

Figure 8.1 Samuel Wale, *Greenwich Hospital*, c.1748 © Coram in the care of the Foundling Museum, London.

INDEX

Index

Index

Index

Index

Index